AF553737

DYNAMICS OF MODERN TOURISM

DYNAMICS OF MODERN TOURISM

Lalita Sharma

CENTRUM PRESS
NEW DELHI-110002 (INDIA)

CENTRUM PRESS
H.O.: 4360/4, Ansari Road, Daryaganj,
New Delhi-110002 (India)
Tel: 23278000, 23261597, 23255577, 23286875

B.O.: No. 1015, Ist Main Road, BSK IIIrd Stage,
IIIrd Phase, IIIrd Block, Bangalore-560085 (INDIA)
Tel: 080-41723429

Email: centrumpress@gmail.com
Visit us at: www.centrumpress.com

Dynamics of Modern Tourism

First Edition, 2010

ISBN 978-93-80540-20-7

PRINTED IN INDIA

Printed at Mehra Offset Press, Delhi

Contents

Preface

The main difference between modern tourism and tourism in the past, is that modern tourism involves the mass availability and mass participation in holidays by what can be regarded as the entire population. This is distinct from tourism before the railway age when there were only two classes of people those who were on a holiday all the time and the masses whom never took a holiday.

The growth of the tourism industry has been driven by economic development. Greater affluence has opened up the possibility to travel for leisure to greater numbers of people. Technical progress - notably the car and air travel - has consistently enabled greater speed, comfort and scope for leisure travellers. Tourism has become big business - by some measures the biggest. It employs 74 million people directly, with tourism-related activities estimated to provide some 200 million jobs.

Modern tourism involves many different types each that in turn have had an impact on the transport means. The different types of tourism can be divided based on the tourist's main interest of their trip.

Author

Chapter 1

Introduction

Modern tourism could be said to have emerged with modern industrial society in the nineteenth century. In this century, industrialisation both spawned the means to travel - initially the railways - and created a growing market amongst the new industrial and professional classes, and amongst the working class, the masses, too. Thomas Cook pioneered leisure travel amongst the middle and working classes in this century. He and his son, John Mason Cook (whose initials JMC are now a brand of Thomas Cook tour operations), took an increasingly broad spectrum of the population to ever more distant destinations. Over the last century and a half the achievement of the industry has been nothing less than the democratisation of leisure travel, from the few deemed worthy, and wealthy enough to partake, to an everyday activity for the majority in developed societies.

The growth of the tourism industry has been driven by economic development. Greater affluence has opened up the possibility to travel for leisure to greater numbers of people. Technical progress - notably the car and air travel - has consistently enabled greater speed, comfort and scope for leisure travellers. Whereas even as recently as forty years ago back-to-back charters were a new innovation, initially confusing to hoteliers and customers, today they are the staple of the big tour operators.

The UK's 'big four', Thomas Cook, Airtours, First Choice and Thomson (now part of TUI, the first European-wide package holiday brand, owned by German conglomerate Pressaug) dominate a market that takes annually some thirty-five million British tourists abroad for their holidays. By supplying *en masse*, such companies have lowered the real cost of holidays, and alongside growing incomes, this has contributed to what Vladimir Raitz, founder of Horizon holidays (the first post-war package holiday company to develop charter flight-based packages) refers to as the package holiday revolution. This growth has been mirrored worldwide, with today some 700 million travelling internationally per year for no other reason than leisure. It is estimated that by 2020, there will be some 1.6 billion international tourists.

Flight to the Sun, written by Raitz, and co-authored by travel expert Roger Bray, reflects on the optimism of the post-war boom in tourism. For travel pioneer Raitz, Wordsworth's often quoted lines captured the mood:

Bliss it was in that dawn to be alive
But to be young was very heaven.

This optimism was shared by the growing number of customers, for whom a shrinking world represented the opportunity to enjoy snow-capped mountains and sun-soaked beaches.

Tourism has become big business - by some measures the biggest. It employs 74 million people directly, with tourism-related activities estimated to provide some 200 million jobs. It provides the largest source of export earnings for countries as diverse as Spain and Barbados. By 2020 it is predicted that tourism expenditure will top US$ 2 trillion, or US$ 5 billion per day. The industry's contribution to global wealth, measured from Gross National Products, is estimated to be 4 per cent directly and 11 per cent including indirect effects.

It has also enjoyed consistent growth in recent decades, decades in which some countries have experienced relative decline in some of their traditional industries. Indeed, attracting tourists has increasingly become a preoccupation of politicians and development planners, evidenced by the rise of 'place marketing' and the intense competition to attract sporting and cultural events, World Heritage Status, City of

Culture status and a host of other events and designations that can assist in improving a country's share of international tourism receipts.

In economic terms, then, Mass Tourism seems self-evidently vitally important. However, it is increasingly discussed less as an economic phenomenon linked to the creation of jobs and investment, or indeed simply as enjoyment, adventure and innocent fun. Rather tourism has increasingly become discussed as a cultural and environmental phenomenon, and more often than not as fraught and destructive.

In this respect the figures for tourism's growth are more likely to be raised in the context of an angst-ridden discussion of its harmful effects than in the celebratory tones characteristic of Thomas Cook 150 years ago, or Vladimir Raitz forty years ago. Wariness rather than celebration typically accompanies accounts of the growth of travel for leisure. It is this emphasis on tourism as a cultural and environmental problem that informs the moralisation of tourism.

This in turn is manifested in a constant denigration of mass package tourism and mass package tourists amongst those for whom such things are deemed unethical. For some, post-war tourism is like Frankenstein's (or perhaps Thomas Cook's) monster, having seemingly run out of control, with dire consequences. The optimism of Raitz, and the association of tourism with innocence, fun and adventure, have been challenged by a mood of pessimism and a sense that moral regulation of pleasure-seeking is necessary in order to preserve environmental and cultural diversity.

The moralisation of tourism involves two mutually reinforcing notions. First, Mass Tourism is deemed to have wrought damage to the environment and to the cultures exposed to it, and hence new types of tourism are proposed that are deemed benign to the environment and benevolent towards other cultures. Second, this ethical tourism is deemed to be better for tourists, too - more enlightening, encouraging respect for other ways of life and a critical reflection on the tourist's own developed society. There are a plethora of terms that academics and those in the industry have applied to this more moral tourism such as ethical tourism, alternative tourism, ecotourism and responsible tourism. Perhaps the term that covers them all, and helps to identify what is distinctive about them taken together, is that coined by industry specialist Ahluwalia Poon - 'New Tourism'. She argues that New Tourism is both an appeal to a certain sense of enlightenment about one's effect on others, and an environmental imperative.

NEW TOURISM - THE SOLUTION

Poon outlined the marketing aspects of New Tourism thus: the holiday must be flexible and must be able to be purchased at prices that are competitive with mass-produced holidays; holidays are not simply aiming at economies of scale, but will be tailored to individual wants; unlike Mass Tourism, production will be driven by the wants of consumers; mass-marketing is no longer the dominant ethos - holidays will be marketed differentially to different needs, incomes, time constraints and travel interests; the holiday is consumed on a large scale by more experienced travellers, more educated, more destination oriented, more independent, more flexible and more green; consumers of New Tourism consider the environment and culture of the destinations they visit to be a key part of the holiday experience.

Poon clearly considers the New Tourist to be the 'thinking tourist' - more educated, independent of mind and aware. Also, from this definition New Tourism could be regarded as post-fordist tourism - tourism that moves away from a standard, mass-produced product towards a flexible, individually tailored one, led by individual demands rather than a homogenous mass market.

Poon's identification of post-Fordist production in holidays has resonance. She quotes the marketing director of British Airways who claims we are seeing 'the end of mass-marketing in the travel business ... we are going to be much more sophisticated in the way we segment our market'. Large tour operators have adapted accordingly. The big four have bought smaller, niche operators to tap into the new markets. In addition, despite the squeeze on so many medium sized tour operators, there has been a large growth in small, specialised operators, claiming to cater for the specific needs of their target market. These operators are often keen to identify with a more moral notion of tourism in their marketing and advertising.

But for Poon, and for many other advocates of New Tourism, it is far more than dry marketing for 'thinking tourists' - it is an ethical imperative; it is ethical tourism. As such it is not simply suggested as an option for prospective tourists, but is advocated as a solution to problems caused by Mass Tourism. Advocacy, by NGOs, campaigns and New Tourism oriented tour operators, is a key feature of New Tourism.

For Poon: 'The tourism industry is in crisis [...] a crisis of mass tourism that has brought social, cultural, economic and environmental havoc in its wake, and it is mass tourism practices that must be radically changed to bring in the new.' The charge that Mass Tourism has had a generally destructive impact on host societies is widely asserted in the context of this advocacy. However, advocates of New Tourism argue that there is a growing market of more ethical tourists who are rejecting mass-produced, homogenous tourism products in favour of tailored holidays that are kinder to the environment and benign to the host culture.

These people perhaps constitute a new school of 'ethical' tourism - the *New Moral Tourism*. The key features of their moralised conception of leisure travel are a search for enlightenment in other places, and a desire to preserve these places in the name of cultural diversity and environmental conservation.

NEW MORAL TOURISM - A PERVASIVE AGENDA

New Moral Tourism is evidenced and expressed in a number of different types of organisation: governments; companies; and a variety of non-governmental organisations.

It is also influential within both popular and academic discussions of contemporary tourism. As such, it is a pervasive agenda. The commitment of global government to reforming the tourism industry, and the tourist, was formalised through the documents that came out of the 1992 United Nations Earth Summit in Rio. Agenda 21 documentation for the tourism industry asserts that, 'the travel and tourism industry has a vested interest in protecting the natural and cultural resources which are the core of its business'.

Elsewhere, the document argues that: 'Travel and Tourism should assist people in leading healthy and productive lives in harmony with nature', the industry should 'contribute to the conservation, protection and restoration of the earth's ecosystem', 'environmental protection should constitute an integral part of the tourism development process' and 'tourism development should recognise and support the identity, culture and interests of indigenous peoples'. *Agenda 21 for the Travel and Tourism Industry* also reflects an impulse for education of tourists. It suggests that publicity for the tourist should promote education for ethical tourism, including in-flight videos, magazine articles, and advice on sick bags.

Whilst the efficacy of Agenda 21 is much debated by grass roots environmentalists, this perspective on tourism has been widely taken up by governments and NGOs. Aid agencies around the world have increasingly financed NGOs engaged in ethical tourism development, seeking to generate a rural development sensitive to the natural environment and culture of recipient communities. In the UK the Department for International Development pioneer 'pro-poor' tourism as a means of relieving rural poverty in the Third World.

They also support schemes to enlighten prospective tourists, for example, through a recent schools video that portrays package tourists in the most unflattering light. USAID, the aid arm of the United States government, also back up the ethical claims of ecotourism by funding it as a means of generating limited development through ecotourism revenues alongside conservation of the natural environment in the Third World. Promoting an appreciation of the value of conservation for the prospective tourist and their hosts are key aims too.

A host of other quasi-governmental organisations concerned with the environment have also developed a commitment to 'sensitive', sustainable tourism development over the last ten to fifteen years. Their definitions of sustainable tourism are general, but often suggest a preservationist emphasis with regard to the environment and culture. For example, the Federation of Nature and National Parks in Europe, in their influential publication *Loving Them to Death?*, define sustainable tourism as an activity which 'maintains the environmental, social and economic integrity and well-being of natural, built and cultural resources *in perpetuity*' (my italics).

This begs the question, central to this critique of tourism's critics, that if they propose to protect nature from the excesses of development, how do they address the poverty and inequality arising from a dearth of development in many parts of the world? Maintaining a society's relationship to its natural environment 'in perpetuity' is hardly likely to tackle this. Opposition to the perceived excesses of Mass Tourism has been evident in recent years, too, amongst religious and cultural organisations.

One event often considered to mark the advent of the global critique of tourism was a conference held in Manila in 1980, convened by a group of religious leaders from developing countries worried about the impact of tourism on local cultures. The 'Manila Statement' boldly asserted that, 'tourism does more harm than good to people and societies in the third world'. The conference also founded the Ecumenical Coalition on Third World Tourism, which has remained highly critical of the tourism industry. A former executive director of the coalition, Koson Srisang, argues that tourism:

> does not benefit the majority of people. Instead it exploits them, pollutes the environment, destroys the ecosystem,

bastardises the culture, robs people of their traditional values and ways of life and subjugates women and children in the abject slavery of prostitution ... [It] epitomises the present unjust world economic order where the few who control wealth and power dictate the terms.

Ecumenical antipathy towards tourism has long been a common theme. The clergy in Britain were vocal in their criticism of the wanton behaviour of early package tourists in the mid-nineteenth century. The Catholic church in Franco's Spain worried about the influence of decadent tourists on Spaniards. Even the Pope recently condemned tourism as 'a kind of subculture that degrades both the tourists and the host community'.

However, the criticisms of modern tourism that hold sway are not those seen as conservative and religious, but rather those presented as radical and secular; they are criticisms expressed through a defence of culture and nature. Hence rather than religious organisations, it tends to be conservation NGOs, campaigns, radical academics and journalists who are in the forefront of criticising Mass Tourism and proposing new, 'ethical' alternatives.

There is a diverse range of NGOs involved in the promotion of what they perceive to be ethical tourism. Global conservation NGOs such as the World Wide Fund For Nature (WWF), the Audubon Society and Conservation International increasingly view ecotourism as a means of winning support, both amongst local populations and more widely, for conservation aims. Ecotourism is at the cutting edge of conservation initiatives as it seems to proffer opportunities for people to benefit from preserving their natural environments rather than changing them.

Its ethical credentials, then, reside in its ability to combine conservation with limited development goals. More traditional forms of tourism are regarded as less ethical as although they generally yield more in the way of economic development they are deemed to be environmentally destructive and culturally problematic. More specific projects aimed at particular destinations or types of tourism include

Alp Action, the Proyecto Ambiental Tenerife, the Save Goa Campaign and numerous others.

In general they highlight the impacts of tourism and lobby against developments they perceive as unethical. The range of goals of these organisations makes any categorisation problematic. However, they often express a disdain for package tourists. For example, the Proyecto Ambiental Tenerife, a project seeking to sustain rural traditions and traditional agriculture on this Spanish island, make the following comment on Mass Tourism:

Mass Tourism was introduced to the island of Tenerife in the 1960s. It made a few local people and many foreigners very rich. It also devastated the rural communities resulting in abandoned terraced farms; beautiful but dilapidated buildings; an age-old culture on the edge of extinction; youth unemployment of 43 per cent. So whilst the Tenerife and Spanish economies have benefited greatly from tourism, this NGO damns the developments as destructive of tradition. This reverence for tradition over change is characteristic of the moralisation of tourism.

British-based Tourism Concern is prominent amongst the campaigning NGOs. They engage in a wide variety of campaigning activities including lobbying the Gambian government to limit all-inclusive resort developments, lobbying travel companies to pull out of Burma due to human rights abuses there and producing educational materials and codes of conduct encouraging young people to be wary of their impact on the places and peoples they may visit.

In Germany, Studienkreis für Tourismus und Entwicklung (Students for Tourism and Responsibility) operate their prestigious 'To Do!' awards. The winners are almost invariably small scale, locally oriented and green. This organisation, typical of others throughout Europe, state in their aims and objectives that they 'support forms of tourism which contribute to intercultural encounter, which allow for joint learning processes, mutual respect as well as respect for cultural diversity and the sustainable use of natural resources'.

In North America, and internationally, The International Ecotourism Society is influential in marketing and promoting the ethical credentials of green holidays. Their role is not just to network with like-minded tourists with a love of the natural world, but to advocate the superiority of eco holidays for both parties concerned: tourists and hosts.

The sciety claim that, 'Ecotravel offers an alternative to many of the negative effects of mass tourism by helping conserve fragile ecosystems, support endangered species and habitats, preserve indigenous cultures and develop sustainable local economies.' They encourage prospective tourists to 'travel with a purpose - a personal purpose and a global one'.

The International Ecotourism Society also work with various development agencies, such as the InterAmerican Development Bank, to advocate ecotourism as an environmentally benign development option.

This trajectory looks likely to develop further - it is an aim of the society to develop this, and it also fits in with the 'greening of aid' through nature-based tourism examined. These and other organisations see raising awareness as a priority. In recent years initiatives with names such as 'Our Holidays, Their Homes', 'Worldwise' and 'Travelling in the Dark' have sought to educate tourists in the UK as to their potential role in environmental and cultural degradation.

Whilst their interest is not restricted to this, there is an emphasis on changing the consumption patterns and the behaviour of holidaymakers in favour of holidays that are deemed benign to the environment and benevolent to the culture of the host. Such organisations have produced ethical codes of conduct, which amount to attempts at a moral regulation of the holidaymaker.

Other NGOs include Kitemark organisations such as the Campaign for Environmentally Responsible Tourism and Green Globe. The former awards their Kitemark to tour operators in the UK they deem to be ethical. Green Globe emerged from the Rio discussions on sustainable development and encourages firms large and small to adapt to the concern over environmental impacts caused by tourists. Calls for ethical tourism feature ever more prominently in the media, too. Journalist Libby Purves argues that 'Tourists should not travel light on morals', and paints a grim picture of the effects of the industry.

The *Guardian* newspaper environment editor, in an article entitled 'Tourism is bad for our health', asserts that Mass Tourism, 'wreak[s] havoc on the environment' and that despite attempts to clean up the industry, 'tourism is essentially and inescapably, environmentally destructive'. Green campaigner and journalist George Monbiot sums up the dim view taken of tourism by media advocates of ethical tourism when he asserts: 'Tourism is, by and large, an unethical activity, which allows us to have fun at everyone else's expense.'

New Moral Tourism is talked up not only as environmentally and culturally benign, as an antidote to Mass Tourism, but also as an 'add-on' to the holiday experience. For example, a new lottery-funded magazine, *Being There*, has recently been launched by British-based campaign Tourism Concern and The Body Shop, aiming to reach 'funky, adventurous, interested and interesting women who want to put something back into the local communities and destinations they visit on holiday'.

For the magazine's supporters, travel is a life-changing experience. Anita Roddick argues that the place you visit 'literally goes from being a holiday destination to a place where you can share, learn and grow'. These sentiments are echoed in the web sites of campaigns and the brochures of many nature-based tour operators. On television, holiday programmes have come in for criticism over their supposed lack of ethical credentials.

A recent report castigates British channel ITV's *Wish You Were Here* for not taking sufficient care to encourage thoughtful behaviour on the part of prospective tourists. The compiler of the report argues: 'Editorial content that meets the growing thirst for a rounded insight into a destination will enable viewers to understand the impact their visit may have on the host country.' In this vein, it is not simply tourism itself that is subject to the critical eye of the New Moral Tourism, but also representations of places.

These are deemed to appeal to our hedonistic streak, which may preclude ethical consideration. Similar points are frequently made with regard to tourist brochures, and even travel guides have been castigated for failing to present what ethical tourism campaigners consider to be an enlightened view. Lonely Planet guidebooks, for example, have recently been subject to a campaign to boycott their Burma guide, on the basis that it encourages travellers to travel to a regime that has used coerced child labour to build up its infrastructure. In fact the guide itself is critical of the regime, too, but takes the view that travellers should decide the ethical issue for themselves. Lonely Planet are also criticised for 'making or breaking' local businesses, depending on whether they are listed in the guides.

THE RESPONSIBLE TRAVELLER

'Of course, *Let's Go* readers aren't stereotypical tourists - the purpose of guidebooks like *Let's Go* is to take you off the beaten track and into those places no coach tour would ever dare venture. Unfortunately, where a backpacker leads, the masses are never very far behind. The past decade has seen one hardcore destination such as Thailand "open up" to tourism - and subsequently lose much of their [sic] appeal. And even in places so remote that they are unlikely to ever become major stops on the global trail, insensitive travellers can still have deleterious effects, from the polluting trail of empty coke cans left behind them to offending local people by their unthinking profligacy and disrespect for local customs. Ironically, perhaps, tourists who fly into a resort and don't leave it for the duration of their stay do the least damage - at least the damage has already been done.

'We're not suggesting that you forget a six month trek in the Andes you've been dreaming of for two weeks in Cancun and Marbella - but [there] are some precautions you can take to make sure that your vacation does the least damage to the environment and the indigenous culture as possible.'

These examples are illustrative of the New Moral Tourism. The holiday is re-presented as an arena for ethical behaviour to the benefit of other peoples and the environment, leading to a holiday experience deemed to be far superior. Many of the above assertions present tourists simply as environmental footprints and cultural impositions. That development has a *creative*, as well as destructive, side is rarely alluded to. Indeed, some of the characterisations of modern tourism seem typically to, as one author points out in relation to a different case, modern travel writing, 'attach the word hideous to man-made things, but never to nature'.

Advocacy of New Moral Tourism is also evident in the commercial sector. A host of companies, spurning the four Ss (Sun, Sea, Sand and Sex) in favour of the three Ts (Travelling, Trekking and Trucking) have set out to appeal to the New Moral Tourist. Their advocacy of ethical tourism is often met with scepticism by the NGOs and campaigns, who question whether their concern to be ethical is genuine or merely a marketing ploy. Nonetheless, many such companies echo the criticisms of package tourism made by the NGOs and express a similar commitment to the environment and the host's culture.

They also display a similar disdain for package tourists. Explore, a trekking holiday company, have advertised their holidays as being for 'people who want more out of their holiday than buckets of cheap wine and a suntan'. Dragoman view their trucking holidays as visiting places that have been 'shunned by the masses who prefer resorts and beaches'. Other brochures set out the important role of their clientele in relation to supporting the culture and environment of their hosts in the Third World.

Encounter Overland regard their customers as 'today's custodians of the ancient relationship between traveller and the native which throughout the world has been the historic basis for peaceful contact'. Preserving the environment is an important motif of most tours of this type - most donate a small portion of the price paid to organisations engaged in wildlife and environmental preservation.

Indeed, the dividing line between private tour operator and conservationist NGO can be a fine one. Discovery Initiatives, for example, works with a number of conservation charities including the World Wide Fund For Nature (WWF), whose Director, Julian Matthews, argues that 'tourism should guarantee that things which draw us now should be the same in 100 years'. Discovery Initiatives donate money to help fund wardens and other resources to help bring about this vision. In similar vein Friends of the Earth have tried to encourage agro-tourism in Cyprus as a counter to the coastal Mass Tourism developments there. Conservation International, a wealthy and influential international conservation NGO, utilises ecotourism as a way to win over local stakeholders to the cause of conservation.

They operate their own ecotours to this end. In north-west Bolivia, ecotourists pay large sums to canoe down the Rio Tuichi to stay in stilted cabins on the edge of a lake in the rainforest. Revenue helps to train local inhabitants as guides, cooks and lodge managers, and contributes to Conservation International's goal of rainforest preservation. Such projects clearly involve an orientation towards the eco-consumer, and hence marketing of ecotourism-for-conservation projects is a growing issue for NGOs.

Another example of the link between the conservation NGOs and the commercial world of marketing is a recent venture on the part of Harold Goodwin, well-known British academic and conservation consultant, who founded *responsibletourism.com* as a means of generating markets for ethical, conservation-based tourism products. Many other organisations, such as The International Ecotourism Society and Tourism Concern, operate similar marketing schemes, helping to bridge the gap between conservation organisations and an eco-conscious clientele.

The growing gap year phenomenon is also influenced by the ethical travel imperative. Gap year travel is growing - in 2000, 22,000 British students deferred their university places, and at the time of writing it is estimated that around 40,000 will take a gap year in 2002 (although many do not carry through their gap year plans).

Travel visas for Australia - a favourite for gappers - have more than doubled in the last five years. Taking time out to travel is, of course, not new and need not represent anything more than the desire to see a bit of the world. However, the gap year, and young people's travels generally, are increasingly linked to being ethical - doing good for other cultures and for the environment - and a growing number of Gap Year Companies have emerged to provide just this for young (and not so young) idealistic gappers. Gap year travel is increasingly discussed as a passport to a sort of global citizenship and to better career prospects. In this vein the World Expeditions Challenge gap year company quote the Chief Executive of the Universities and Colleges Admissions Service:

Whatever you might choose to do in your year out, you can be sure you'll not only develop a range of valuable skills, but also have a personally enriching experience, the benefits of which are now widely recognised by universities and colleges. Another gap year company, Trekforce, organise 'adventure with a purpose' for prospective customers.

The projects are focussed on conservation in the Third World, such as rainforest conservation, the construction of a jaguar research centre, work preserving coral reefs in Belize and orang-utan conservation in Borneo. Raleigh International made the news in the UK in 2000 when Prince William took part in a project, which included helping in the building of a wooden cabin in rural Peru.

The much-publicised gap year taken by Prince William and the experience of many others suggest that gap years can be exciting and unique experiences for those inclined to such work. However, the claims to be contributing to these poor societies may be more circumspect. Projects based around preserving the environment are, in truth, unlikely to help in liberating people from poverty. Their ethical credentials seem to come from the *personal* (but very limited) role an individual can play in development, and from a sense of personal mission accompanying such pursuits.

What all the pronouncements from this variety of organisations and individuals point towards is a profoundly negative view of the development of Mass Tourism, and also an appeal, implicit or explicit, for tourists to change their lifestyle and regard their holidays in a different way. It is held that host communities - their environment and culture - and indeed the tourists too, will be the losers if this does not happen.

It is suggested that the tourist also benefits from the New Moral Tourism approach by being engaged in something more meaningful and more enlightening than typical package holidays. The influence of these sentiments constitutes the moralisation of tourism.

MORAL MESSAGE

Some people have questioned the importance of New Tourism, observing that package holidays remain popular in spite of the assault on their ethical credentials. The extent to which Poon and others identify a sea change in the tourism industry is debatable. The World Tourism Organisation (WTO), picking up on Poon's terminology, estimate that New Tourism will remain below 10 per cent of total tourism for the foreseeable future. In both the developed and developing worlds, New Tourism is peripheral. Also, independent travel and tailor-made tours have always been an option for those who did not want to travel with the package holiday companies (provided, of course, that they could afford it). New Moral Tourism is perhaps not really all that new.

There is, however, evidence of a growth in market segments that we might associate with the moralisation of tourism. According to the World Resources Institute, whilst tourism grew by 4 per cent in the early 1990s, 'nature travel' grew at a rate of 10-30 per cent. World Tourism Organisation estimates show global spending on the more narrowly defined ecotourism market increasing at a rate of 20 per cent per year, about five times the rate for tourism generally.

However, leaving aside the newness of New Moral Tourism in terms of *practice,* it is evident that there is much that is new and changing in terms of the *debates* around tourism. Whilst we may not all be New Moral Tourists, the moralisation of tourism profoundly colours the debates about the future of the industry, and how tourists see themselves. The rise in codes of conduct critical guides promoting ethical tourism (titles such as *The Good Tourist, The Green Travel Guide, Community Tourism Guide* etc.) and the increase in campaign and NGO activity around the issues illustrates that the New Moral Tourism is a prominent moral agenda. The weight given to ecotourism in the burgeoning number of college and university courses featuring tourism, and the talking up of ethical tourism in the media, also points in the same direction.

HOLIDAY SNAPS

'We all joke about going to a Costa, meeting the neighbours, eating fish and chips and drinking English beer, and as this concept becomes more pronounced and the Costas lose their appeal, a new breed of traveller is emerging. Going independent, travelling further in to the interior, choosing somewhere "unspoilt", and demanding more: more ethnic experiences, more genuine culture, more understanding of the people they meet. And they don't want to harm the environment they travel to.'

Even large companies have sought to identify themselves with the environmental and cultural critique of Mass Tourism. For example, British Airways sponsored a recent publication, *The Green Travel Guide,* which was explicitly critical of the growth of tourism - ironically, a growth facilitated by BA, Europe's largest airline. Their advertisment in the guide warns us that, 'It's no use being the world's favourite airline if there's nowhere left worth visiting.'

Green campaigners writing in the same publication would undoubtedly blame BA themselves for this state of affairs! STA Travel, a large travel agency catering for the much maligned backpacker and other young travellers, has sponsored a 'Code for Young Travellers' put together by campaigners from Tourism Concern. That a commercial company should be advising their potential customers on what to consume and how to behave is ironic given the dictum 'the customer is always right' - this perhaps should be replaced by '*our* customers are always right' for the purveyors of ethical advice.

Both of the examples given here, along with the adoption of ethical environment friendly Kitemarks, and numerous other initiatives, reflect an impulse within the industry to be self-critical and engage with the ethical agenda.

The breadth of deference to the ethical agenda has resulted in an air of moral authority for the New Moral Tourism - it is often simply assumed we must all agree. For example, in *The Green Travel Guide*, Greg Neale, the *Sunday Telegraph* environment correspondent, informs us that:

Surely we know the damage that modern day mass transport and tourism does: polluted beachlines, once undisturbed hillsides now scarred by the paths of numberless walkers, package holiday jet planes churning out more pollution into the atmosphere, formerly tranquil fishing villages now concrete canyons that reverberate every summer's evening to the beery brayings of tee-shirted tourists. Presumably, resorts such as Torremolinos come into this category - a place that fifty years ago was a poor, dusty fishing village ('picturesque') and now is a fun-lovers', sun-seekers' mecca ('a monstrosity' in the words of this guide).

A key aspect of New Moral Tourism, then, is *advocacy* - new forms of tourist behaviour (or 'tourism practice') are advocated by a range of public, civil society and commercial organisations with growing influence on the agenda. The advocates have taken the moral high ground. Hence whilst much tourism continues as before, there is a certain etiquette that many are prepared to buy in to - the assumptions implicit in New Moral Tourism are rarely challenged.

CULTURAL ASSUMPTIONS

Amongst these assumptions is the question of individualism. Poon clearly regards her New Tourist as more 'individual' - less simply 'following the crowd', a view shared by other advocates of New Moral Tourism. Mass Tourism has long been caricatured as lacking in individualism. The title of one influential book, *The Golden Hordes*, captures the pejorative depiction of package tourists. Another author argues that the growth of alternative tourism is based on a 'search for spontaneity, enhanced interpersonal relations, creativity, authenticity, solidarity and social and ecological harmony', with Mass Tourism seen as running counter to these worthy aims.

Poon, who coined the term 'New Tourism', sees Mass Tourism as being 'consumed *en masse* in a similar, robot-like and routine manner, with a lack of consideration for the norms, culture and environment of the host country visited'. These characterisations present holidaymakers as people clearly lacking in the ability to be discerning in what they buy and what they do. New Tourists on the other hand go for more tailored holidays, suited to their own individual needs.

But because many people like a similar environment for their holidays does not make them any less individual, any more than an adventure tourist travelling to a remote Pacific Island becomes a unique individual. New Moral Tourism makes a rather condescending value judgement of how other people choose to spend their money and their leisure time.

New Moral Tourists are presented as being 'people-centred' - interested in the people and the cultures they encounter on their travels.

By implication, and often explicitly, Mass Tourists are less people-centred - they are, instead, regarded as 'self-centred', living in a 'tourist bubble'. In this vein prominent Green activist and journalist George Monbiot argues that tourists 'remain firmly behind barriers - be they windows of a coach, the walls of a hotel or the lens of a camera'. Whilst holidays are fleeting visits, and the context of a cash relationship is not always conducive to friendships, one suspects that many tourists who have made friends and mixed easily on holiday would question this.

Compared to the Mass Tourists in their 'tourist bubble', New Moral Tourism is seen as an 'add-on' to the tourist experience. One author says that alternative tourism is tourism that 'sets out to be consistent with natural, social and community values and which allows both host and guest to enjoy positive and worthwhile interaction and shared experiences'.

Again, the implication here is that mainstream package holidays are none of these things. The author suggests guided nature walks, bicycle tours, camel safaris, bird safaris and an increase in domestic tourism as worthy alternatives to package tours.

The most well-known marketing typology developed specifically in relation to tourism shares this outlook. Plogg's typology, named after its marketing consultant author, Stanley Plogg, sees tourists as existing along a spectrum, with 'allocentrics' at one end and 'psychocentrics' at the other. Allocentrics are outward-oriented people - interested in people and places. Psychocentrics are concerned with self-gratification - comfort, safety and convenience. It is no surprise that New Moral Tourists are usually seen as Plogg's allocentrics, whilst package tourists are perceived to be psychocentrics.

Whilst Plogg's typology may or may not be a useful device for establishing target markets and selling holidays, his broader assumptions about people are unconvincing. One could argue that New Moral Tourism can reflect a distinct disillusionment with 'people' - family, people at work, people in the neighbourhood and perhaps humanity. After all, is not ecotourism (often at the 'very moral' end of the spectrum) all about eschewing people in favour of a natural high? The New Moral Tourist may be alienated from modern life, seeking respite from 'people' by immersing themselves in nature, or communing with people whose existence is viewed as 'at one with nature'.

This response to the pressures of modern life could be regarded as introspective in that it can be accompanied by a self-conscious search for selfhood. The other cultures and environments avidly sought out by 'allocentric' eco-travellers may comprise a stage for this working out of this modern angst. The Mass Tourist, on the other hand, enjoys conviviality, crowds ... people.

So which of the two are 'people-centred'? In fact it is possible to reverse some of Plogg's assumptions and arrive at a typology that is at least as convincing as Plogg's own. Whilst the New Moral Tourist may be self-consciously allocentric, perhaps it is the mass package tourist who can lay claim to being more 'people-centred'. The New Moral Tourist, on the other hand, subscribes to the Romantic notion that the self is to be found not in society but in solitudinous contemplation of nature.

Also New Moral Tourists are 'thinking tourists', concerned with the culture and environment of their hosts. Their 'mass' counterparts are caricatured as unthinking and blind to both the damage they do and the better time they could be having if only they would adopt more ethical practices.

For my honeymoon in 1997 we stayed in a flat on Mijas Costa on the Costa del Sol for a fortnight. We had a wonderful time, dividing our holiday between the coastal resorts and towns and villages inland. On returning, a workmate asked me where we had been. 'Southern Spain' I replied. The Costa del Sol sounded a bit common. Whilst Costa del Sol evokes 'crude mass tourism', Southern Spain evokes 'culture'.

'Oh, whereabouts? Did you go to Granada?' Horrified at my lack of cultural capital, I searched for an answer that would keep me in the camp of traveller, and out of that of Mass Tourist. 'Well, we stayed in Mijas - beautiful little place set back from the coast. Lots of tourists, but even more character.' 'Oh how lovely - we've been there, too.' Phew, I thought. My credibility teetered on a knife edge, but I'd come through it. 'We even went to a bullfight ... errr ...'. I floundered as I realised that for the 'thinking' tourist, bullfights are not 'culture' but barbarism.

One author refers to the way tourists are typically

referred to in the third person, and commonly regarded as 'lemmings'. 'We do not know why mass tourists move, but we do know that, at certain times of the year, they all start moving - and we have a fair idea of the destination.' It is in this fashion that the advocates of ethical tourism regard their 'unethical' counterparts - acting as an unthinking mass. But because some people do not engage with the moral tourism agenda, and are not preoccupied with ethical issues related to their consumption of leisure travel, does not make them any less 'thinking'. It may be that they do not consider a holiday as a vehicle for doing good (or bad for that matter).

Whether New Moral Tourism makes us think is debatable anyway. One author suggests that the interpretation of eco-sites should 'seek(s) to reveal meaning and stimulate a cognitive and emotional response. This response should impel people into reconsidering their value base and behaviour.' Eco-holidays and various other niches focussed on 'nature' and 'culture' explicitly share this educative aim. However, the meaning we are to have revealed to us is simply assumed to be the overriding value of the natural environment and the richness of cultural diversity.

It is simply assumed that our 'value base' needs shifting in the direction of reverence for our host's way of life. UN advisor Hector Ceballos-Lascurain, often credited as the originator of the term 'ecotourism', echoes this preachy character of New Moral Tourism: 'The person who practices ecotourism will eventually acquire a consciousness that will convert him into someone keenly interested in conservation issues.'

If education is the aim, the focus on the culture of the host society may actually create a barrier. A typical view is that of the Managing Director of travel company Concerning India: 'I do not claim to understand India, only to enjoy and respect its many virtues ...'. 'Respect' is often invoked in the advocacy of New Moral Tourism to indicate a deference to the culture of the host community. 'They' are deemed so different to 'us' that we cannot know them or make judgements about their society, we can only respect the differences that define us. What we actually learn through this deference is questionable - presumably to claim to be able to understand the history or culture of places visited would run the risk of being accused of cultural arrogance or a lack of 'respect'.

The barrier to education is strengthened by the implicit message of New Moral Tourism to consider one's insignificance in the face of the vast expanse of nature, or the fascinating but bewildering experience of cultures different from one's own. We are encouraged to contemplate the limits of rationality and progress in favour of a celebration of nature and contemplation of spirituality - this is central to the philosophy of ecotourism, the principal moralised brand of leisure travel.

There is little room here for critical insight. Even in its own terms of reference - the need to be more informed on our travels about people and places - New Moral Tourism is a stifling etiquette that presents a barrier to discovery.

Two dozen British tourists paid £250 each to take part in Explore Worldwide's Nile Clean-Up Trip in Egypt, picking up dirty toilet paper. Explore Worldwide brochures promise 'the opportunity to meet ethnic or tribal peoples' (Explore Worldwide).Discover the World suggests travel can be 'tainted with unease' and it promises packages that can be 'enjoyed with a clear conscience'. (Discover the World).

The stated purpose of the Earthwatch Institute's Amazonian Cultural Traditions volunteering holiday is to record the rich oral traditions of the people of Pirabas 'threatened by the cannonade of modern culture, namely television' (Earthwatch Institute).

MORAL OR MASS

Many of the cultural assumptions of New Moral Tourism, then, are expressed through distancing these new forms of tourism from mass, package tourism. Responsible tourism, ethical tourism and new tourism - these labels, whilst broad, clearly suggest the previous existence of irresponsible tourism, unethical tourism and old tourism (Mass Tourism), and are attempts to counter these with more moral products. In fact, it may be more useful to consider New Moral Tourism in terms of what it is not, rather than trying to pin down what it is.

New Moral Tourism is defined *against* Mass Tourism - according to one author it originated in 'a worldwide reaction against mass tourism'. A slightly less categorical assertion, although expressing a similar sentiment, comes from two prominent authors in the field: 'By the 1990s, there is a sense that the public has become "tired" of the crowds, weary of jetlag, awakened to the evidences of pollution, and in search of something new.'

The stereotypical associations of tourism in its mass form - crude, homogenous, insensitive to hosts, involving resorts that alter the landscape, crowded, frivolous - are railed against by the advocates of a New Moral Tourism.Hence New Moral Tourism and Mass Tourism can be seen as a series of oppositions.

For the new moral tourist, mass tourism is characterised by:

- *Sameness*: It does not involve experiencing cultural differences, being based around a mass-marketed and consumed product in resort complexes, purpose-built for tourists.
- *Crudeness*: It involves a lack of self-restraint - alcohol, sex and sunbathing, perhaps in excess.
- *Destructive*: Mass tourism is deemed to be destructive in two senses.

It is seen as paying scant regard to the environmental consequences of tourism. It is also held to involve the imposition of the tourist's culture on to the host, as the former has little interest in the latter. They are there as self-seeking/ pleasure-seeking subjects.

In contrast to this New Moral Tourists associate themselves with:

- *Difference*: The new moral tourist wants to experience cultural and environmental difference and to encourage and sustain that difference. This is done for altruistic motives - Mass Tourism is seen as being bad for the host - but also through a certain deference to the host culture which is held in esteem.

- *Cultural sophistication*: The new moral tourist takes the trouble to learn about the host's culture and language. Aware of the importance of cultural difference in the host-tourist encounter, the New Moral Tourist adopts a cautious approach, and is sensitive with regard to their behaviour.
- *Constructive*: The new moral tourist, where possible, will try to be constructive with regard to local cultures and environments.

This will involve, for example, buying craft goods from local traders rather than souvenirs (possibly mass-produced, using imported materials) as such goods encourage the preservation of the local culture rather than support a western one. New Moral Tourists may themselves get involved with activities to preserve and sustain a particular way of life, through work on projects, although such assistance may also be in the form of financial support for NGOs and charities, which is sometimes included in the tour cost.

We have, then, two tourism types, the latter opposed to the former:

Mass tourism	New moral tourism
Sameness	Difference
Crude	Sensitive
Destructive	Constructive
Modern	Critical of modern 'progress'

These oppositions may be schematic, in that tourism could rarely be characterised as either one or the other. Nevertheless they are the ideological parameters within which tourism discourse, and the self-understanding of the New Moral Tourist, lies. This 'ideal' New Moral Tourist is not a straw man. He encapsulates an important trend that has come to influence how we understand tourism.

The New Moral Tourism defines itself against its Other, Mass Tourism. Here, Mass Tourism is more than a reference to numbers of tourists - it is also, and more crucially, about a *type* of tourist, and a particular type of person. The use of the term 'mass' in the context of Mass Tourism, when not used in a purely descriptive sense, tends to carry pejorative connotations. Mass Tourism is an exemplar of mass consumption in modern, industrial, mass society, and mass consumption is eschewed by the New Moral Tourist.

'The code of utilitarian pleasure means we have to evaluate our vacation time by what we have accomplished - what did we learn, what spiritual or emotional breakthroughs were achieved, what new sensations were experienced? And the only way we can award ourselves points is by seeking out the unfamiliar sights, cultivating above-average pleasures. Therefore Bobos go to incredible lengths to distinguish themselves from passive, non-industrious tourists who pile in and out of tour buses at the old warhorse sights.

Since the tourists carry cameras, Bobo travellers are embarrassed to. Since tourists sit around the most famous squares, Bobo travellers spend enormous amounts of time at obscure ones watching non tourist oriented pastimes, which usually involve a bunch of old men rolling metal balls.'

It is instructive to consider briefly the usage of the term 'mass' in this broader context. Ideas of mass society developed in the latter half of the nineteenth century. They reflected the reality of industrialisation, large conglomerations of people in cities and an attendant fear of the masses - especially when they were organised and politicised. Uses of the term 'masses' at this time carried negative connotations.

Generally, the term was used to describe the multitude of 'common' people, perceived as lacking in education, cleanliness and civility. A further association was with disorder - the mass could easily become the rioting mob, acting without recourse to rationality. Finally there was a paternal element to elite conceptions of the masses - they lacked civility, and were therefore in need of civilisation and culture.

These ideas were reflected in the view of early package tourists in Britain and elsewhere. Thomas Cook's first tours were temperance trips, promoting the virtues of abstinence and Godliness. Cook himself held a paternal view of his customers, and he was quite prepared to comment on what he considered their uncouth behaviour. In turn, Cook's critics castigated him for enabling the 'uncultured' masses to partake of leisure travel.

The association of mass with a new type of social form, mass society, was first made by Herbert Blumer in the 1930s. For Blumer, mass society was the object, not the subject of society. The ability of the masses to think critically and act rationally came a poor second to the sense that they were *acted upon*. Mass culture makes us, rather than the other way round, is the logic of this conceptualisation.

The masses lack individuality - they are not the rulers of their own destiny, but dupes of voracious advertising. Blumer's view of mass society, whilst it is contested, is important in shaping the post Second World War conception of mass consumerism, and it is a strong undercurrent in the criticisms of modern Mass Tourism.

New Moral Tourism is, then, a crusade against a particular characterisation of Mass Tourism, and the Mass Tourist. Raymond Williams' comment that 'There are no such things as masses, only ways of seeing people as masses' is pertinent. The mass can also be considered the many with a common goal - either threatening or worthy of championing. In the past negative conceptions of the masses would have been contested by political movements and trades unions that stood for the masses, or tempered by a sense that growing affluence for the masses was a sign of progress. Cook himself defended his tours from the critics on this latter basis. However, today, in the absence of a common goal, and without the sense that more opportunities for people to travel is part of human progress, they can be presented as a homogenous, unthinking mass, patronised and talked down to by the self-appointed spokespersons of new, ethical tourism.

ANTI-MODERN MORALS

As well as a slight on tourists, New Moral Tourism also

stands against modernity and transformative economic development.

In the view of the New Moral Tourism advocate, for 'transformative', read 'destructive'. The places most often characterised as having been destroyed by Mass Tourism are the Spanish Costas - especially the Costa del Sol. From the Monty Python comedy sketch featuring 'Brits' abroad drinking Watneys Red Barrel and singing 'Torremolinos' to the predictable disparagement from Rough Guide and Lonely Planet guidebook authors, the Costa del Sol has long been stereotypical Mass Tourism.

One author asserts an unequivocal view of Mass Tourism developments such as those in the popular Mediterranean resorts:

The building of high-rise hotels on beach frontages is an environmental impact of tourism that achieves headline status. This kind of obvious environmental rape is now less common than it was during the rapid growth periods of the 1960s and 1970s.

The high-rise represents mass society - catering for many people, a common standard of accommodation, and the beach front represents a natural encounter between the land and the sea. The latter is sacrosanct for the critics. It is worthy of note that this characterisation of high-rise hotels conveniently located for the beach as 'rape' is not the assertion of environmental campaign literature, but appears in the most widely read textbook on the tourism industry.

Another commentator on the tourism industry makes a similar point in relation to the development of tourism in the Algarve in Portugal:

This frenzied activity is how it must have been in the South Wales valleys at the start of the industrial revolution: endless digging, building and labouring. In those days the commodities were coal, iron and steel. In the Algarve today they labour for tourism. But the results are similar. Clifftop by clifftop, beach by beach, valley by valley - the natural beauty of the countryside is being eroded. No dark satanic mills or slag heaps, perhaps, but the landscape here is being disfigured just as badly by tower blocks of hotels and apartments.

Not only does this author bemoan 'disfigurement' (like 'rape', implying that nature has human characteristics) of the environment, without any sense that something may be gained, too, from this, but he distances himself from industrial development *per se* on the grounds that it erodes natural beauty. Such emotive assertions, made without qualification, reflect the 'pro-environment-anti-people' character of the critique of 'old' Mass Tourism. And whilst the Costas are iconic of Mass Tourism, package holidays generally are criticised for their effects on the environments and cultures of the destinations.

The critique of modern society implicit in New Moral Tourism is also evident in the idea of a 'post-modern tourist, or 'post-tourist', invoked by John Urry and Maxine Feiffer. The post-tourist reacts against modernism, central to which is 'the view of the public as a homogenous mass'. Urry argues that the weakness of the working class and the growth of the middle class heighten this 'anti-mass' sentiment.

One could go further. Regardless of the size of the various social classes, however one might define them, it is the decline of *collectivity*, embodied in political projects of Left and Right, trades unions, church and community that may reinforce the type of individualism exercised by the post-tourist. Moreover, postmodernism's rejection of the idea of progress stands against modernity, and mass consumption in the form of Mass Tourism is exemplary of modernity.

An example of the anti-modern emphasis of New Moral Tourism is the UnTourist network, which appeared in Australia in the 1990s. UnTourists are explicitly seeking out the antithesis of the modern societies:

We sought out all the most discerning, untouristy people we knew - the insiders, the writers, the foodies, the fishermen, the sailors, the farmers, the culture buffs, the historians and the savvy locals - they helped to hunt out the best of everything the destination could offer in things to do, see, eat, buy, and in places to stay.

This self-conscious search for the 'backstage regions' - those hidden from the less discerning tourist - is characteristic of the New Moral Tourism.

And this is not simply a question of lifestyle - UnTourism is also linked to 'giving something back' to the hosts:

Mass tourism is about infrastructure (big hotels, souvenir shops, garish promotions and the fast buck) whereas Untourism is about caring for people, maintaining unspoiled environments, authenticity and value for money ... If untourists won't go to places created solely to soak up the tourist dollar, preferring to see and do what the locals do ... there will be less room to spoil what is natural, authentic and/or special about a place.

So for this type of tourist, whom sociologist Peter Corrigan argues are becoming more commonplace, taking a stand against modern values (and Mass Tourism) through leisure travel is good for the environment, the communities visited, and, as a more moral form of activity, good for the tourist too.

SUSTAINABLE TOURISM

Much of the scepticism of previous forms of Mass Tourism development is couched in terms of its lack of 'sustainability'.

As with so many other phenomena - housing, communities, economy, architecture etc. - tourism has acquired the prefix 'sustainable'. Broadly speaking, certain types of tourism have become strongly associated with being sustainable, and others unsustainable. Typically, ecotourism, nature tourism, green tourism, alternative tourism etc., whilst critically regarded, are placed under the rubric 'sustainable', whilst the package holidays that dominate the market are rarely associated with sustainability.

Of course some would argue that Mass Tourism can be sustainable too, and that to focus upon a relatively small section of the tourism market - New Tourism - is to miss the point. But a glance at academic literature, brochures and the literature from relevant NGOs shows that there is a casual association between sustainability and New Moral Tourism brands such as ecotourism that is rarely challenged. This suggests a congruence between the two, at least in the way the term is used.

Sustainable tourism's parental concept, sustainable development, is the aim, apparently, of all manner of organisations, in the commercial world, the public sector and also amongst NGOs. But whilst it is an agenda that is widely bought in to, there is relatively little agreement about precisely what it is.

The most common, underpinning, definition of sustainable development is that established in the UN report *Our Common Future* in 1987, and popularised at the UN Earth Summit in Rio in 1992: 'development that meets the needs of the present without compromising the ability of future generations to meet their own needs'. It is generally seen as a response to previous and current forms of growth, deemed to have put the ability of future generations to meet their needs in jeopardy. Development, it is held, has proceeded apace with scant regard for the environment or for its effect on the cultures of the world. There are, it is considered, increasingly pressing environmental and cultural limits to growth.

The association of New Moral Tourism with sustainable tourism, or the 'moralisation' of sustainable tourism, is not surprising. The breadth of usage of its parental concept, sustainable development, seems to have obscured any coherence - the term can be moulded to fit one's preference. Sustainability has always lacked conceptual clarity, and been interpreted in different ways, and may even be seen as inherently contradictory.

Its contradictory nature comes out of its attempt to reconcile development and the environment, which for some expresses the problem itself, rather than a solution to a problem. Such a view holds that 'sustainability', at least in the way it is interpreted in the advocacy of New Moral Tourism, and 'development' are in fact mutually contradictory concepts.

One definition of sustainable tourism suggests that the nature-growth contradiction at the heart of sustainable development has been resolved here in terms of nature. The definition given by the Federation of Nature and National Parks in Europe is activity that 'maintains the environmental, social and economic integrity and well-being of natural, built and cultural resources *in perpetuity*' (my italics). Clearly such assertions reflect a preservationist emphasis not just with regard to the natural environment but also to culture. It is an emphasis characteristic of New Moral Tourism.

Indeed, rarely can a term have been so overused as the mantra 'sustainable development' - one source notes that over seventy definitions have been proposed. One definition of sustainable development is that it involves the 'management of air, water, soil, minerals and living species including man, so as to achieve the highest sustainable quality of life'.

This amounts to saying that that which is sustainable is, ... sustainable. It leaves unresolved the question of how we judge this, what our priorities are with regard to the environment and the extent to which we are critical or celebratory about previous patterns of development. Hence without irony, institutions and individuals as diverse as George Bush, the International Monetary Fund, Friends of the Earth and Prince Charles have invoked sustainable development.

From this, it should be no surprise that definitions of sustainable tourism have become numerous, too. It also remains a vague term, one that can be used in a variety of circumstances by a variety of people to convey a variety of meanings. It is a term that can easily be moralised, especially in a climate of cultural uncertainty and environmental angst.

But despite the lack of coherence, it is common to discuss the strength of sustainable tourism as being in its assumption that man is indivisible from the environment. It is viewed as a progressive approach, countering perceived arrogance on the part of humanity in its approach to the natural world. However, this seemingly holistic approach, that views humanity as a part of nature, ignores the reality that all human development has involved a greater ability to harness the natural world for human ends.

Upholding this as progressive does not imply ignoring environmental problems, or seeing the environment in purely instrumental terms, but involves a recognition that humanity is a distinctive and dominant part of nature, with the capacity to organise and transform the natural world around human ends.

It is also notable that sustainable tourism has tended to develop increasingly as a *socio-environmental* category, with an emphasis on *people* as well as the effect of development on *ecological processes*. Hence sustainable tourism has developed a profound sensitivity towards cultural change, change in how communities relate to their environments. In the context of tourism, Third World communities are often viewed as guardians of precious environments, and their cultures deemed sustainable on this basis. This view has profound implications for how we view the potential to develop poor societies, whose poverty is defined by a reliance on their immediate natural environment.

ECOTOURISM - AN EXAMPLE OF NEW MORAL TOURISM

As one might expect, given the morally loaded nature of the debate, there is little agreement about precisely what constitutes any of the New Moral Tourism brands. There are many different types of tourism that shelter under the 'ethical' umbrella. Green tourism, ecotourism, alternative tourism, sustainable tourism and community tourism are just a few of these. The plethora of categories confirms that, in reality, there is confusion as to what is and is not new and ethical - what is ethical to one advocate of New Moral Tourism may not be to another.

Ecotourism is strongly associated with being a more ethical form of tourism and is more often than not at the forefront of the moralisation of tourism. The term itself is less than fifteen years old, and since its invention few can agree on a precise definition. For some it is simply tourism to relatively undisturbed areas to appreciate the scenery and wildlife. However, others argue that ecotourism should involve assisting in environmental preservation and developing an environmental conscience - it has a purpose well beyond satisfying the desires of the consumer.

A recent dispute over whether fishing could be categorised as ecotourism, revolving around whether it is 'consumptive' or not (the argument was initially around whether the fish should be thrown back, and subsequently over whether they feel pain) is indicative of the nit-picking principles of some zealous ecotourism advocates. More vitally, the originator of the term, Hector Ceballos-Lascurain, saw ecotourism as a means of developing eco-consciousness. It is hence a market segment with a mission - to educate tourists and hosts to lead better lives, more in harmony with nature.

In their 1989 video 'The Environmental Tourist', the Audubon Society, America's foremost environmental advocates, describe ecotourism not as a particular set of practices but as a 'travel ethic'. This chimes with the notion of tourism as having a higher moral purpose, rooted in what is essentially an aspect of lifestyle. This drawing together of lifestyle, and a certain morality linked to the elevation of a certain sense of culture and nature, is central to the moralisation of tourism. It is the common feature that unites the various niches that feature in the search for a new, ethical tourism. They are united in their trepidation at tourism's (and potentially their own) effect on cultural diversity and on the natural environment, and see what we buy and how we behave as a means of exercising more ethical, moral judgement.

One academic paper on the subject of ecotourism to the Ladakh Farms Project in India argues that, for ecotourists, travel can mean a lot more than a leisure activity. It might form part of a broader philosophical reflection relating to the self and nature. It might involve trying to find answers to many of the problems experienced when living in a westernised, industrialised country.

The authors quote the following personal communication to illustrate this:

Many people who have spent time in this ancient culture have found it a life-changing experience. They have come away with a recognition that a life closer to nature is not necessarily one of back-breaking toil. They have been inspired by a new faith in human nature and have often left Ladakh with renewed optimism about the possibility for change in western society.

Visitors to the project, run by the International Society for Ecology and Culture, are encouraged to work and raise the status of subsistence agriculture. According to its advocates, visitors

have an important role in demystifying the image of the luxury and leisure filled lives that people experience in so-called 'developed' countries. Visitors are expected to educate themselves to educate their hosts through reading *Ancient Futures: Learning from Ladakh* by Helen Norberg Haydn.

Whilst this is perhaps an extreme example of New Moral Tourism, it nonetheless illustrates a number of its important features. First, the rejection of 'western' development and the moral elevation of rural, subsistence, 'sustainable' lifestyles is a common factor.

New Moral Tourism is in this sense part of a broader critique of modern society that morally elevates tradition above development as a response to the perceived destructive nature of the latter. However, an irony in the Ladakh Project is that, as the project admits, the crisis arises in part because many younger members of Ladakh society are/heading for the towns and cities, presumably less impressed with the benefits of a rural, 'sustainable' life than their western advocates.

Second, the ecotourist seeks enlightenment from the experience. The learning of profound truths, absent in developed societies that are considered superficial, makes ecotourism enriching for the tourist in the view of New Moral Tourism. Whether enlightenment equates to education is doubtful. It would seem that the reverence and 'respect' for tradition provide an obstacle to a critical examination of the grinding poverty of the people of Ladakh.

Third, the Project hopes to enlighten others as to the benefits of a life closer to nature. In this case this applies not only to other prospective tourists, but also to the local people themselves, including those voting with their feet and leaving for the cities. New Moral Tourism, then, is not simply another choice for prospective tourists, but is advocated as a more moral form of behaviour for all of us.

Tourism is becoming increasingly moralised. On the one hand, certain types of tourism, and tourist, are considered unethical, as they fail to recognise a *particular* notion of environmental and cultural risk. On the other, the new, ethical alternatives are seen as not only better from the perspective of the host societies, but also better for the tourists themselves. Consumer choices over what kind of holiday one prefers are transformed into moral choices, seen as having significant consequences for one's host, and also for oneself.

Whilst it is the case that distinct 'new tourism' markets remain relatively small, the moralisation of tourism is a pervasive, fluid agenda, colouring the way we see contemporary leisure travel. It casts a shadow over the growth of leisure travel, a growth that one may have assumed would be viewed in more upbeat fashion. It also questions the notion of innocent fun, traditionally associated with holidays. Simply pleasing oneself has become moral terrain.

Chapter 2

New Moral Tourism

The claims of certain forms of tourism to be more moral are not only rooted in the ideological developments referred to. They are also reflected in the conception of nature-based, culturally sensitive tourism as an exemplary development tool, especially in the Third World. Mass Tourism's impact on development is deemed to be disappointing and highly problematic from a cultural and environmental perspective.

It is considered that New Moral Tourism types, however, such as ecotourism and community tourism, are able to bring together the previously antagonistic goals of development and conservation. This chapter examines the claims made for New Moral Tourism in the field of development.

NEW MORAL TOURISM AS DEVELOPMENT

It is widely argued that whilst Mass Tourism has brought problems in its wake, new types of tourism such as ecotourism and community tourism are beneficial with regard to development in the Third World. The claims that these types of tourism are ethical are based on their professed capacity to meet conservation aims whilst providing benefits for communities.

Ecotourism, community tourism, nature tourism and so on are not only part of the etiquette of the New Moral Tourism movement but have become the focus of various NGOs and campaigns, new and old, to achieve this goal, especially in the world's poorer countries. They attract considerable aid funding through governmental and supragovernmental aid organisations too.

The tourism-for-conservation agenda is an important one. *The Green Travel Guide* argues that, 'tourism can be a powerful force for conservation' and notes that there are more than 5,000 national parks, wildlife sanctuaries and reserves around the world today, many depending on tourism for financial support. USAID, the aid arm of the United States government, for example, use ecotourism as a strategic tool for 'environmentally responsible development' in more than a dozen countries.

Conservation International, a big and wealthy player in international conservation, utilise it in seventeen out of the twenty-five countries in which they operate. In the UK the Department for International Development run a scheme promoting what they refer to as 'pro-poor tourism', aiming to help the very poorest in rural parts of the Third World by attracting tourists appreciative of the undisturbed environment.

Such an approach is now commonplace within the NGO and aid world. NGOs, scientific organisations and conservation organisations, such as the WWF, Nature Conservancy, the Audubon Society, the Sierra Club and the Earthwatch Institute promote ecotourism for similar reasons. It extends to smaller campaigns and NGOs, too. The US-based International Eco-Tourism Society propose ecotourism as a boon to Third World countries threatened by what they perceive to be harmful development. Ecotourism, they believe, can achieve both conservation and development, two goals often considered to be antithetical. Similarly, influential campaign Tourism Concern see community tourism as an ethical alternative to what they regard as damaging Mass Tourism.

The conservation-oriented NGOs especially have tended to benefit from what has been termed the 'greening of aid' - the tendency to attach environmental conditions or emphasis to Third World aid. They are also considered characteristic of a growing 'civil society', having grown greatly in number and in influence. They have acted as powerful vehicles for the transference of environmentalist thinking into the arena of development policy, and it is here that nature-based tourism is considered innovative.

TOURISM AND ENVIRONMENT

How can tourism, castigated as a problem, and even as imperialism, in its 'mass' form, become advocated as a solution in its 'new' forms? One author answers this succinctly in a paper titled 'Tourism and Natural Heritage, a Symbiotic Relationship?'. Harold Goodwin argues against the view that tourism, like any other industry, is likely to be in conflict with the natural environment. Rather, he argues, it has a special role to play in development.

Nature tourism, depending as it does on a desire to experience areas of perceived natural beauty and distinction, can provide funds to manage and maintain these areas. Consumers may be prepared to pay considerable amounts of money in order to experience 'untouched' environments. This money can then be used, in part, to encourage people local to the area to co-operate in the conservation of their environment.

This perspective is important as it questions, as Goodwin points out, the perception that there is necessarily a tension between development and the environment. Put simply, some may see industrial development as vital for creating jobs and wealth, whilst others may point to the environmental impact of such development.

Prioritising one means neglecting the other - a 'win-lose' scenario. Tourism, it is argued, is one form of development that can go some way to resolving this tension - if it is the right kind of tourism, managed in the right way.

(from questions and answers on ecotravel, from US conservationists the Audubon Society's 'The Ethics of Ecotravel')

Question: There's a boom in ecotravel and adventure travel. Should we visit wild places, or should we leave them alone?

Answer: There are fragile environments, such as areas of the Amazon, Alaska, or Siberia, that have never supported much human life and should be zoned for no visitation. But it's another story in places that are already inhabited. These areas are going to be developed one way or another. Americans need to understand that the world's population is increasing and that international environmental destruction is happening at an alarming rate. We can't tell local people that they can't profit from their own natural areas, and tourism represents a far nicer alternative than, say, logging or strip mining.

Question: What about the impact we have on local people?

Answer: We may feel guilty about visiting a place, but thousands of people are literally begging for ecotourism to come to their areas. The money that is generated goes a long way. More important is that once the people see how much we care about their place and how they can benefit from that, keeping it wild becomes more important to them as well. Every member of Audubon is an emissary for conservation.

Hence tourism is sometimes suggested as a less damaging form of development by environmentalists who fear the Third World may be committing 'ecocide' through logging or other activities that use up natural resources in their struggle to survive. For NGOs and governmental agencies concerned with the environment *and* development, it provides an apparent solution; or in the words of USAID a 'win-win' situation. The community can earn money from tourists appreciative of the natural environment, and this money can support the community in their existing way of life.

The direct benefits to the local populations concerned may include the opportunity to work in conservation, salaries paid from aid funds, revenue from ecotourism, and sometimes infrastructural benefits such as schools and medical facilities.

The material benefits are evident. In a sense it is true that everyone wins - the environment is preserved, and local people benefit. The 'UN Year of Ecotourism' in 2002, marks the growing prominence of this strategy.

Table. Examples of Projects Supporting Ecotourism as a Means Towards Integrated Conservation and Development.

Country	Name of project	Donors involved	Special features
Belize	Rio brave conservation and management area	Various american and british donors, private sponsors	Education and research-related ecotourism successfully managed by an NGO (Programme for Belize)
Brazil	Proecotour	Inter american development Bank (IDB)	Large-scale ecotourism programme covering the entire Amazon, financing infrastructure, private investments, marketing studies, private sector capacity building (in preparation)
Honduras	Ecotourism development in protected area system	UN development programme (UNDP)/global environment facility (GEF), world bank	Area selection according to tourism potential; ecotourism facilities, training and promotion, NGO capacity building
Central America	Promotion of sustainable development through tourism (FODESTUR)	German Agency for Technical Cooperation (GTZ)	Facilitation of regional stakeholder co-operation and creation of regional ecotourism routes (Ruta Verde)
Cameroon	National ecotourism strategy	German Agency for Technical Cooperation (GTZ)	National ecotourism strategy focussing on stakeholder participation, protected areas and local communities (in preparation)
Namibia	Namibian community based tourism Association (NACOBTA)	Swedish international development cooperation agency (SIDA), worldwide Fund for Nature (WWF)/US agency for International development (USAID), various European donors	Community tourism development based on Communal Area Conservancies; community funds, training and marketing
Tanzania	Cultural tourism programme	Dutch development organisation (SNV)	Development of ecotourism products in indigenous communities near protected areas, capacity building and institutional strengthening; marketing through National Tourist Board

One lauded example of this approach is the aid-funded Communal Areas Management Programme for Indigenous Resources (Campfire) that operates in Zimbabwe. Here limited game hunting and ecotourism are organised for tourists, with the revenues contributing to supporting the rural populations in these areas.

The environment - the wildlife and its environs - are preserved, and the population can benefit through the tourism revenues. Rather than being a problem, then, such tourism is put forward as *appropriate development*; as a solution, in rural Zimbabwe.

It is worth asking the question as to whether this symbiosis is *per se* a good thing in this context. The holistic approach advocated by Goodwin and central to the claims of New Moral Tourism looks at the relationship between people and nature, and makes a virtue out of not separating the two. People, it is held, are a part of nature, and their relationship to it is key to sustainability.

The New Moral Tourism philosophy of community involvement is presented as benevolent to rural populations reliant on the land - they are able to gain some benefits and 'live in harmony with parks'. But why not, in so far as environments are vital (be it for tourism, the economy or science), separate people from their environment? Why not offer them something better than a life close to nature? People are part of nature, but the dominant part. Humanity has developed on the basis of harnessing nature and organising it around needs and wants.

There is nothing moral or positive in encouraging specific groups of people to remain in a traditional relationship to their land, rather it seems to reflect low horizons as to what is possible with regard to development. Surely, it is one manifestation of a narrow development agenda that should be challenged rather than lauded as innovative and even moral.

TOURISM AND CULTURE

And just as tourism can be seen to have a symbiotic relationship with the environment, so too with culture. Local cultures can attract tourism, generate revenue and potentially make those cultures viable. These 'traditional' cultures are typically seen as 'very green' by environmentalists. Advocates of New Moral Tourism engage in a self-conscious attempt to promote the inter-generational passage of culture, in terms of craft skill and religious beliefs etc. There is an unstated assumption that such a project is worthy - that encouraging cultural diversity around the world, promoting local identity, is desirable and very much part of an imperative of sustainable development.

Such cultural tourism in the Third World may be on the one hand simply buying into a desire for 'culture', or a sense of spirituality on the part of the tourist - it can be good business. However, it is considered to be much more than this. It is also held to contribute to the imperative to conserve cultures and cultural diversity.

The relationship of tourism to the environment on the one hand and culture on the other, are really two sides of the same coin. Modern environmental thinking regards traditional, rural cultures as exemplary of more sustainable practice with regard to the environment. By this reasoning, anything that supports traditional cultures is good for the environment and anything that conserves the environment is good for these cultures. Such a perspective is evident at the highest levels of global environmental governance. Principle 22 of the Rio Declaration on Environment and Development states that:

Indigenous populations and their communities and other local communities have a vital role in environmental management and development because of their knowledge and traditional practices. Cultural tourism along these lines has been endorsed at the highest levels of global government. For World Bank President James Wolfensohn, 'culture can be justified for tourism, for industry and for employment, but it must be seen as an essential element in preserving and enhancing national pride and spirit'. Schemes that key into cultural tourism markets in order to engender development often make reference to this broader perspective of cultural conservation or, in this case, 'enhancing national spirit'. However, the relationship between tourism and culture is seen as being a fragile one. UNESCO points to the potential in, but also to the cautious attitude needed towards, utilising cultural tourism in this way:

Cultural Tourism can encourage the revival of traditions and the restoration of sites and monuments. But unbridled tourism can have the opposite effect. Here there is a real dilemma. Is there not a risk that the boom in cultural tourism, by the sheer weight of numbers involved, may harbour the seed of its own destruction by eroding the very cultures and sites that are its stock in trade?

Elsewhere the acceptance of tourism's role in cultural conservation is rather more grudging than cautious. Egyptologist Rainer Stadelman argues that, 'Tourism is already a catastrophe. But we have to admit that without tourism there would be no public interest, and without that, there would be no money for our work.' What is important here is tourism's role in maintaining aspects of culture through *making culture pay*.

Advocates of New Moral Tourism bemoan the demise of cultural diversity due to broader economic and social trends, and see New Tourism, be it sometimes grudgingly, as a way of turning interest in different cultures into a means of encouraging their viability. Tourism is in such circumstances portrayed as a necessary evil.

However, much of the advocacy of tourism's role in maintaining culture is more upbeat than this. One author lists potential positive impacts of cultural tourism: building community pride, enhancing a sense of identity, encouraging revival or maintenance of traditional crafts, enhancing external support for minority groups and preservation of their culture, broadening community horizons, enhancing local and external appreciation and support for cultural heritage.

One important expression of the discussion of culture and tourism's ability to aid in its conservation is the UNESCO list of sites designated as World Heritage Sites. The rapid expansion of the World Heritage list is one result of a profound sense of unease with what is regarded as 'cultural levelling' - seen as the increasing dominance of a homogenous, global culture that sweeps diversity away.

Mass Tourism is seen as complicit in this. These sites are predominantly 'cultural' rather than 'natural' in that they generally relate to the built environment as an expression of human cultures. Towns, villages as well as monuments, buildings etc. can be designated as World Heritage Sites.

Designation can be important, and is much sought after as it can assist in the promotion of tourism to an area - people are more likely to want to visit a World Heritage Site. Applications to become a World Heritage Site if accepted carry an obligation to preserve the sight, and use revenue gained from this status to assist in this. Hence the awarding of World Heritage Status is an example of tourism contributing to the maintenance of important aspects of cultural diversity. As one UNESCO report has it, tourism can 'help keep alive' and even 'encourage the revival of traditional cultures'.

As part of a BBC series on 'Great Railway Journeys', American actor and ambassador for the UN Danny Glover travelled on a train towards Kita in Mali as part of his journey in central Africa.

On the train he met two women traders. One had red eyes through crying - they had fared badly on this trip. She said it as a matter of honour that she was returning empty-handed. She recounted to Glover that she had sons who wanted to go to America, and asked whether he could help.

Glover's trip went on to visit a group of the Doggon people. On seeing the musical celebration of the hunt, Glover commented that 'they have a powerful sense of who they are, and where they come from' even if they were poor.

He watched the Doggon mask dances, unchanged over many generations except that they now attracted some tourist dollars. Glover had a Doggon mask in his American home and felt a connection with the people he was visiting.

Danny Glover's wonderment at the culture he

encountered - his sensitivity and attempts to empathise with his hosts - could have meant little to the women on the train desperate for money, desperate to see their sons get to America. And the Doggon chief explained to Glover that he was fearful that education, not tourism or commercialisation, would put paid to the old traditions.

A clear example of the promotion of passing culture down, one generation to the next, is the UCOTA (Ugandan Community Tourism Association) project. This project oversees the 'Heritage Trail' scheme developed by British charity Action For Conservation Through Tourism (ACT).

It posits tourism as a way of conserving ancient cultures, rather than principally the environment or wildlife. The Heritage Trail is organised around the four ancient kingdoms within Uganda, stressing the diversity within the country and the possibilities for attracting tourists interested in this. Here, the theme is 'making culture pay' rather than 'making nature pay'. Moreover, strengthening and even reviving of cultural identities is an explicit aim of the Heritage Trail.

In is worth noting in passing that the Heritage Trail scheme is in part a reaction to the collapse of the gorilla watching market in Uganda, an activity that had previously attracted aid funding. Gorilla watching, however, has suffered greatly since the tragic murders of tourists near the Rwandan border in 1998.

The collapse of this risky market raises a question over the application of the term 'sustainable tourism' to such a scheme. Reliance on the natural world in this way is often fraught with uncertainties especially in places such as Uganda's borders, where conflicts over resources are played out. Gorilla tourism may have helped to sustain the gorilla population, but proved to be totally unsustainable for the Ugandan economy.

THE RISE OF 'COMMUNITY'

The view that tourism can combine development with conservation of the environment and cultures is significant given the criticisms made of some conservation projects in the past. For example, in 1994, the World Wide Fund For Nature (WWF) used the slogan: 'He's destroying his own rain forest. To stop him, do you send in the army or an anthropologist?' in a fund-raising advertisement. This approach was rightly criticised for its assumption that 'the west knows best' with regard to the value of the rainforest, and its assumption that the solution lay with the outside expert rather than the local population. One NGO, Survival International, pointed out that this slogan implied a 'nature first' approach, with local people pushed into the background.

A further example is that of the wildlife sanctuary developed in the Ngorogoro crater in Tanzania in the 1980s. Here the nomadic inhabitants of the crater, the Masai, were pressured and offered inducements to leave the crater, and they agreed to leave to live on its edge. They subsequently found it difficult to subsist here, yet were unable to return to the more fertile soil in the crater.

The project responsible for this was condemned by environmentalists and others close to the Masai and knowledgeable about their way of life. The Masai were victims of the conservation-first approach, which left them without the most basic means of subsistence.

Indeed, such criticisms of environmental NGOs are not uncommon. Writing in 1991, one author goes so far as to describe US environmental institutions as tending 'to see environmental protection in isolation from the social context, ... [They] would soon convert Costa Rica's forests into fenced-off Green museums surrounded by starving peasant families'.

The conservation-oriented NGOs, then, have been accused of putting the environment before people; a 'win-lose' scenario. It is in response to this sort of criticism that many of the NGOs have reformulated and re-presented their projects using the language of 'community' and 'culture' alongside that of 'environment' and 'nature'. Conservation International, World Wide Fund For Nature and other major NGOs, previously criticised for a form of conservation that ignored local populations, are now keen to trumpet their community credentials, as are smaller NGOs and campaigns.

More precisely, they explicitly link environmental concern with the wellbeing of the local community. If the environment is conserved, the viability of a rural existence dependent on that environment is also improved. This is, then, the holistic approach adopted by today's NGOs.

It draws together environment and culture, the former being central to the latter for poor rural communities, rather than treating the two in isolation. Nature-based tourism has a key role here in generating benefits for communities derived from conservation.

The clearest expression of the moral authority of 'community' over nature *per se* is the growth of community tourism. Ecotourism, a few years ago the vogue for tourism-for-conservation projects, now has its critics within the milieu of NGOs and campaigning organisations. It is important, they argue, for tourism, as any other form of development, to be sensitive first and foremost to *community* needs.

Today community tourism is considered by many to be the state of the art in ethical tourism. Community tourism has been most clearly set out by British campaigning group Tourism Concern, who see it as 'people first' rather than 'environment first'. Their *Community Tourism Guide* offers a brief analysis of this type of tourism and lists holidays that conform to this.

They define community tourism as that which 'involves genuine community participation and benefits'. *The Community Tourism Guide* goes on to argue: 'It is only by putting people at the centre of the picture that true conservation solutions will be found.'

This is revealing - conservation remains the aim, but local communities have to be brought onside. But what if a community did not want to put the author's 'true conservation solutions' first?

What if they prefer to leave the community in search of more lucrative jobs in hotels and in the cities? What if they view their culture as restrictive? What if they want to break away from the poverty in their community? Community tourism provides answers for conservationists confronted with the accusation that they are only concerned with the environment, but fewer to the question of development itself.

'People first' community tourism puts an emphasis on community democracy - involving the community in decision making. However, democracy presupposes that there are substantially different options for people to choose freely between. .In the poor rural communities where community tourism is mainly advocated, these choices do not exist. Instead agendas are set by those offering aid or investment.

Perhaps we have championing of community tourism abroad precisely because of the sense that community has diminished in the developed world through urbanisation, mobility and globalisation of culture. So why not go in search of the missing elements of the modern existence? Tourists can buy community-based holidays staying in rural villages throughout the Third World.

There is no reason why people should not enjoy this type of holiday, or why it might not be an appropriate development option in certain circumstances. However, community tourism, like ecotourism, is more than a holiday. It has become part of a degraded development agenda that cannot see beyond development as Third World societies living off their natural resources.

The community tourism agenda has been widely adopted by major conservation-oriented NGOs, governmental aid organisations and campaigns. Ecotourism is rhetorically no longer solely about conservation of the environment - there has to be seen to be consultation with and benefits for the local community - 'ecommunity tourism', perhaps? The International Ecotourism Society define ecotourism as 'responsible travel to natural areas that conserves the environment *and improves the well-being of local people*'.

USAID support projects that claim to integrate conservation and development activities in many Third World countries. These, they claim, provide alternatives to encroaching into protected areas to hunt, log and farm. Furthermore, 'a new group of stakeholders with a vested interest in protecting parks' is created. It is clearly important for them to offer benefits to host communities, as 'potential local resistance to setting aside forest and fishing areas for conservation can often be softened by employment and income-producing opportunities Ecotourism can generate'.

This suggests that sponsorship of ecotourism is after all to do with environmental imperatives, and that the small economic benefits to communities are instrumental to this aim - to clear the way for its acceptance within developing world communities.

In similar fashion, Conservation International argue that 'All projects need to integrate the conservation of neighbouring ecosystems with the creation of economic opportunities for local residents ...'. Furthermore, 'the development of an Eco Tourism project depends on building a local constituency that has a vested economic interest in protecting their natural resources'.

Community participation is also sometimes seen as having an educative function for the host population as well as for the tourist. Erlet Cater argues that community involvement 'extends beyond economic survival, environmental awareness and sociocultural integrity to allow *appreciation by the community of their own resources*' (my italics). Ecotourism, then, preaches conservation ethics to host populations, and provides material incentives to back this up. Not dissimilar to this are the Wildlife Clubs established by some NGOs in parts of rural Africa to promote a sense of the value of wildlife conservation amongst children.

WWF: 'tourism to protect natural areas, as a means of economic gain through natural resource preservation ...'

The International Ecotourism Society: 'Purposeful travel to natural areas to understand the culture and natural history of the environment, taking care not to alter the integrity of the ecosystem, while producing economic opportunities to make the conservation of natural resources beneficial to local people.'

PATA (Pacific Area Tourism Association): 'The Eco Tourist practices a non-consumptive use of wildlife and natural resources and contributes to the local area through labour or financial means aimed at directly benefiting the conservation issues in general, and to the specific needs of the locals.'

International Union for the Conservation of Nature (IUCN): 'Ecotourism is environmentally responsible travel and visitation to relatively undisturbed natural areas, in order to enjoy and appreciate nature (and any accompanying cultural features - both past and present) that promotes conservation, has low negative visitor impacts, and provides for beneficial active socioeconomic involvement of local populations.'

It is not surprising that the community tourism agenda, incorporating the language of culture and community, has been taken up so widely by the advocates of ecotourism. It is no more than a subtler version of the same eco-first philosophy. As Tourism Concern's *Community Tourism Guide* states:

If conservationists want [communities] to say 'no' to harmful development, they must offer them alternative means of feeding their families. Tourism may be that alternative. In many places, tourism is a central pillar of emerging alliances between local communities and conservation organisations.

But benefits of this sort come at a price, be they labelled ecotourism or community tourism. The role of poor rural communities as guardians of the environment is, in a sense, reinforced. The choice they are faced with is to accept aid or investment on the terms offered, or not at all. The aid is effectively tied to a particular conception of what these societies are capable of achieving. The relationship of poor, rural communities in the Third World to their environment remains intact, but now this relationship is viewed not as limiting their economic prospects but as a successful example of development.

CAMPFIRE

One of the most discussed, celebrated, and occasionally criticised, community tourism projects is the Communal Areas Management Programme for Indigenous Resources (Campfire) project in Zimbabwe (mentioned earlier). A brief examination of the project reveals the problems and limitations of New Moral Tourism as a development tool.

Campfire was introduced in rural parts of Zimbabwe in the late 1980s. The project effectively encourages wildlife conservation, but on the basis of establishing opportunities for the local communities to benefit from it. The two stated aims of Campfire are: to conserve natural resources in the communal areas; to increase income-earning opportunities in poor communities.

The aim is to make nature pay; to establish the natural heritage as a viable basis for the local economy. Primarily 'making nature pay' is to be achieved by allowing limited hunting tourism, the bounties from which contribute towards community benefits and the control of wildlife numbers. Indigenous hunting is outlawed. Simply, the bounties paid by hunter tourists, it is argued, can generate more value for local communities than the meat from animals they hunt themselves. In effect, then, tourism generates income that enables local communities to live in harmony with wildlife and their natural environment.

A village elder has explained the scheme thus: It is as if we are farming wild animals, but instead of getting meat and skins for them, we get money that the tourists pay to see them. That is why we must look after our wild animals.

Such schemes facilitate some economic development, but one that is based on the existing relationship of the population to the land. Benefits can be delivered, but the limits on these are set by an imperative to maintain the people's way of life defined by their relationship to the natural environment. Hence in a sense development is redefined as working around rather than in any way challenging people's direct dependence on the land.

Like the village elder quoted, we tend to define the success of such development projects by what they deliver to the local populations. In the case of Campfire there is some debate on its performance. However, it is worth also considering what such forms of aid implicitly rule out for that population. The kind of thoroughgoing development that would increase the independence of local people from their immediate environment is discounted as unrealistic or, commonly, inappropriate.

Campfire is funded through a variety of governmental and non-governmental aid agencies. It involves a complex system of administration, the shape of which is itself revealing. The Zimbabwean Department of National Parks and Wildlife Management (DNPWM) works closely with a variety of NGOs including the WWF and the Zimbabwe Trust.

At a national level the Ministry of Local Government, Rural and Urban Development (MLGRUD) are concerned with income generation and are legally responsible for the management of wildlife within limits set by the DNPWM, whose primary role is conservation. At a local level, Rural District Councils (RDCs) play a key role in implementation.

Whilst community participation is well established within the Campfire literature, some have questioned the reality. One report suggests that the aim is 'not to allow local communities to choose what to do with "their wildlife", but to teach them how to manage it in the manner DNPWM sees fit'. DNPWM has the sanction of withdrawing Campfire status if their policy is not complied with.

Campfire is less a case of 'co-management', as claimed, and more a case of 'persuasion'. Ultimately that power to persuade is strong, backed up by the financial authority of the NGOs. It is not fanciful to suggest that poor communities will accept the limited benefits of Campfire on the terms available, rather than questioning this at the risk of cutting off these benefits.

The process is driven from the northern NGOs, their conception of wildlife and the community's relationship to it - it is the western NGOs that provide the finance for Campfire. Whilst it is true that the Zimbabwean government ministry is centrally involved through the DNPWM, there is in fact a special Campfire unit within this department which has tended to bypass local DNPWM offices. Instead, the Zimbabwean trust, an NGO, has set up its own network of regional and local offices which liaise directly with participating RDCs.

One report describes this process thus: 'The general trend in Campfire has been to set up its own set of structures, which operate in conjunction with, but separate from, the existing central and local government structures.' This process extends not only to RDCs but also to wards and villages, which are supposed to set up special ward wildlife committees, including both 'traditional' and 'modern' leaders.

A question rarely posed about this and other such projects is the extent to which they may be establishing lines of authority and finance that bypass and potentially undermine a country's existing structures of governance. For example, USAID have channelled aid directly to the local level, to the RDCs, rather than through the DNPWM at a national level.

If this is the case, it would suggest that Campfire may not be contributing to *political* capacity development, but undermining national sovereign structures. Put simply, if local areas identify with structures other than the Zimbabwean government for sources for finance, this may weaken the authority and efficacy of the government.

Campfire has delivered tangible gains to participating communities. These include the building of schools and health centres. Yet there is also evidence that benefits have been very limited in scope and variable in different regions. Moreover, the basis of the benefits has been to tie rural communities to the task of natural resource management - they effectively receive benefits in return for co-operating and assisting in the management of wildlife. Yet in an important sense it is their relationship to their natural environment that defines their poverty. The relationship between people and their environment is not in any sense transformed, but instead is reinforced, and subsidised, through aid funding and the hunting bounties of wealthy tourists.

It may be argued by some that rural Third World communities have very little other than their natural resource endowment upon which to base their development prospects, but the point is that talking up this sort of development as 'sustainable' or 'appropriate' at best makes a virtue out of a necessity and at worst lowers development aspirations by tying them to the land. Put another way, it may be the case that regions in the Third World have a comparative advantage in 'nature', but this is precisely what defines their Third World status. Organising development around this involves a very limited conception of development.

Another way to view projects such as Campfire is as a form of tied aid. Tied aid has been widely criticised as being as much about supporting one's own economy as benefiting developing countries, as the aid is conditional on purchasing from the donor country. Clare Short, Britain's Minister at the Department for International Development, has spoken out against it. Yet here considerable sums of aid to Zimbabwe are tied, not to purchases, but to a conservation philosophy generated in the milieu of western NGOs, increasingly fêted by western governments.

Advocates of ecotourism and community tourism see such schemes as morally superior to Mass Tourism because of their ability to generate environmentally sensitive development. But this resides on a particular view of development and of the developing world. In reality New Moral Tourism is no more of a solution to less-developed status than more traditional forms of tourism. Indeed, it carries a set of assumptions that may be more limiting to the aspirations for development in the Third World. Zimbabwe has a gross national product per person of around US$ 650 compared with US$ 14,000 for the UK. Championing development on the basis of the existing relationship between people and their environment rules out the kind of transformative economic development that could make inroads into such gross inequality.

'The first Campfire tourism project to be fully run by local communities. Sunungukai, in northern Zimbabwe on the edge of the Umfurudzi Safari Area, consists of four traditional style chalets and offers rugged hiking, fishing, birdwatching and wildlife plus the chance to see Bushman paintings, meet traditional healers, experience village life and buy local crafts. The camp is run by a locally elected committee. $10 per night.'

SOLOMON ISLANDS

The Solomon Islands provide a good example of the 'tourism for conservation' approach. The development charity Oxfam, under their 'Community Aid Abroad' scheme, offers tourists the chance to 'celebrate and preserve the unique biodiversity of the rainforests' and 'enjoy the warm hospitality of remote village communities and share their mountain lifestyle which has evolved in harmony with the rainforest ecosystem'. Ecotourism is seen as an important source of income in this area as it supports 'their desire to preserve, not destroy the forest'.

Of course, the chance to visit the Solomon Islands is one many would relish. However, it seems to be tied here to discouraging the inhabitants of the island from acting in a manner deemed damaging to the natural environment. Aid given on this basis embodies a conception of the Solomon Islands as a bastion of nature, and this view may have implication for how wider developments are viewed; developments that may be deemed destructive of nature.

CENTRAL GHANA PROJECT

Another fêted tourism-for-conservation project is Conservation International's Central Ghana Project. The project received the sought-after British Airways Tourism For Tomorrow award in 1999. Whilst other forms of industrial development, it is argued, may damage the environment, 'Ecotourism continues to be a positive alternative to destroying Ghana's rainforest.

Ecotourism can help create jobs and business opportunities for local communities while building appreciation for a country's natural heritage and culture.' The project includes an interpretative exhibit, 'Hidden Connections', highlighting the biological and cultural connections between the rainforest and people. Yet it is worth asking what this 'natural heritage and culture' actually represents. These 'biological and cultural connections' are presented almost as a natural order of things. It is an order that eschews change and involves abject poverty for the majority.

It would seem that a particular conception of culture is presented, one that is only holistic in the sense that it ties people to the limits of the land and rules out any change in the relationship between people and their land. The aid creates some benefits for some people, but at the expense of defining a large swathe of the country as a 'conservation area'. The limited horizons implicit in this version of culture are all too evident in a country lacking basic industries; a country being forced to live off its natural capital.

BELIZE

Belize is well known as a haven for nature, and has a high profile as an eco-tourism destination. This is not surprising given that well over 40 per cent of its land mass has been given over to reserves and conservation areas, established by wealthy environmental NGOs. These NGOs wield immense power over the shape of the Belize economy - ecotourism figures prominently, as it is regarded as less damaging than the ways the people of Belize made a living prior to the reserves.

One author describes the environmentalists active in Belize as the 'New Missionaries', exuding a moral authority to preserve nature, with the communities on Belize something of an afterthought. The shaping of Belize by environmental NGOs is evident in the relocation of Maya residents to make way for the Cockscomb jaguar sanctuary, with the hiring of a local schoolteacher as sanctuary director as part of the deal.

The US-based Audubon Society, by agreement, established the Belize Audubon Society, which administers eight protected areas established under the National Parks Systems Act. NGOs and environmental groups have played a key role in shaping the Belize economy in an image acceptable to their own ecocentric view.

Having established ecotourism as a key industry in Belize, environmentalists have been able to manipulate eco-sentiment to pressure the Belize government to stop developments unfavourable to the environmental agenda. Some groups publicised the logging of Belize's Columbia Forest Reserve in the US and organised a campaign of letters, faxes and e-mails from 'would-be' tourists to Belize, saying they would be going elsewhere until the logging stopped.

PRO-POOR TOURISM

In the UK, the Department for International Development (DfID) also sponsors a scheme to promote small-scale, sustainable tourism in the Third World. The literature sees tourism as a means of addressing the 'pro-poor' agenda to establish basic needs for the world's poorest people. One of the justifications given for utilising tourism in this way is that, 'Tourism products can be built on natural resources and culture, which are often the only significant assets the poor have.'

This lack of resources defines their underdeveloped status. The pro-poor tourism approach works around this to engender a limited development in rural areas. Such a development can hardly be held up and celebrated; it seems to reflect rather low horizons within the development debate over what is possible.

Indeed, one department workshop paper begins with a quote from the World Wide Fund For Nature suggesting that nature constrains the extent to which poverty can be tackled: 'Sustainable Tourism is tourism and associated infrastructures that, both now and in the future, operate within *natural* capacities for the regeneration and future productivity of natural resources' (my italics).

Yet in what sense are there natural limits in the fashion implied? The limits to development in the Third World are better regarded as *social* in nature rather than rooted in natural processes.

They are a product of unequal economic and political relationships, and more immediately, the burden of debt and the dearth of inward investment and of aid itself. Few in the more developed countries live within limits defined by their specific relationship to their immediate environment in the way the Department for International Development's advisors seem to be advocating here in the name of sustainability.

The pro-poor initiative is also discussed in terms of new benefits for the poor. Of these, 'Economic benefits are only one (very important) component - social, environmental and cultural costs and benefits also need to be taken into account.' One of these cultural impacts is that tourism may employ more women than men, thus creating greater quality between the sexes in the areas concerned. Whilst in the abstract greater equality must be a good thing, the attempt to engineer equality through aid in this way must itself raise some ethical questions.

'Pro-poor tourism' takes issue with what it rightly sees as 'a defensive or protectionist approach: "preserving local culture", "minimising costs"' in the language of sustainable tourism.

Pro-poor tourism seeks to expand opportunities. In addition, it sees itself as a broader approach than community-based tourism, because it also prioritises the links between the poor community and the formal sector. As such pro-poor tourism has much to be said for it as an approach to tackling rural poverty.

However, it too reflects low horizons on the development front. Rather than constituting an attempt to liberate people from the constraints of their environment, pro-poor tourism organises around these constraints. Worthy, perhaps, but hardly an inspiring vision of what is possible.

There is nothing wrong with ecotourism as a commercially viable way of making money. However, as with the DfID scheme, it has come to appear as the form of tourism associated with innovative development, and has been taken up by a variety of NGOs with this justification. When ecotourism is presented as a dynamic development strategy, it is important to point out that it offers relatively little in the way of benefits.

Moreover the outlook behind ecotourism, that views human development only in terms of the pre-existing relationship between man and nature, precludes a discussion of broader developmental needs.

That ecotourism can be celebrated and presented in an upbeat way as a means to development suggests that some have lowered their sights with regard to development possibilities. Real development requires transformation of the relationship to the natural world. Ecotourism development projects take the relationship as it exists and institutionalises it through lines of funding from the developed world.

The projects mentioned are examples of a broader trend that involves New Moral Tourism as a tool in development, or to be more precise, integrated conservation and development. The impulse to encourage Third World states to adopt conservation is far from new. However, the discourse and the practice are very different today from the past.

In the past colonial attitudes to conservation tended to see the west as superior, and as such with the authority to impose its own solutions without recourse to consultation. These solutions included the imposition of national parks and game reserves, in line with the colonial conception of, for example, Africa as a haven for wilderness and wildlife (alongside its role as a source of cheap raw materials and its strategic importance). The reserves served to meet the recreational need of the colonisers. Many of the same 'natural' areas remain a priority for tourism-for-conservation projects today.

Post independence, national parks and reserves were generally not a priority for newly liberated African states that sought to shed Third World status through wide-scale economic development.

Some western environmentalists tried to encourage the Third World to see 'the virtue of living off the income of their natural resources, not the capital'. In many ways, the growth of tourism-for-conservation strategies represents the victory of environmental concern over the development ambitions of many of Africa's post-colonial regimes. One author puts this down to the growing importance of the tourism industry and the growing ability of environmental NGOs such as Conservation International, WWF, Nature Conservancy, Smithsonian Institute and government agencies such as USAID to shift priorities through lines of funding. One could add to this the failure of national development projects in Africa. It is only in this context that 'living off natural resources' can be presented to Africans and others in the Third World in any kind of positive manner.

In contrast to the colonial period, today advocates of New Moral Tourism present themselves as defenders of cultural diversity in poor rural areas of the Third World. Globalisation must be resisted and diverse cultures must survive the modern assault, it is held. The advocates of New Moral Tourism see themselves as radicals, at the cutting edge of development, and are strongly critical of colonial attitudes to the Third World.

Yet their defence of culture and the environment carries assumptions that help perpetuate the inequality established in the colonial era. Indeed, in the name of defending cultural diversity, equality barely gets a look in. The language of diversity has become a bastion against change. Development, appropriate development, is limited to that which is possible *given* existing culture; culture expressing the relationship between people and their environment.

SUSTAINABLE DEVELOPMENT

The nature-based tourism adopted by NGOs is generally discussed as being sustainable, both in its own terms and with reference to Mass Tourism, as it is based on the conservation of natural resources rather than their transformation. It is worth referring to the most commonplace definition of sustainable development - that originating in the Brundtland Commission, and popularised at the UN Rio Earth Summit in 1992, to consider the implications of this.

Here, sustainable development is defined as, 'development that meets the needs of the present without compromising the ability of future generations to meet their own needs'.

In the USA GNP per capita is $29,240 whilst in Kenya it is $964 (allowing for estimated differences in purchasing power). Are the needs of either country's population met? And who is to decide what these 'needs' are? The UN? Or perhaps the World Bank, who service the 'needs' of developed economies by removing greater wealth from Africa through debt repayments than is injected in through meagre aid budgets? This reality - that some people meet their needs by preventing others from meeting theirs - is overlooked.

In fact, there is an emphasis in sustainable development circles on meeting '*basic* needs'. Basic needs - the absolute minimum that people need to survive - are obviously a priority. Ecotourism can provide revenue to help provide for these basic needs.

However, it also seems to preclude going far beyond basic needs, as to do so would contradict the environmental conservation agenda that is at the heart of Campfire and other projects seeking to utilise tourism as a development tool. Needs over and above basic ones may conflict with the priority given to the environment. They would involve transformative change on the scale that is ruled out as damaging to the environmental and diluting of cultures.

NEW MORAL TOURISM'S ECONOMIC CLAIMS

The arguments in favour of New Moral Tourism as a development tool are not restricted to its claimed benign characteristics for culture and the environment. Alongside this it is argued to possess positive characteristics for economic development relative to more mainstream multinational-led hotel and resort development.

Community tourism, ecotourism and related new tourisms present smallness of scale as central to their advantages. Small, more personal and, importantly, locally owned businesses are seen as more beneficial to the local population. Indeed, smallness of scale has always been an important plank of environmental thinking, epitomised by

Schumacher's *Small is Beautiful* written in the early 1970s. In this context it is important to consider the benefits of small-scale tourism.

Advocates argue that it can deliver greater gains to local populations, as it is based within communities and is therefore more likely to draw upon locally owned businesses in accommodation, food, crafts etc. The argument goes that $10 spent within an eco- or community tour will go further than $10 spent on a traditional package.

Formally there is, of course, a case for this. Undoubtedly large, foreign-owned hotels have shareholders to worry about, and have no obligation to reinvest in the areas in which they are based. They typically repatriate much of the profit made and often prefer standardisation to local sourcing. Wages may be low for locally recruited staff, whilst managerial staff from the hotel company's base country may be more handsomely paid. On the other hand, an ecotourist purchasing locally produced crafts directly from the people who made them may be fairly confident that their money goes to local people.

Yet large hotels enable large numbers of people to visit, therefore whilst a dollar for dollar comparison may flatter community tourism, the potential to generate foreign exchange is much greater for more mainstream hotels. Community tourism and ecotourism, by their very nature, must involve small numbers of people (usually in rural areas) and therefore the overall impact is limited.

Also, when the community tourism dollar does accrue to local populations, this is more likely to be in the informal economy, and in craft production. The extent to which this can contribute to development on any wide-scale level has itself to be questioned. Indeed, in extreme ecotourism, based in the wilderness, there may be nothing to spend money on anyway.

Polly Pattullo rightly argues in *Last Resorts: the Cost of Tourism in the Caribbean* that an important limitation of tourism's development potential is its failure to link up with local suppliers. She cites examples in the Caribbean where

Irish potatoes and Florida orange juice take precedence over domestically grown yam, breadfruit, mangoes and bananas. Various initiatives have tried to create more linkages within Caribbean economies, such as the 1992 'Time For Action' initiative of the West Indian Commission. This document urged that 'agriculture, manufacturing and tourism be developed on a symbiotic basis'.

Pattullo identifies a vital point - that if tourism is to have the greatest beneficial effect, then other related industries need to develop. Yet the large-scale transfers of capital needed to bring this about have never materialised. Also, the development of a broader range of industries that tourism could complement in a more diversified economy would require the very things advocates of New Moral Tourism eschew - modern industry utilising modern technology, and on a large scale.

In place of this, New Moral Tourism cites greater self-sufficiency through linkages to the local economy in terms of crafts and 'sustainable' agricultural produce. The latter usually refer to production processes that are economically inefficient and labour intensive. Stephen Page points out that 'the more self-sufficient an economy, the greater the revenue retained', and hence the greater the multiplier - the knock-on impact of tourist spending. This is true, formally, but ultimately trade is beneficial. It is the basis on which trade takes place that is problematic. Self-sufficiency is not a virtue in and of itself - economies isolated from the world economy are amongst the poorest.

Critics of multinational investment-led tourism development, typically in resorts and hotels, cite a low multiplier effect, lack of linkages with local industries, low wages and a reliance on foreign capital as evidence of its limitations. Yet in a sense these things comprise the meaning of 'less developed' or 'Third World' - the inability to trade on any sort of equal basis, lack of local capital and a capitalist class, lack of auxiliary and complementary industries.

What does the new approach represent in relation to this imperfect state of affairs? In many ways it is more of a retreat than an advance. Tourism development in the past may have carried many limiting features, but New Moral Tourism turns away from development itself.

Mass Tourism is no panacea, but it is an industry, like any other, that can and does improve the lot of people where it is located. It can bring substantial benefits to developing economies. One (rare) author prepared to explicitly defend Mass Tourism cites the Dominican Republic, that has in the last twenty-five years built a tourism industry based on all-inclusives, as an example.

All-inclusives are, for New Moral Tourists, the worst, least ethical forms of tourism as they are large scale and focus on the comforts of the guests rather than the needs of the environment or community directly. But because of their large scale and orientation towards the market they attract many tourists - some 2.6 million in 1999, generating US$ 2.5 billion in revenue and 140,000 direct jobs. This represents around 15 per cent of GDP and 30 per cent of export earnings in the Dominican Republic.

No one would argue that tourism in the Dominican Republic is about to transform this poor country. However, the country is a lot better off with than without its Mass Tourism industry. Moreover ecotourism can provide nowhere near the same levels of foreign exchange earnings or job creation.

One might also cite The Gambia as a country that has benefited from Mass Tourism. The Gambia receives around 85,000 international tourists annually, with tourism accounting for about 11 per cent of GDP and some 7,000 jobs directly and indirectly. In the absence of regular scheduled services, the regular charter holiday flights have created an important transport link with knock-on effects on the economy.

Yet opposing the hotel-based all-inclusive holiday developments commonplace in The Gambia has become a *cause célèbre* for western advocates of New Moral Tourism, concerned over the corrosive impact on culture as well as the limited economic effect. Gambia remains amongst the poorest countries in Africa, but it is likely it would be poorer still if tourism development had been subject to the restrictions desired by the New Moral Tourism lobby.

Mass Tourism has played a significant role in generating development in countries such as Spain. There, broader industrial growth and the integration of Spain into the world economy in the 1960s and 1970s set the context in which revenue from tourism contributed to the transformation of the Spanish economy.

Such positive contextual factors are not evident in the Dominican Republic today. This suggests that it is the broader context of the Dominican Republic that limits the effect of tourism development, rather than the type of tourism itself. Broader economic and political factors determine the possibilities, or lack of them, for tourism to contribute to economic transformation.

It is difficult to accept that small-scale tourism has anything significant to offer the development agenda. In attempting to improve on the development performance of the traditional sector, community tourism simply replaces old problems with new ones - high leakages are replaced with low foreign exchange potential. More importantly, in reacting to the injustices evident in the way large multinational businesses operate, the advocates of New Moral Tourism turn away from substantial developments towards those that create few 'negative impacts'. The problem is that they succeed in producing few positive ones either.

Impacts are generally interpreted in a negative fashion anyway by the New Moral Tourism - environmental change is interpreted as environmental destruction and cultural change is seen as being in a negative direction. Moreover, the negative consequences accruing to some people in the course of tourism development are customarily elevated above the positive consequences of tourism-led development for many others.

One report reminds us of 'the many dangers that lurk behind the cash that travellers inject into the world economy', and that it 'wreak[s] havoc with local cultures and environments'. Development based upon tourism undoubtedly brings uncertainties and insecurities, leaves some as winners and others as losers and creates problems with regard to the environment - although havoc is surely too strong a word.

However, alongside the 'havoc' come new opportunities. Development is both a process of destruction and creation simultaneously. New Tourism advocates focus on destruction, and fails to recognise the benefits accruing from development.

Finally, it is worth stressing that this conservation agenda that purports to offer development through nature-based tourism is rarely a matter of free choice for Third World countries. North-South relations are characterised by an intense inequality in political and economic life. Third World debt and the fortress approach to travellers from the Third World coming to the west are facets of this. Many of the same institutions championing tourism as a means of achieving 'win-win' - USAID, the United Nations, the World Bank - are the same ones enforcing debt repayments, presiding over structural adjustment programmes and denying access to richer countries to Third World peoples.

Structural adjustment programmes, organised through the World Bank, IMF and United Nations, are a key feature of this inequality. Structural adjustment effectively means that some developing world countries can benefit from better terms on their debt, but that in turn the country must follow a particular set of economic policies. One author argues that the creditor organisations 'virtually control the economies' of many developing countries. These policies in general involve an opening up to international investment and competition. In this way the rich can pull rank on the poorer nations through managing the process of debt repayment and debt write-offs.

Of course, this may be viewed as an eminently sensible option. The conditions put on the assistance may be seen as ensuring better governance and greater economic growth. However, it amounts to an infringement of sovereignty. Moreover the debt situation is a consequence of the subservient position of the South in the first place - it is an expression of the subjugation of the poorer nations by the rich. To 'offer' to write off debts in this way is less an act of generosity and more one of imposing one's will using debt as leverage.

Some of the very institutions presiding over this state of affairs are keen to promote ecotourism and conservation generally as a benefit for Third World environments and societies.

The hypocrisy is stunning. The use of New Moral Tourism to promote a more green form of development is advocated by the UN ... yet aid budgets of UN members remain miserly.

A number of prominent conservation schemes operate through debt for nature swaps. These operate on principles similar to the structural adjustment programmes. The swaps operate by large international NGOs purchasing debt that Third World countries owe to commercial banks. The banks will sell at a discounted rate, as they may consider the chances of repayment to be uncertain.

The Third World government then effectively owes the NGO instead of the bank. The NGOs renegotiate the debt on more favourable terms for the country, normally over a longer period and the interest on the bonds now held by the NGO is used to support conservation programmes. Conservation areas established are typically sites for the development of ecotourism of some kind, as a means of making these areas more economically viable. On maturity of these bonds, the principal can act as an endowment for the local NGO operation.

For the conservation NGOs this mechanism enables them to promote conservation in the countries concerned. This is in part a response to the conservation imperative generally, but also there is a concern that pressure to service debt repayments has pushed Third World countries into environmentally unsustainable practices such as logging, clearing forests for cash crops and cattle grazing, part of a drive to produce exportable goods to help the debt situation.

Table. Examples of Debt for Nature Swaps.

Date	Country	Cost $	Purchaser	Face value of debt $	Conservation funds $	Total external debt $
1989	Madagascar	950,000	WWF	2.1m	2.1m	3.9b
1990	Madagascar	2.5m	CI	5m	5m	
1990	Madagascar	446,000	WWF	919,000	919,000	
1989	Zambia	454,000	WWF	2.3m	2.3m	7.2b
1991	Ghana	250,000	CI/SI/DDC	1m	1m	10.5b
CI = Conservation International DDC = Debt For Development Coalition SI = Smithsonian Institute WWF = World Wildlife Fund M = millions/b = billions (US)						

Debt for nature swaps may be seen in the context of the 'win-win' scenario set out earlier - they deliver environmental conservation and some debt is written off at the same time. However, the debt reduction is conditional on a limited transference of sovereignty to the NGO concerned. Also, it is tied to an acceptance of turning over swathes of territory to national parks and other conservation areas.

These areas can generate further finance through ecotourism. Ecotourism revenue can provide the incentive for local communities to support these schemes - it is how, as set out earlier, the NGOs can win friends and influence people. Ultimately, though, the assistance is given on condition that it contributes to reinforcing a pre-existing relationship to the land in rural areas - conservation is the aim, substantial development is eschewed.

The debt for nature swaps shows how the broader inequalities between North and South enable NGOs to establish a conservation agenda in the Third World. The idea that by tagging ecotourism on to conservation in some way makes this a 'development' agenda too is to diminish the idea of development still further.

RE-PRESENTING TOURISM

Tourism is being recast as an arena for moral proscription and critical self-awareness. I have argued that this version of tourism is not a progressive development, as its advocates claim.

Rather, it is a recipe for wariness and personal guilt in an arena traditionally associated with innocence, fun and a footloose and fancy free attitude.

The root of the modern critique of tourism is to see the relationship between people and nature as brittle. Tourism has been a prime target for environmental concern, because for the tourist the environment is often part of what they enjoy, often in large numbers. The tremendous growth of opportunities to travel and enjoy the environment - the beach, warm climates, snow-covered mountains - is regarded by the critics as a threat.

The critique has also moved on to increasingly present the relationship between different peoples, host and tourist, as adversarial. Each is defined by their different cultures, with the emphasis on *different*. There has been a boom in advice for the tourist, presupposing that they require guidelines and codes to negotiate this world of difference. Accompanying this, a dim view is taken of those who ignore the advice and treat a holiday as just a holiday.

The result of this is that tourism is changing, and not for the better. In different times package tourism was more likely to have been regarded simply as a welcome respite from the rigours and proscriptions of everyday life. Today, wariness and caution better describe the sentiment encouraged by the New Moral Tourism. Our holidays have become a vessel into which we are encouraged to pour environmental angst and fears of globalisation. New Moral Tourists travel with a sense of personal mission, as tourism is recast as philanthropy towards the hosts and a 'unique experience' for the tourist.

The ire directed against tourism is misplaced. The growth of Mass Tourism has been a mark of real progress in modern society. Many can travel abroad for leisure when only a couple of generations ago foreign travel was a rarity for most people. New opportunities have opened up as the holiday companies have expanded to ever more destinations. This has not been at the expense of those hosting the growing numbers of tourists.

Tourism to the resorts on the Spanish Costas - for tourism's critics surely near the top of the 'unethical' list - have contributed to economic growth that has enabled the Spanish themselves to travel increasingly as tourists. Indeed, Torremolinos can no longer be viewed as a colony of British lager louts with little thought for locals - a large proportion of tourists late on in the season are the Spanish themselves.

In poorer countries the gulf between tourist and host is more marked. The response to this from advocates of New Moral Tourism is to call for more 'sensitive' tourism - tourism that tries to avoid displays of wealth such as comfortable hotels and cameras. But whilst tourism may bring together people with different access to wealth and opportunity, it did not create this inequality. Get rid of the all-inclusive resorts, the conspicuous displays of wealth and privilege, and poor people are if anything worse off.

It is true that tourism can bring together people of very different backgrounds - the ultra-rich and the poor, the latter perhaps cleaning rooms for the former in some grand hotel. But for the most part, tourists are ordinary people seeking out good weather, good food, fun and perhaps a little taste of a different way of life. It is probably something they have worked and saved hard for. The portrayal of tourists, still today, as rather thoughtless people who contribute to the exploitation of the places they visit, is belittling.

It also trivialises any discussion of poverty and how to tackle it. In fact, the solutions offered up by the New Moral Tourism lobby are less concerned with material wealth and more with cultural difference. More often than not a preoccupation with the latter gets in the way of addressing the dearth of the former (or even seeing it as a dearth at all). Campaigners for New Moral Tourism like to champion the cause of those who have lost out in some way from resort developments. Yet they are reticent to balance this against the many benefits derived from tourism developments. Their agenda is preservationist not only with regard to the natural world, but also with regard to culture. Individuals and their aspirations for a better life are distorted by the preoccupation with an iconic *culture,* cast in china, in need of protection from other cultures, other people.

Whilst the moralisation of tourism sees only the differences between people, we should regard travel, for leisure, for education or for business, as part of a common culture. This is not in the sense that we all engage in it, but that there can be few who do not have the *aspiration* to travel for leisure. Aspiration is important - it provides a link between culture as *what is* and culture as *what could be.* But culture in the latter sense is often obscured by a debate that assumes the differences between peoples as their defining characteristic, even in the prosaic realm of leisure travel.

And what of the backpackers - the tourists who see themselves as travellers? As we have seen, they have in many ways joined the ranks of the package tourists in the eyes of the critics. They, too, are held responsible for commercialising cultures around the world and damaging environments.

Joseph Conrad described the origins of his thirst for travel thus, in *The Heart of Darkness*:

Now when I was a little chap I had a passion for maps. I would look for hours at South America, or Africa, or Australia, and lose myself in the glories of exploration. At that time there were many blank spaces on the earth, and when I saw one that looked particularly inviting on a map (but they all look like that) I would put my finger on it and say, 'When I grow up I will go there.'

The spirit of this passage has inspired many, and although there are no more 'blank spaces' on the earth, the desire to travel remains strong. Pete Smith, a 28-year-old manager for the specialist youth travel company STA Travel, sees hundreds of customers every month buying round-the-world tickets and booking short breaks to every continent. He recalls his father telling him about his one trip abroad, a three-day coach journey to Barcelona.

The Sombrero he brought back still adorns the family living room wall. For Pete himself, New York had a mythical quality in his teenage years - a city synonymous with music and the movies - the 'city that never sleeps'. Yet now short breaks across the Atlantic are commonplace for his customers, and he is planning a trip to the Big Apple. Such is the growth of international travel. My three-year-old son has a Children's Map of Europe from Stanfords Map shop in London on his wall, and has already decided that Lapland, at the very edge of the map (and with a picture of Santa and his reindeer), is one place he would like to go!

The moral baggage associated with travel now threatens to shackle a spirit of adventure for travellers young and old. As travel has become a focus for moral codes, something has been lost along the way. If travel is to really be a 'life-expanding activity', or a 'unique experience' of any kind, then it has to rely on the individual, be they reckless or sensitive, impulsive or well prepared.

Attempts to formalise codes of conduct, and the constant appeals for deference to the interests of the host's 'environment' and 'culture' only contribute to a spirit of caution rather than one of adventure and discovery. Today's young travellers are counselled to be New Moral Tourists - travel is to be wary, cautious and condemnatory of those who favour the resorts.

Tourism looks set to continue to grow. Notably, parts of Asia are increasingly getting the travel bug, and the economic growth to realise the ambition to travel. Even in the Third World, where people's aspirations for travel are confounded by poverty and immigration laws, numbers able to travel as tourists are increasing, be it slowly. How we interpret this growth is an open question. Is tourism to be an angst-ridden pursuit, a necessary evil, something we do but wish others wouldn't (hell, when it comes to holidays, is always other people), or is it to be guilt-free enjoyment? There is no need to make a grand case for package tourism, rooted in some supposed positive effect on tolerance, worldliness or as the World Travel and Tourism Council bizarrely claim in its effect on promoting world peace. John F. Kennedy once stated that, 'Travel has become one of the great forces for peace and understanding in our times.'

Yet to misquote a popular analysis, there have been more people killed in wars since the advent of Mass Tourism than in any other period in history, so Kennedy was wide of the mark. In fact tourism has no great moral claims to be made for it. It is not the aim here to counter the doom merchants with a celebration of leisure travel as the high point of human culture, or a boon to cultural tolerance (although the aspiration and growing ability to travel are worthy of celebration).

Tourism need only be about enjoyment, and requires no other justification. As for the moralising about tourist behaviour, how people choose to enjoy themselves is a matter for them. Some may have a preference for solitude above conviviality, the wilderness above the resort, but New Moral Tourism is disingenuous in dressing this up as having a moral basis.

Of course, footloose international travel remains, globally, the prerogative of the few, not the many. But given the chance, few would choose to stay at home. And whether abroad is Bombay or even Benidorm, that aspiration is something to be salvaged from the angst-ridden commentaries on tourism, and celebrated.

Chapter 3

Authenticity, Tourism, and Self-Discovery

During the summer of 2001, the Tourist Authority of Thailand (TAT, formerly TCT) aired a new commercial to promote its "Amazing Thailand" year. As the commercial opened, a robot sat with its back to a tree in a vaguely tropical setting. Its chrome head nodded a bit, as if it was napping. An icon at the lower edge of the screen identified the location of the forest as "Amazing Thailand." Cut to the robot in a market, the robot dancing in a nightclub, the robot at a Buddhist temple. Its movements are—as expected for a robot—stiff and hesitating, its face is an expressionless metal mask.

Cut to the robot at night on the back of an old-looking boat floating down a misty river with dense forest on both sides. The robot is waving at a group of old Thai villagers who have crowded on to a dock to wave back at it. The robot puts its hands together in a wai (a traditional Thai greeting and farewell) and bows its head.

The villagers return the wai, and as we cut back to the robot, we see that he has changed into a young white man, appearing somewhere between the ages of eighteen and twenty-five, with a backwards-turned baseball cap. His head rises up, and he has a profoundly content expression on his face as he sees the villagers with his human eyes. Cut to a black screen with the logo and slogan: "Amazing Thailand".

In other words, in the TAT advertisement, the white tourist, alienated from his human identity back at home, rediscovers it through a moment of genuine interaction and shared sentiment with a misty and traditional Thai village. He escapes the other automatons and discovers a hidden world whose inhabitants are human and help him to become truly human, although significantly he does not become Thai, but farang. He has not immersed his alienated self into Thai society to become adopted into Thainess, but rather through interaction with Thais he re-asserts his masculinity and whiteness.

Here, I will use the TAT commercial as a starting point to examine the trope of self-discovery in tourist-related literature dealing with Thailand. I will begin by examining theories of tourism and the problem of authenticity, and then go on to look at two specific instances of tourism in Thailand: "ethnic" tourism, in Valene Smith's term, where the tourist adventure is an apparently unironic search for "untouched" tribal areas in the Chiang Mai region of Thailand; and sex tourism in Bangkok, where tropes of rebirth and a rediscovery of masculinity are echoed both in tourist's diaries and in fiction written by and for expatriates living in Bangkok.

THE TOURIST

The foundational works on the ethnography of tourism (not, it is to be noted, tourist ethnographies) appeared in the late 1970s, as anthropology took a turn for the reflexive and self-critical. These attempt to define who a tourist is, and what they do, and whether what they do is ultimately good or bad for the "toured". Maxine Feifer, citing in part the Shorter Oxford English Dictionary, describes the tourist as "'one who travels for pleasure or culture' ... Yet nobody wants to be called a tourist". While I will begin with the tourist traveling for "pleasure," I ultimately want to conclude with the tourist traveling for "culture", more specifically, traveling for self-identity. Through immersion in the other, the tourist seeks an authentic self-image.

The tourist space is one where the rules of work space do not apply: what is appropriate when one is touring is often what is not appropriate when one is working. Time, for the stereotypical wage laborer/petty bourgeoisie, is divided into two poles: time spent working, and leisure time, corresponding to Leach's profane and sacred time, respectively. When on vacation, the tourist is seeking a break from the constrictions that everyday life places upon him: the tourist, when touring, is searching for an alternate identity that can, upon a return home, be reincorporated into the self, thereby offering transcendence.

Writing on the subject of identity, Daniel Miller cites two shopping malls in Great Britain as spaces in which a shopper's "identity is discovered and refined". In his example, shoppers from different ethnic and class backgrounds saw "dual aspects and potentials of themselves" (ibid.) in the products that they consumed, regardless of the class or ethnic orientation of the shopping site: upper-class consumers identified aspects of themselves (a shared Englishness, a lack of pretension, for example) in a working-class shopping centre, and working-class consumers at an upper-class shopping centre saw upper-class potentials of themselves.

In each case, shoppers shopping "outside" their own demographic, rather than feeling alienated, instead drew lines of comparison and commonality. While I do not feel that culture or a tourist experience is "consumed" in the same way as goods in a shopping mall, the formation of identity through consumption is part of the process that occurs with the tourists in my examples from Thailand: tourists identify parts of themselves in the others that they meet and re-flame their own identities accordingly.

The act of tourism, of "doing" Africa, the Middle East, or Southeast Asia, is a collection and expansion of cosmopolitanism for the bourgeoisie tourist. A country visited is a country added to a list of status symbols. But one cannot say one has England under one's belt if all they have seen of the country is Heathrow airport. The robot is not transformed back into the baseball cap-wearing backpacker instantly upon arrival in Thailand.

The tourist must interact with the country in whatever form of authenticity is required: primitive tribes, wild animals, Buddhist meditation, or Patpong sex workers, in a meaningful manner, the tourist must find authenticity and respond appropriately.

THE QUEST FOR THE AUTHENTIC

Tourism and authenticity, especially in the two examples from Thailand I will analyse, are linked. The tourist seeks out the authentic, and despises the fellow tourist who accepts a shallow, "touristic" image. According to MacCannell: "the rhetoric of tourism is full of manifestations of the importance of the authenticity of the relationship between tourists and what they see", and "touristic shame is not based on being a tourist but on not being tourist enough ... on a failure to see everything the way it ought to be seen".

MacCannell argues that alienation in modern labour has dispossessed "modern man" from authenticity, that "modern man has been condemned to look elsewhere, everywhere, for his authenticity, to see if he can catch a glimpse of it reflected in the simplicity, poverty, chastity, or purity of others". In seeking this authenticity, the tourist has a preformed image of what the authentic Other should look like, fed through movies, National Geographic, slides from relatives' travels, and documentaries on PBS or the Travel Channel.

According to Dennison Nash, "Such [tourist] places must be different enough to satisfy the tourist impulse. Such differences, however, must be compatible with the touristic needs of specific metropolitan centers ... [they must show] compatibility with metropolitan dreams". The tourist space is not just an enclave of the, in Nash's words, "metropolitan centre"—the source of tourists—in the periphery—the destination of tourists, but rather a space where the centre's fantasies and constructions of the periphery are embodied by peripheral actors themselves.

Feifer quotes an advertisement in London's weekly Time Out travel magazine: "Mai Hong Song in the golden triangle—opium country—of Thailand, where you can meet both sides in the guerrilla war on a 'trip down the By river, which will make you think you've just changed places with a character from Apocalypse Now'". An authentic experience, therefore, is just like the movies.

But the tourist is aware that authenticity can be faked: the tourist and the industry are locked in an arms race of style, where the tourist reaches for ever more powerful abilities of discernment, and the tourist industry attempts to stage more and more believable displays of authenticity. MacCannell, following Goffman's idea of "back" and "front," gives an entire spectrum of authenticity, based on the "implicit distinction between false fronts and intimate reality".

For example, an airport poster or display would be a true "front" space, which few take as truly "authentic"; a faux-tribal dance arranged at a tourist-oriented dinner (the famous northern Thai kantoke) would be a "touristic front"; a hill-tribe village accustomed to and prepared for the arrival of backpackers would be farther "back" but still prepared for and in some ways arranged for tourists.

Similarly, one could graft a hierarchy of tourists, with package tours at the "front", moving towards lone backpackers, and finally including a hazy zone where ethnographers, expatriates, and tour guides themselves mix somewhere towards the "back" half. Tourists reaching for these more elusive "back" zones often cast themselves as ethnographers, dispensing canny advice or small glossaries of local words.

Both would-be canny tourists and ethnographers pride themselves on being able to penetrate touristic veils to arrive at something real beneath, something which has a bearing on who the tourist/ethnographer actually, authentically, is. It should be noted that when I speak of "authenticity," I do not propose that such a thing is present outside of the perception of the tourist.

In this chapter, I am not proposing that a reified authenticity actually exists; instead, I am discussing the concept of authenticity as it is imagined by the tourist. For the tourist, then, an understanding of true identity of the toured (or the ethnographed), is therefore key to the discovery of the true identity of the tourist. The robot that learns how to authentically wai becomes capable of separating the true from the false.

REDISCOVERING AUTHENTIC HUMANITY

In northern Thailand, ethnic tourism focuses around a number of ethnically distinct minorities who generally live in the highlands. These groups are discursively lumped together in the Thai term chao khao—generally translated into English as "hill tribes". The term chao khao is associated with a homogenizing description that depicts them as being interesting, colorful, but ultimately destructive newcomers to the Thai nation. According to a Chiang Mai-based and tourist-oriented magazine, Welcome to Chiangmai and Chiangrai:

Over 100 years ago, the Hilltribe peoples migrated south from China into what are now Burma, Laos, Vietnam, and Thailand. The six major tribes are the Karen (Kariang, Yang), the Hmong (Meo), the Yao (Mien), the Akha (Ekaw), the Lisu (Lisaw), and the Lahu (Mussur). The main profession of all these tribes is farming, and all of them tend to migrate whenever they feel that the soil at their present location is becoming depleted (Welcome to Chiangmai and Chiangrai, 2004).

The casting of chao khao as destructive (if colorful) migrants is not limited to the tourist literature. Such a representation permeates government policy towards the hill tribes as well. According to Peter Kunstadter: "an equation tends to be drawn [in Thai national discourse] in which 'hill people' equals Meo [Hmong], that is, recently immigrant, opium-growing nomadic swiddeners who are possibly Communist".

According to one Thai guide leading tours from Chiang Mai, the government gives [the chao khao] the land, so the only way they can keep that land is through tourism. The news that the Thai government is graciously allowing them to stay would be news indeed to most Akha, Karen, Lisu, or Lahu villages, especially as some of these groups have resided in the area for several centuries. After being framed as chao khao, a framing that both homogenizes and de-politicizes the group, the diversity within the category can be safely used to market ethnic tourism to the tourist.

The tourist is cast as a cross between an ethnographer and a stamp collector, urged to visit each tribe to understand distinct ways of life, and then receive a sense of satisfaction that they have properly "done Northern Thailand". An online tourist guide to Northern Thailand lists the appropriate tribes to see as well as contributing to the "newcomer" label described above as well a constructing them as being perfect tourist hosts:

Hilltribe peoples migrated over 100 years ago from the southern part of China into Laos, Myanmar (Burma), Vietnam and Thailand. They have preserved their way of life with little change for over thousand years. Comprising seven major tribes, KAREN, HMONG (MEO), YAO, LISU, LAHU, LAWA and AKHA, each has its own distinct culture, religion, language, art and colorful style of dress, these people make their homes in the highlands. The main profession of all these tribes is farming. All the tribes are hospitable and welcome visitors to their villages, providing them with the opportunity to see and experience their way of life (Thailine 2004).

Erik Cohen describes the presentation of hill tribes in tourist-oriented signs and brochures, and lists the characteristics ascribed to them. Most often, the chao khao are "primitive," which Cohen describes "almost as the touristic trademark of the hill tribes".

They are "natural" and "remote", a characteristic of hill tribe villages that is exaggerated by many hill tribe advertisements (ibid.). In short, they are presented in these places as being utterly authentic, representing humanity without modernity, a trait that, for MacCannell, serves as a means of delineating modernity itself: "These displaced forms [of 'pre-modern' peoples commodified for museums] ... establish in consciousness the definition and boundary of modernity by rendering concrete and immediate that which modernity isn't".

If, as MacCannell argues, modernity is ultimately alienating and inauthentic, a visit to the chao khao is an encounter with a person utterly untainted by the world. Except, of course, for the fact that they are not. Villages are connected by dirt and then asphalt roads to local centres. "Untainted" tribesmen may beg for money or tobacco.

Possibly worst of all from the tourist's point of view, there may be other robots along on the journey of self-discovery, for in the touristic experience, as Graburn writes, "to share is to lose power". Cohen describes the dilemma that Thai tour guides to heavily tourist-visited hill tribe villages face: "whether to help in the construction of 'tourist space' and interpret it as authentic, or to admit frankly the existing discrepancies" and then, presumably, suggest a farther-off site.

THE OTHER HILL PEOPLE

As travelers in search of human authenticity in the pre-modern, hill tribe tourists in Chiang Mai display continuous anxiety over the authenticity of tribal sites. Because of the stigma that the label "tourist" carries, such tourists generally refer to themselves as "travelers", "visitors", or, the term I use here, "trekkers". A resource written by trekkers and other tourists more concerned with authenticity, the Lonely Planet travel guide cautions:

Chiang Mai is a good base for mountain treks, and just about every guesthouse advertises treks to visit the hill tribes who live in the surrounding area. You may want to think twice about joining such an excursion if you have qualms about interrupting the traditional patterns of life in hill-tribe areas. This part of Thailand is considerably overtrekked and some hill-tribe villages have been turned into little more than human zoos.

According to Lonely Planet, the trekker is explicitly not interested in a human zoo, and a trekker should only do tourist things if forced: "A fairly touristy Hmong hill-tribe village [near Doi Suthep] is worth visiting—especially if you won't have the chance to make it out to a more remote village—and the locals sell Hmong handicrafts". While the guide suggests that a visit to this Hmong village is better than nothing, the Hmong here do not display "traditional patterns of life". Unspoken is the assumption that neither do the Thais nor do the tourists or trekkers themselves. In Chiang Mai and Chiang Rai, I had the opportunity to speak with several tourists who had recently visited or were planning visits to chao khao villages. The anxiety professed by Lonely Planet was echoed nearly verbatim by many of these tourists, especially the worry over "cultural zoos". In each case, the tourists defended their own actions while in the village or in selecting a tour to travel to the village.

A significant feature of this interaction was the strict avoidance of the term "tourist". As MacCannell writes: "I think it significant that people who are actually in accord are struggling to distance themselves via this moral stereotype of the tourist". In other words, continual distancing of self (as "trekker", "ethnographer", or, as we will see, "old hand") from the label "tourist" is a key feature of tourist identity.

One tourist expressed her anxiety over her own complicity in the commodification of culture, claiming that the village was a "human zoo", and that while she attempted to be (in her mind) respectful, others on the tour did not care about the sensitivities that local people may have had.

Another trekker, who had gone with a package tour, also referred to anxiety over the effect of the tourists on the locals, claiming that while some of them can be like human zoos, the one she was on was one of the "good ones". In each case, the trekker is invested, both monetarily and socially, in the creating of her trip as a positive and restorative one, each trekker attempts to display her ability to distinguish the difference between authenticity and none, as well as her proficiency in acting appropriately, and each trekker displayed her disgust at other tourists who had no such sensitivity.

The robot-becoming-human image is the one marketed for trekkers, and it is the one they have come to find. Even though they largely remain skeptical over whether or not an authentic encounter can take place, many of them, having invested time and money in the travel, allow themselves to feel as though they have achieved authenticity as a state of mind.

Such an authenticity is a reinscription of the self, often marked by the acquiring of a tattoo, jewellery, or even a tribal-language name. This ability to dabble in Otherness requires a subject position that is entirely unmarked: in this particular case, whiteness. The farang tourists can acquire a taste of what they imagine to be an "authentic" life—they can see the real world—and then return to London, California, or Stockholm unproblematically.

As a transition from discussing chao khao tourism to discussing sex tourism, I will address one writer who engages in both. Cleo Odzer, an anthropologist who has written about sex work in Thailand, closes her account of Patpong sex workers with a description of a Chiang Mai-based chao khao tour:

With six other people in my group, I'd trekked for two days into the territory of an indigenous mountain tribe. Wearing ancient dress with beaded headgear; the tribal people welcomed us and taught us folk dances. In an interlaced ring of natives and tourists, we stomped and clapped round a fire.

When the guide distributed blankets for us to bed down on the ground, my trailmates went off to sleep ... When only the night creatures could be heard hooting and gnawing, the guide and I went to his personal hut made of bamboo and thatch by that mysterious tribe in that exotic jungle on a mountain somewhere near Burma... Thailand was a paradise for Western women too.

Odzer here accepts without even the anxiety of the Chiang Mai tourists the Orientalized "authenticity" of the unnamed "tribal" people. Their garb is "ancient", the dances are "folk dances". The fire is enough to create a specter of authenticity for Odzer and she does not see any underlying commodification of dress and dance. The tribal people "welcome" her.

Through the context of her experiences in Thailand, Odzer discovers herself, specifically, her sexuality: "I wasn't thinking too much about Hoi.

Or Nok, Pong, Tik, Chat, and the other Patpong prostitutes [that she has come to Thailand to study]. Instead, I thought of the Thai men I'd known [i.e., slept with]—Jek, Toom, Em, and the Chiang Mai trail guide I'd spent a memorable night with on a mountain top". Odzer has discovered her authentic self, framed in a pseudo-feminist context, as a Western woman through both sex and an authentic encounter with the exotic.

She, like the robot, has learned how to, as she imagines it, properly interact—although in her case this means to sleep with multiple partners in various cities in Thailand—and has therefore discovered herself as a gendered, sexualized person, more importantly, a white woman, claiming a space that white men typically claim. Gender, Sexuality, and Authenticity

THE THAI SEX TOURIST INDUSTRY

The TAT's 2004 promotion slogan was titled either "Unseen Thailand" or "Unseen Paradise", depending on whether the site was visited in Thai or English, respectively. "Unseen Thailand" has a banner displaying waterfalls, mountainous landscapes, and blue rivers. The English-language "Unseen Paradise" is a promotion of fifty resorts that, according to the TAT, are unspoiled by tourism (the paradox of an "unseen" tourist resort is left unacknowledged).

On the "Unseen Paradise" website, the central picture is a Thai woman, her back, smeared with mud or sand, to the camera, looking halfway over her shoulder at a temple-style painting of a traditional Thai dancer. Both the dancer and the woman are topless. The caption beneath reads: "Heaven is now possible and right here within your grasp".

Beyond the irony of displaying lush photographs of landscapes while subsequently suggesting that no one has ever seen them, the website geared towards foreign travelers sells a sexualized image while the Thai-language site does not: the sex industry for Thais is not connected to tourism and does not rest upon the same Orientalized image.

As the international reputation of Thailand as a sex tourist destination pervades the discourse surrounding Thailand as a sex tourist destination, an enormous number of foreign visitors come to Thailand expressly for the sex industry.

Studies of sex work in Thailand have focused on two poles of the practice: condemning the industry as "a violation of women's human rights", or focusing on the agency of women involved in the sex industry, to ones citing prostitution as purely "an entrepreneurial decision". Studies of the industry often conclude with a policy suggestion: the Thai government should tighten prosecution of prostitution, the Thai government should legalize prostitution, or the Thai government should be harsh on traffickers but easier on sex workers.

Here, however, I would like to focus on the sex tourists themselves, their constructions of what they are doing, and how this relates to their self-identity. I will draw specifically upon two main sources: My Wife in Bangkok, by Rory O'Merry (1990), an autobiographical account of a sex tourist in Patpong; and the novels of Christopher Moore (1993), an expatriate living in Bangkok writing fictionalized accounts of expatriates living in Bangkok who have intimate (and mercenary) connections with the Bangkok sex industry.

Farang sex tourists, according to much the literature, are often taken aback by what Erik Cohen calls the "open-ended" nature of prostitution in Thailand, a term that he uses to mean prostitution which may not be immediately recognizable as such or distinguishable from a purely romantic relationship. As such they are confronted with a fundamental problem of how to determine authenticity within their relationship. As Erik Cohen writes:

For many foreigners, particularly middle-aged married or divorced men, the encounter with open-ended prostitution in Thailand is on the order of a revelation. Many become infatuated with Thai women and strongly attracted to girls they initially picked up from a bar or coffee shop for the night.

Being tourists, however, their stay in Thailand is ordinarily brief and, [sic] they inevitably face a difficult problem: many would like to extend the liaison beyond their departure; but they are also aware that the girls worked in bars or a coffee shop when they had first met, and will probably return there again to engage in sexual liaisons with other men. The farangs' problem becomes one of how to safeguard the relationship.

The foreign men therefore feel the need to become experts at authenticity; each of the authors examined here displays the distinction between being able to determine authenticity and being victim to "staged" authenticity as central.

O'Merry arrives on the scene looking for a photographic subject to document. Thinking of Buddhism, he arrives at the World Fellowship of Buddhists and receives a brochure entitled Meditation Temples in Thailand. He writes: "Now that I was actually in the Far East, somehow this all seemed very depressing, so I went for a walk. I wound up in a place called the Bier-Kutsche," a sex tourist destination.

Here, he meets Pidang, a sex worker, and goes back to his hotel with her. His move from an interest in religious meditation towards participating in the sex trade is entirely unreflexive, accepting as natural the fact that a farang male in Thailand would partake: "Let's face it, most of the 2,000,000 men who go to Thailand will spend a minimum of 500 baht on a bar girl". This move, from an interest in religion to an interest in sex, is one that will be reflected in each of my examples from this section.

But something strikes O'Merry as unique in his experience with the Thai sex industry: "Somehow I didn't feel as if I'd spent the night with a prostitute". O'Merry has performed exactly as Cohen's farang sex tourist has: he has fallen for the "staged authenticity" of "open-ended" sex work. O'Merry's confusion initially stems from the fact that Pidang does not immediately ask for money. Following Cohen's model, O'Merry is confused by Pidang's behaviour and seeming affection for him: "I've seen a lot of hookers in my life, but she looked much more like a housewife".

O'Merry plays along, seeming to accept that his relationship with Pidang is not a commercial one. They move in together, and Pidang requests a stipend in order to, as she tells O'Merry, care for her son. The conflicts over money in O'Merry's mind are not that between a sex worker and her client, but rather between a Thai husband and wife, and he naturalizes the commercial relationship in which he is enmeshed: "A Thai man must buy lots of things for his wife, so he'd better work. If he does, he gets pussy. If not, she goes somewhere else and finds a new man—Thai style!". For O'Merry, his relationship with Pidang is the first step to "becoming a Thai".

This claim to "native" identity is one often made among tourists approaching the more "back" region of the tourist spectrum: it is one that the chaa khao tourists are searching for (although rarely find), and it is one heard all too often in ethnographic circles from ethnographers who have recently returned from the field and have felt that their two years in situ affords them a "native" identity. This identity is notably fluid: O'Merry can claim to be both Thai and also white, but Pidang cannot make the same claim regardless of her familiarity with farang customs.

O'Merry, after having achieved his status as Thai expert, drops the diary style and addresses the reader directly, giving a list of "Go-Go bar Etiquette" and listing bars and shows that he found particularly interesting. O'Merry also cautions the farang visitor on his conduct:

Some men who come to Thailand are really unhinged by the freedom and make fools of themselves. I have seen two farang, surrounded by lovely women, fight it out over a fairly ordinary one.... They disgraced themselves, not just in front of the Thai women, but in front of males from all over the world.

According to Julia O'Connell Davidson, male sex tourists are often dissatisfied with their ability to conform to Western ideas of masculinity and sexuality at home while women, to many sex tourists in Thailand, have an intrinsic market value based on their physical appearance.

Therefore, to sleep with many attractive women, especially under the illusion that these relations are not monetarily related, is to increase one's own self-worth. O'Merry's main critique of these men is that they are fighting over something that is only "fairly ordinary", or rather value-less. They have not achieved the discerning eye that O'Merry has.

What is worse, is that they have shown their ignorance "in front of males from all over the world", they have proved their lack of (according to O'Merry) masculine knowledge at exactly the space where it is being enacted. Unable to tell "authentically" beautiful Thai sex workers from others, they are merely tourists. He, on the other hand, can see authenticity and interact authentically; he has become, in effect, the Bangkok Old Hand, the hero of Moore's novels.

Of Old Hands and Hard Cores

The division between the tourist who accepts "staged" authenticity and one who has a more "backstage" view is articulated by Christopher Moore, who, according to the back cover of his novels: "has discovered a lost generation of Westerners living in the East". This "lost generation" is comprised of "third-shift farangs" (white) American and European men who have come to Thailand after meeting with failure at home, and "old hands" or "hardcores", (white) American and European men who have stayed long enough in Thailand to become acclimated. These latter are, as Moore describes on the back cover, "conditioned for urban survival".

Annette Hamilton describes the trope of the Bangkok Old Hand from Moore (and others) as:

The exile or expatriate habitue of the bars of the capital, a man of the world who finds an addictive pleasure in the hotbeds of sin where he spends his flee time and an awareness of a heightened form of 'being alive' unavailable elsewhere.... The experience of this kind of life has been transformative, opening up a register of truth for the male subject; in this place he was able to become himself, to realise himself, to express fully his deepest desires (Hamilton 1997, p. 151).

Moore makes the latter point explicitly: he describes his experienced male characters as "hardcores", meaning that their identity is tied into a sexual identity that everyday people would not understand: "Calvino was a hardcore and what worked him up [sexually], like most hardcores, remained a disturbing mystery". Being "hardcore" is closely tied to being an "old hand". Calvino continually tells farang men who have arrived directly from the United States (or Germany), "This is Bangkok", followed by a piece of sage advice. Calvino singles out Hutton, a fleshly-arrived American, for much of this lecturing.

When Hutton is murdered, Calvino takes it upon himself to discover the killer, with the help of Hutton's live-in sex worker, Noi, with whom Calvino has already, long ago, had sex. Moore draws a distinct line between those farang who are taken in by "staged" authenticity and those who are not: "Old hands saw through the superficial image of Thailand", whereas Hutton naively attempts to rescue Noi from a life of prostitution: "Hutton had bought her out, fallen in love, and made the traditional farang one-man rescue mission into the never-never heartland of the Bangkok sex world. If Hutton had lived long enough, he would have understood that the kind of people who worked and camped out in the Love Nest Bar could never be saved".

Here, Hutton serves as the negative example for the "old hand", the "third-shift farang": "third-shift farang arrived in Thailand because the third-shift worker's rumor mill had hooked them with the promise they [sic] might advance into a first-shift life in a tropic paradise ... In Bangkok, you could start over and no one would suspect, except the old hands, that you were a third-shifter".

For the old hand, "Bangkok was a step on a new path to some personal redemption that the old religion of home never offered", implying that, unlike Moore's sex workers, the sex tourist is actually the one that, in Moore's view, both needs and is capable of salvation. The mention of religion here is significant: Moore's protagonists are looking for personal redemption and renewal, but one which Christianity is unable to fulfill, but before this rebirth one has to truly know the city. Calvino, and by proxy Moore, sees the Bangkok sex industry in its "authentic" manner; having done this, he is fundamentally changed.

According to Hamilton, Moore is articulating "the sustaining masculine identity available in this world [i.e., Bangkok], which contrasts, implicitly or explicitly, with the lack of a similar sense of being 'at home', that is, in 'the West'". For Hutton, the United States was where he met two men who ridiculed him publicly on a bus as a failure. For Calvino, his daughter asks him to come back to the United States, and he responds by advising her about the Buddhist teachings related to "letting go", an echo of O'Merry's initial shift from an interest in Buddhism to an interest in commercial sex. In either case, a return to the United States is impossible.

Without a return to the United States, Moore's old hands are not "tourists", they do not complete the tour and return home, although these fictional characters serve as ideal-types for the sex tourist, especially, like O'Merry, the long-term sex tourist. However, Moore's characters make little connections outside of the tourist space of Patpong, and mostly exist within a circle of fellow expatriates, "bar girls", and the occasional Thai police officer.

The characters and the expatriate community of Bangkok that Moore represents (his "lost generation") remain floating in the "staged" space of Patpong, that area designed for tourism—as Nash writes, designed for "compatibility with metropolitan dreams", in other words, an area staged with a certain exoticised and Orientalized image of what it is supposed to be: a place crafted to be the imagined image resting in the mind of the tourist. The process that creates the floating world that sex tourists and hill-tribe trekkers inhabit is not a static one. When the tourist leaves, the sex worker or chao khao remains, having had one more glimpse into what these farang want from them. They—the toured, as opposed to the tourist—adapt and change, molding their interaction to fit the image the tourist carries with them to Thailand.

This process is similar, but not quite, to what Bhabha describes as mimicry: creating "a reformed, recognizable Other, as a subject of a difference that is almost the same, but not quite". Yet while Bhabha is referring to colonial subjects emulating (yet always, deliberately, inadequately) the colonists, here, Pidang is attempting to fit to what she perceives O'Merry wants—the exoticised image that O'Merry imagines, not O'Merry himself or a woman from his hometown.

This difference, the fact that she is "almost the same, but not quite" both encompasses her value to O'Merry as well as places her at the bottom of a hierarchy: she is the toured, not the tourist, and as I have mentioned previously, O'Merry's claim to knowledge of Thailand is far less controversial than Pidang's claim to knowledge of Europe.

By seeing through this mimicry, Moore and other expatriate writers make their claim for being able to see the authentic world. Patpong is simply the place where the facade is at its most shallow. A classic example is the concept, advocated by all of these authors, that sex is always an economic transaction. For the sex tourist, the ability to see through "open-ended" prostitution exposes deceptions that were deeper and more difficult to penetrate in the countries from whence they have come.

Jack Reynolds voices a fictional sex worker's thoughts: "She believes he has insulted her, because he asked her to sleep with him for nothing '[a]s if she were a very low girl with no self-respect at all. Only the lowest girls slept with men for nothing—for love, as the foreigners said—but she was a very high girl, she had a price, and if a man liked her he would show his respect by paying that price'". Similarly, Moore's Calvino states "the only free sex is the sex that you pay for", and O'Merry claims that "I've paid every woman in one way or another [for sex]". Prostitution, for sex tourists, is mapped on to every sexual relationship, and the sex tourists are simply acting normally and honestly, and Patpong is the site at which such relationships are more "authentically" presented.

THE MASCULINE GAZE AND REBIRTH

The "World Sex Guide" is a country-specific online guide to prostitution written by one anonymous author and a number of equally unnamed contributors. Their presentation of the sex industry in Thailand epitomizes the trope of rebirth and rediscovery present in Thai tourist literature:

> Sex is, for me, the fountain of youth. With variety, a man of any age can enjoy many women every day. This really isn't possible in many places but Thailand. Youth, grace, petiteness, sweetness, friendliness, understanding, enthusiasm and pure fun are the norm. That just isn't true in our drab, grey, boring, cold Western countries where that Christian work ethic pervades our lives (World Sex Guide 2004).

In this passage, Thailand becomes the source of alienated labour—the "Christian work ethic"—is something suffered by the tourist, not by the worker. Thai women's subjectivities are hidden. The one-way gaze of masculinity is present in the other authors as well. O'Merry's photographs are the most explicit example of the masculine gaze, one divorced from reflexivity and positionality.

Aside from Pidang's seminude picture on the cover of the book, inside are numerous photographs of Thai go-go dancers or Pidang in various states of undress, but none of O'Merry himself. Moore does in text what O'Merry has done in photographs. Each description of Thai women describes their bodies in meticulous detail, each description of farang men is cursory.

When Thai sex workers speak English in Moore's books, their speech is broken and laden with errors; when farangs speak Thai, the Thai is transliterated into perfect English. Hence, the tourist world is one of absolute confidence, as Rosalind Morris writes "The woman translates, gives the foreign man access to the local world, renders him competent both in terms of his masculinity and in terms of his foreignness".

The invisible gaze is central to tourist identity, especially with sex tourist masculinity, and the invisible gaze is tied to the tourists' identity as someone who can distinguish. According to Bourdieu: "Everything in the genesis of the female habitus and in the social conditions of its actualization combines to make the female experience of the body the limiting case of the universal experience of the body-for-others, constantly exposed to the objectification performed by the gaze and the discourse of others". The women are marked, they are "sex workers", "prostitutes", or infantilized "girls", explicitly distinguished from other women, whereas the sex tourists are "men", or "farangs" in order to distinguish them from Thai men.

Women are present for display, objectified as commodities with physical features quantifiable into baht: "Only guys like Hutton looked at Noi as an irreplaceable human being, but Hutton was dead". The touristic anxiety comes about as that display is interpreted: am I seeing this right?, the tourist wonders, as he does not have to wonder if he is seen.

Fundamentally, the authenticity that the sex tourist seeks is not that of Patpong, Chiang Mai's "kamphaeng din" area, or other such sites. Sex tourists may see these areas as doubtfully "real" (like Brad), or as shallow facades overlaying an underlying trueness (like Moore), but in each case they allow the tourist to realise a more important authenticity: his own.

These men, suffering from age or anomie at home, are able to perform a (pre-imagined, pre-packaged) narrative of restoration and rejuvenation, where they, even in such a questionably authentic place, are able to discover their authentic selves as competent, masculine, and desirable (for money or status if not out of physical attraction). This is the self-identity that they bring home from the tour: themselves.

AMBIVALENCE AND SEX WORK

Brad was a wealthy young British man who had been convinced by a website that his teeth fillings were full of mercury that was leaking into his bloodstream and causing him to become depressed. Luckily, this website also sold medication to cure this depression, so he purchased quite a bit of this medication and came to Thailand in order to find himself. My partner and I befriended Brad in a tea shop in Chiang Mai, and we discussed his experiences in Northern Thailand for many afternoons.

Brad had recently met someone, a young Thai woman from Isaan at a local bar. While he was very excited over their budding relationship, he was concerned about her should he have to return to England: she had told him that she had come to the bar feeling lonely after a bad relationship and wanting to "be bad", and that should he leave, she might go out again—her friends were continually going and sleeping with different partners each night, and it was an end to the path that she saw herself on should Brad leave.

From Brad's story, I quickly implied that his new girlfriend was more than likely engaging in open-ended prostitution with him, yet Brad was full of doubt on the issue. While he agreed that the bar where he met his girlfriend was "not the sort of place where you [meaning myself and my partner] should go", he was happy to have saved her from such a place, and was also happy at his good fortune to catch her on [as she said] the first night she had gone there.

Brad also saw his experience "saving" this woman as a chance to redeem himself for having been born wealthy. He had been given quite a lot of money as inheritance from his family, and through giving it to this woman, he would be accruing karma—Brad had also been reading a book on Thai Buddhism, and expressed his relationship to the religion (in his case, consisting of visiting temples, meditating at home, and reading this book) as restoring his lost "balance".

The medication that he was taking for his alleged poisoning required him to work on restoring balance, and he cited meditation and riding a motorbike as being two things that would help him to clean his bloodstream.

Through his interaction with this woman, Brad has cast himself as his own conception of a masculine, heroic man, with an added pseudo-Buddhist twist. Brad had been poisoned (a diagnosis that, it should be noted, came from a website and not from a doctor) by the rapacity and greed of the West, requiring that he flee.

Arriving with an idea of the spiritually pure East in mind, Brad can escape his home identity as an unemployed, depressed man who is approaching his mid-thirties, and find his "true" nature, one which has been linked to Thailand all along. He finds in the Thai other aspects of himself that have been, in his mind, repressed by British society.

The invocation of Buddhism by O'Merry, Moore's Calvino, and Brad provide a map to how foreign tourists perceive Thailand and the "East". In searching for a self-definition, these farangs have all initially turned towards religion and retain a stated interest in Buddhism.

O'Merry does not elaborate on his connection to Buddhism other than calling the World Fellowship of Buddhists "depressing", and I do not know how much of Moore's fictional character reflects his or others' experiences, but Brad's contact with Buddhism was only cursory. Brad visited local temples, occasionally would wai the Buddha images, but did not (and largely could not, outside of English-language areas in the temples) communicate with monks or those worshipping at the temple.

Yet the fact that it is cursory should not dissuade discussion of his relationship to the religion. Mauss mentions the widespread use of foreign religions in magic, as that which is not understood has power expressly because it is not understood.

For Brad, this was Buddhism's significance: it was a blank slate upon which he could cast his own narrative of self-discovery. His connection to Buddhism was, like his relationship with the Thai woman, a way in which he could re-define himself through using a signifier—Thailand—whose signified was supplied by Brad himself.

The canny tourist, trekker or old hand, becomes one who discerns authenticity and can subsequently act accordingly. In the case of tourists in Thailand, class, race, and other divisions between tourists themselves are overwritten by the profound class differences between the Other(s) that they have come to tour, especially in the two cases presented here. Divisions that do remain include length of stay and breadth of "authentic" experience.

As tourists move into a more discerning self-identity, the question remains: what happens to these tourists upon their return? When the tourist is thrust back into the world of alienated labour and inauthentic experiences, how much of the identity of "discerner of authenticity" remains? What happens to the hardcore-ness of a returned "hardcore" when he ceases to, in Moore's words, "always have women throwing themselves at [him]"?

To answer such a question would require fieldwork among returned tourists to Thailand, data that I do not have. However, much of the tourist literature implies a return to an automaton-like state: the young man was a robot when he arrived, and he must have become a robot in some manner, so the robot must re-emerge. Graburn suggests that the experience of touring for the tourist is "more 'real' than 'real life'", an experience founded upon this re-creation of the self: "[When we return from touring,] We step back into our former roles ... often with a sense of culture shock. We inherit our past selves like an heir to the estate of a deceased person who has to pick up the threads, for we are not ourselves. We are a new person who has gone through recreation and, if we do not feel renewed, the whole point of tourism has been missed".

The model of tourism presented here is one wherein the tourist imagines an authenticity, travels to a place where that authenticity has been (more or less) created by actors associated with the local tourist industry, acquires an ability to distinguish between levels of this authenticity, and assumes a new identity to add to his (or her) own, one recognized as being a more "true" one, even though this identity and indeed the "authenticity" discovered has far more to do with the tourist's own imagination than what is to be found in Thailand.

Chapter 4

Community Based Heritage Eco-Cultural Tourism

As we enter into the next millennium and the birth of a new global era, we are confronting the urgent need for local/regional/national/international peace and security more than in the past. This may be broadly ascribed to the increasing conflicts arising out of social, economic, religious and political factors. The widening gap between the haves and have-nots, have further accelerated these conflicts. Hence, we are seeking universal human rights and universal human progress and prosperity.

One powerful indicator of such a development is the fact that more people are traveling from more countries than ever before, making travel and tourism the worlds largest industry. Its growth is expected to continue with globalization and as people everywhere seem determined to exercise their right to travel and to make their world a more familiar place in the spirit of peace and friendship.

Tourism itself has always been a peace-based industry and may be considered as a Global Peace Industry. In the face of current human population increases and worldwide ecological degradation, intact and healthy ecosystems are becoming the world's most sought-after tourism destinations. Culture and Heritage besides peace and harmony in such areas attract special groups of tourists, who demand quality products.

THREATS TO PEACE AND SUSTAINABILITY

Peace and sustainability, considered as the indicators of

development are threatened due to a myriad of conflicts—Social, Economic, political, cultural and Environmental. These conflicts usually confront multiple and diverse stakeholders such as state institutions, religious organizations, communities, indigenous ethnic groups, local institutions, private development and non-government organizations, international organizations, and many other players.

Wide differences in culture, knowledge, power, influence, and resources characterize these groups. Even though most conflicts essentially develop in a local framework, they are also frequently connected at regional, national and even international levels, transcending political and geographical boundaries including non-represented interests (e.g. future generations). Such complexity explains, in part, the lack of sustained attention that conflicts receive.

In addition, many conflicts in India are often dealt with unprofessionally and result in frustrations, violence, greater inequities, and negative impacts on quality of life, economic and social processes and in the natural resources themselves. The most common methods of intervention in conflicts tend to be centralized, hierarchical, and sectorial, with a predominantly technical and adversarial (judicial) and at times political. Seldom do they achieve a reasonable level of satisfaction for all interested parties.

Hence, we are urgently in need of alternative paradigms for development—we are moving from the narrower 'reductionist', 'reactive' and 'bureaucratic' approaches to 'wholistic/Integrated or Systems' view of looking at issues, 'pro-active' policies and 'participatory' strategies. How quick and how effective we are in reorienting ourselves according to these shifting paradigms will determine our sustainable futures.

THE IMPORTANCE OF THE TOURISM SECTOR AS THE PROMOTER OF PEACE AND SUSTAINABILITY

The word 'conflict' carries negative connotations. It is often thought of as the opposite of cooperation and peace, and is most commonly associated with violence or the threat of violence. This view of conflict is not always helpful. In many settings it should be seen as a potential force for positive social change—its presence a visible demonstration of society adapting to a new political, economic or physical environment. A potential non-violent approach to solve these conflicts at the least social/economic/Environmental costs may be through evolving alternative tourism strategies.

In the midst of growing tensions and worries everywhere "Getting away from it all," is understandably popular. With so many wonderful places in the world, prices of international travel falling, and the stresses and strains of everyday life increasing, more people are traveling.

And as the population grows and incomes rise in many societies, the trend is steeply up. In 2000, international tourist arrivals reached an all time high of 698 million, an increase of 7.4 % that was double the growth rate of 1999, according to the World Tourism Organization. Tourism sector employs 11 per cent of the global workforce—over 200 million people—either directly or indirectly.

THE TOURISM SECTOR IN INDIA

India's tourism potentials are immense - with a large variety ranging from rich cultural diversity, world-renowned historical, religious, heritage and architectural monuments, unique fairs, festivals, folklore and folk dances besides the costumes and customs to wildlife sanctuaries with exquisite flora and fauna. Besides, there are cool hill stations and long stretches of sunny beaches all round the peninsula.

The diversity is not only in climate but is all pervasive and as J. Nehru put it, "India is a land of contrasts—with the rural tranquility of simplicity and urban bustle, pomp and show". Added to this, there are plenty of traditional arts and crafts to carry back as souvenirs; Indian hospitality and variety induce tourists to make repeated visits.

India's wide choice of adventure sports ranges from the daring to the exotic—trekking, camping, rock climbing, white water rafting, skating, air/water gliding, etc. In spite of such attractions, tourist arrivals in India are less than 1% of the world arrivals. Tourism in India is different from other sectors by some special characteristics that include:

A wider variety of stake-holders but with lack of communication and coordination.

Uniformity of artificial structures in Tourism areas does not blend with the natural diversity of undisturbed areas. Inter-sectoral linkages and complexity with several intangible costs and benefits; conflicts leading to problems in analysis, monitoring and coordination; mixed priorities and conflicts, make cooperation & participation difficult.

Research on tourism especially on policy and planning has been given low priority—as a result, it is poorly studied & understood as a sector in general and its Environmental & Social/Cultural impacts in particular; hence, we are confronted with fragmented & poorly coordinated policies, riddled with ad-hoc decisions for short term gains at the cost of long term sustainability.

Multiplier effect is prominent—can enhance poverty alleviation and alternative livelihoods; but is rarely understood by the planners and the implementing agencies. Seasonality in Tourist influx has implications for carrying capacity analysis and Tourism policy/planning/ implementation, but rarely taken into account by the planners/policy makers.

Spatial and temporal dimensions—implications for Physical planning:

Positive & negative feed backs—implications for absorbing capacity, carrying capacity, Sustainability, and resilience; a typical tourism cycle would involve—Exploration/development/consolidation/stagnation/decline/ rejuvenation; however, negative impacts, on a cumulative basis destroy the resource base, affecting the natural, cultural, and Heritage attractions, culminating in declining tourism trends.

Life supporting systems are impacted, culminating in debates on Ecological integrity Vs Economic security. 'Profit maximization' is the prime motto of Tourism enterprises (irrespective of whether they are private or Govt. sector undertakings) and hence, tourism is largely out of control for planners; some impacts are irreversible and hence tourism itself is affected due to degradation in Environmental health/ quality.

The Ecological impacts of tourism are more on Common Property Resources—air, soil and ground water, leading to tragedy of the commons as they are treated as 'open access commons'. Lack of know how and trained man power in Govt. agencies on Eco-cultural tourism lead to lack of appreciation and Govt. support for community based initiatives.

Tourism industry is fundamentally dependent on the diversity and quality of the natural and cultural resources. Hence, it has grater reasons to conserve/protect the same. But are we giving adequate attention/priorities for natural and cultural resources while planning and implementing tourism projects in India?

Though tourism is India's one of the largest foreign exchange earners and one among the fastest growing industries, the natural resource base that supports tourism is "heavily stressed" in and around the main tourist destination areas. In spite of the overwhelming technological and information revolution, we have trapped ourselves in a vicious circle of self-destruction by adopting the typical "boom and bust" tourism paths paved by the ill-conceived and unplanned/uncontrolled mass tourism, promoted for short-term profit maximization at the cost of degradation in Environmental quality. Ironically, this in turn, ultimately detracts the tourists and destroys the Tourism industry itself.

The question is whether we, in the blind pursuit of rapid Economic growth and earning more foreign exchange Q an afford to sacrifice thc higher Environmental quality and Our rich cultural Heritage upon which tourism so strongly depends. Though we have already learnt many bitter lessons, we tend to overlook them. Changes in the physical, spatial, and socio-economic structure of a tourist area as well as the existence of several, sometimes burdensome, environmental/ social problems testify to the presence of these conflicts and the crying need for evolving appropriate strategies to sustainably manage the Environmental quality, and to improve the local livelihood opportunities.

However, the researchers as well as policy makers in India largely ignore the inseparable links between the Environmental quality (EQ), sustainability, peace and tourism and pay little attention to participation of local communities, by focusing only on setting up infrastructures, promoting marketing strategies and make only adhoc/piece meal efforts to improve the EQ, sustainability and peace in the destination areas.

This is self-evident from the "tell-tale symptoms" or "indicators" such as garbage dumps, foul smell, very high rates of pollution, overexploitation of natural resources, alienation of local communities, increasing conflicts and violence in several destination areas. The industry has learned these bitter lessons only after the irreversible damages have already set in.

Examples can be seen every where the mass tourism went out of control—starting from Ooty and Kodai lakes in the South to Dal lake in the North; from Kovalam in the South to Goa in the North; even our nation's pride Taj Mahal is not spared! As a result, tourism has become a dirty word amongst many communities, environmental groups and human rights campaigners. This is really unfortunate as the tourism sector has greater potential to enhance local livelihoods, if it is properly planned.

THE ILLS OF THE TOURISM INDUSTRY

Though tourism could lead to a variety of potential benefits, uncontrolled mass tourism, the most predominant form of tourism today, inevitably increases the already existing conflicts, besides creating new ones. Tourism's voracious appetite for basic resources—land, water and energy—has meant that the tourism industry and Government Agencies are increasingly finding themselves opposed over land rights and water rights by local people. Lack of access by locals to public beaches, violation by hotels of environmental regulations, and heavy-handed tactics by local authorities to free-up beach areas for hotels' use, have all been cited in legal disputes throughout the world.

For instance, three quarters of the sand dunes on the Mediterranean coast between Spain and Sicily have now disappeared, largely because of the construction of hotels and holiday flats. One of the most famous long-term tourism protests has been in Goa, India. With one five-star hotel consuming as much water as five local villages and one five-star tourist consuming 28 times more electricity per day than a local Goan, local discontent over resource-use is understandable.

Thus, the modern world is characterized by mass concentrations of people, mass production, and mass activities. Diversity and beauty of land and life are more and more replaced by uniformity and ugliness. Human settlements in their mad rush for development have turned beautiful tree-clad landscapes into desolate concrete jungles, and fertile lands with diverse native vegetation are increasingly destroyed by monocultures. Tourism is no exception to this general rule.

THE GREEN SIGNALS

Over the last decade, understanding of these complex and interconnected issues by the world tourism industry, tourists, governments and communities has increased as indicated by the evolution of numerous alternative forms of tourism such as 'green' tourism, 'alternative' tourism, 'responsible' tourism, 'sustainable' tourism, 'eco' tourism, 'eco-cultural' tourism (ECT), 'eco-development' tourism, 'Heritage eco-cultural' tourism (HECT), 'community' tourism, "ethical' tourism, 'fair-trade' tourism and even, most recently, the particularly un-catchy, 'pro-poor' tourism(PPT).

Unfortunately, we, in India have not sufficiently re-oriented ourselves, to meet the future international market demand for these specialized forms of tourism.

The concept of sustainable tourism should not be confused with ECT. According to WTO, all tourism activities, be they geared to holidays, business, conferences, congresses or fairs, health, adventure or ECT itself, must be sustainable.

This means that the planning and development of tourism infrastructure, its subsequent operation and also its marketing should focus on environmental, social, cultural and economic sustainability criteria, so as to ensure that neither the natural environment nor the socio-cultural fabric of the host communities will be impaired by the arrival/activities of tourists; on the contrary, enterprises, as well as the communities in which they operate, should benefit from tourism, both economically and culturally.

Eco-tourism, a growing trend, is the most commonly understood term as tourism that focuses on an appreciation of the environment. In 1993 the World Tourism Organisation (WTO) estimated nature tourism generates 7 per cent of all international travel expenditure. More recent research reveals this is now much higher, accounting for 20 per cent of international travel in the Asia-Pacific region and some areas, such as South Africa, experiencing a massive growth in visitors to game and nature reserves, of over 100 per cent annually. Research by The International Ecotourism Society (TIES) reveals that coo-tourists are likely to be higher spenders on their holidays than 'ordinary' mass tourists. And high spending, nature-loving, responsible tourists are undoubtedly an attractive option for governments looking for ways of earning foreign exchange.

The recent Amman Declaration on Peace Through Tourism (8-11 November 2000) reflects many of the strategies discussed above and has recognised that peace is an essential precondition for travel and tourism and all aspects of human growth and development. Hence, it has recommended the development of tourism as a global vehicle for promoting understanding, trust and goodwill among peoples of the world through an appropriate political and economic framework.

THE NEW THREATS

The alternative tourism strategies, evolved in response to the concern for the Ecology, culture, Heritage and local livelihoods, have created both new opportunities as well as new threats. One of eco-tourism's first problems is one of definition. Although, there are several definitions, there is no certification system to abide by or international monitoring body. The term can be used by anyone at anytime for anything from a small-scale locally run rainforest lodge where the money goes to support a local community, to a large, luxury, foreign-owned resort which has little community involvement and uses masses of natural resources.

Eco-tourists may even visit areas of national beauty and wildlife significance without realizing that local people have been evicted from the area in order for eco-tourism to be developed, as has happened in East Africa, India, Southern Africa and many other destinations.

Ill-conceived and/or ill-planned Eco-tourism, as practiced now by a majority of the business communities has caused serious, irreversible negative impacts in environmentally and culturally sensitive areas, even in countries that are well known as eco-tourism destinations like Belize or Costa Rica.

The Malaysian-based Third World Network working with the Thailand-based Tourism Information Monitoring team (TIM-team) cite examples throughout Asia, including the eco-tourism policy promoted by the tourism working group under the Greater Mekong Sub-region (GMS) development scheme, led by the Asian Development Bank, which covers a vast area across Burma, Cambodia, Laos, Thailand, Vietnam and Yunnan/China.

They are riddled with several problems relating to accusations of 'human zoos' being created and financial exploitation of hill tribe villages by outside tour operators. Besides, the increasing link of eco-tourism to the multi-million dollar biotechnology industry through bio-piracy in key eco-tourist sites like rainforests, and the use of eco-tourism by the World Bank's Social Investment Project to support massive development projects, some involving logging operations are becoming common in many developing countries. The revolution in information and communication technologies would enable both the promoters and the tourists to exploit the hidden potentials ECT in a region, more efficiently than ever. However, the lack of discipline of government and the escalating demand for growth will undermine efforts to create sustainable eco-tourism economies that are small but beautiful.

Under extreme conditions of land grabbing and unplanned structures, it may create concrete jungles, surrounded by degraded vegetation, thus destroying the once tranquil zones. Hence, we have to be extremely careful while promoting ECT.

Despite these problems, an International Year of Ecotourism (IYE) was declared by the United Nations for 2002. This will be co-ordinated by the WTO and UNEP and a range of activities held, including a World Ecotourism Summit from 19-22 May 2002 in Quebec, Canada plus various regional conferences. Oliver Hillel, the UNEP tourism programme co-ordinator sees the IYE as a chance to "assess what eco-tourism is, or can be, rather than only a promotional event for UN member governments, for the private sector and for recipients of development aid."

It is clear to many that nature-based tourism is presently seen as one of the most lucrative niche markets, and powerful transnational corporations are likely to exploit the IYE to dictate their own definitions and rules of eco-tourism on society, while people-centred initiatives will be squeezed out and marginalised.

While the commitment of the tourism industry in India to tackle these complex issues seems limited, a few smaller operators are keen to work closely with local people in order for the communities to support their business and out of an honest desire to protect environments and optimise benefits to local people. However, such small operators lack the know-how to tackle the issues involved. As a result, alternative tourism strategies for which India has a greater potential, make up a very small proportion of overall tourism facilities.

THE POTENTIAL ALTERNATIVES

In any outdoor tourism activity, human experience,

knowledge, expectation, and socio-cultural contexts interact with environmental elements and environments as entities to produce an outcome that affects both the humans and the environment. Thus, sustainable tourism development depends in many important ways on the proper handling of the relationships between Tourism and the Environment. Sustainability, Peace and Environmental quality occupy the central table in the wake of global terrorism.

Greater sustainability of the tourism would mean more regional products, less noise and emissions, lesser solid wastes and appropriate sewage treatment measures, creation of jobs, lesser social conflicts/violence by learning to live in harmony and higher quality of life for the local populations well as improved quality of holidays for the guest. The conventional mass tourism, by its very nature cannot cater to these demands. Hence, alternative tourism strategies are emerging.

Sustainable tourism is defined (WTTC, WTO and Earth council, 1996) as "Tourism that meets the needs of the present tourists and host regions while protecting and enhancing opportunity for the future. It is envisaged as leading to management of all resources in such a way that economic, social and aesthetic needs can be fulfilled while maintaining cultural integrity, essential ecological processes, bio-Diversity and life supporting systems (soil, air and water)". Thus, it has the inbuilt mechanism for promoting peace and harmony among the tourism stakeholders.

A related alternative is Eco-cultural Tourism (ECT). ECT activities are offered by a large and wide variety of operators, and practiced by an even larger array of tourists. While there is no single universal definition for ECT, its general characteristics can be summarized as follows:

All nature-based forms of tourism in which the main motivation of the tourists is the observation and appreciation for admiring, enjoying and/or studying nature as well as the traditional cultures and Heritage (both past and present) prevailing in relatively undisturbed or uncontaminated natural areas.

It contains participatory, interactive, educational and interpretation features.

It is generally, but not exclusively organized for environmentally, socially conscious small groups by specialized and small, locally owned businesses. Foreign operators of varying sizes also organize, operate and/or market ECT tours, generally for small groups. It minimizes negative impacts upon the natural and socio-cultural environment.

Heritage Eco-cultural Tourism (HECT) is a newly emerging type of alternative tourism. When Heritage of the destination areas can be exploited along with the local Ecological and cultural attractions, we have a case for Heritage Eco-cultural Tourism.

Heritage embraces magnificent natural, indigenous and historic landscapes (natural or man-made), wildlife and healthy, intact ecosystems, historical elements (that has helped to shape the regional/national identity), cultural elements and human values, shaping regional, national, global identity; it also incorporates a strong connection to 'place'; that is, people come to the place by choice, they are somehow transformed by it, and they choose to identify themselves with it even if they don't live there.

This may be because of the outstanding universal value of the areas visited from the point of view of science, conservation or natural beauty.

Historical places, objects and manifestations of cultural, scientific, symbolic, spiritual and religious values are important expressions of the culture, identity and religious beliefs of societies. Their role and importance, particularly in the light of the need for cultural identity and continuity in a rapidly changing world, need to be promoted. Tourists are actively seeking such lost values. They come hoping for a profound psychic or spiritual experience in some quiet corners of the destination areas. Hence, we have greater responsibility to conserve the cultural Heritage areas.

HECT, by its very design is ideally suitable for this purpose.

The following are the key potential benefits of HECT:

Protection and active conservation of natural and built heritage resources, justified by their own intrinsic value for posterity and the revenue which visitors contribute.

Enhancement of the natural and built environment to meet rising quality standards necessary to sustain modern travel and tourism.

Reconstruction for visitor usage of urban environments and environments degraded by the industrial practices of former extractive and manufacturing industries.

Establishment of attractive environments for tourism destinations, for residents as much as visitors, which may support other compatible new economic activities, from agriculture and fishing to service and manufacturing industries.

Creation of economic value and protection for resources which otherwise have no perceived value to residents, or represent a cost rather than a benefit- livelihood opportunities—micro-enterprises?

Opportunity to communicate and interpret the values of natural and built heritage and of cultural inheritance of residents of visited areas.

Effective management of visitors within an environment so that it can support long-term economic development and repeat visits.

Research and development of good environmental practices and management systems to influence the operation of travel and tourism businesses as well as visitor behaviour at destinations.

Opportunities, through the direct customer contacts that all travel and tourism businesses have, for operators to communicate and interpret the values of natural and built heritage and culture to visitors, thus helping to create a new generation of responsible consumers

The available knowledge indicate that the following may be considered as the major criteria for selecting HECT sites:

Geography—proximity to mass-tourism sites; sufficiently closer for easy accessibility but adequately away from motorable roads and other human disturbances. Climate & Ecology—microclimates/habitats conducive enough for the tourists without any need for artificial comforts

Rarity & Uniqueness—Ecosystems like mountains, rivers, mangroves, coral reefs and islands endowed with unspoiled beauty, unique culture and Heritage.

Infrastructure—only reasonable—to the barest minimum but with desirable conditions—hygienic ethnic food (locally produced/prepared), protected water supply, natural ventilation and local architecture.

Diversity—higher habitat/community/Ecosystem/cultural (food, cloth, architecture, crafts, festivals etc.)—diversity and purity—potentials/opportunities for viewing/appreciating more attractive species/cultures as well as Heritage elements; Potentials for a variety of nature/adventure tourism activities such as camping for wildlife observation, traditional healing camps, caving, bird-watching, trekking, rock-climbing, mountain biking, skating, para-gliding, wind-surfing, funky jumping, canopy walkways, white water rafting, snorkeling, scuba diving, recreational fishing

Unpolluted/relatively undisturbed areas with higher Environmental quality—in contrast to polluted/degraded landscapes/seascapes

Minimum health/safety risks—to avoid costly demands from the tourists

Opportunities for Environmental Education & interpretation—for all the stake-holders

Opportunities for generating and sustaining new livelihoods—to cater to the demands of the tourists—e.g. Apiculture (the science and art of raising honey bees), agriculture, horticulture, floriculture, community dairy/ piggery/poultry, preparation of Ethnic foods, rich diversity of arts and crafts.

Community cooperation- to make and enforce their own decisions on eco-tourism development.

Presence of dedicated NGOs—for catalyzing cooperation.

Cooperation of other stake-holders—Govt. and other institutions—their policies, programmes and goals.

Marketing opportunities—potentials for targeting different types of eco-tourists (hardcore, dedicated, mainstream and casual); marketing linkages and potentials.

The HECT will enable the tourists as well as the local communities to find ways to live sustainably, and in peace with nature, Cultural Heritage and intact, functioning ecosystems. More importantly, we will be reconnecting ourselves with our forgotten treasure of the diverse culture and Heritage of the bygone era. In this process, tourism will promote peace and sustainability by closer mutualistic interactions between tourists and the local communities.

Among the several organizations that could be involved in the promotion of HECT, mention must be made of UNESCO (World Heritage sites programme) and the International Institute for Peace through Tourism (IIPT) at international levels and the Indian National Trust for the promotion of Arts and Cultural Heritage (INTACH) at the national level. The Indian Tourism Development Corporation (ITDC) and the State Tourism Development Corporations have to recognise the potentials of HECT and reorient themselves to the tasks ahead.

Broad guidelines for promoting HECT strategies may be modified and adopted from UNEP (1995) that has prescribed Environmental codes of conduct for tourism and Gonsalves' (1991) paper on guidelines for alternative tourism for the third world. The adoption of the Global Code of Ethics for Tourism, the Green Globe programme (WWF, 2000), the ECOTEL Certification awarded by HVS Eco Services, Certification Programs for Sustainable Tourism and Eco-tourism, Exemplary Practices by Canadian Tourism Commission (1999), The National Eco-tourism Accreditation Programme of the Eco-tourism Association of Australia and the Australian Tourism Operators Association and equitable community participation in tourism are a few other such initiatives to name, globally.

Recently, Mastny (2002) from World Watch Institute has provided policy guidelines with examples for sustainable tourism. The recently emerging pro-poor tourism approaches, have to be ideally integrated into HECT. Caribbean island. It is an island-state much like many others in this region of the world: Its beaches are white, its people are black, its skies and waters are blue, its mountains are green, and its birds and fishes and flowers are every colour in the rainbow.

Its roads were laid out when land transportation was by way of horseback or donkey cart or on foot. Its legislature meets in a dignified one hundred-fifty year old stone building painted the colour of lime juice. Its school children wear uniforms and appear to the American visitor to be anachronistically neat and well-behaved. It is an interesting place.

Its history is interesting, too. Virtually the entire native-born population today is made up of the descendants of Africans, brought to the Caribbean in chains by European colonialists to labour in the mines and on the plantations. Europeans conquered the Caribbean islands in the 16th century. They established trading outposts, plantations, and mines throughout the region. The commerce that ensued introduced tomatoes to Italy, potatoes to Ireland, and sugar and horses to the Americas. It also introduced the plantation system of agricultural production based on African slavery to the Americas.

After a series of slave uprisings throughout the Caribbean, the practice of slavery was ended on this island in the 1840s. In the twentieth century, the descendants of slaves gained in social and political strength; in the second half of the twentieth century, blacks came to control the government, and have done so for several decades. From these islands have come music, poetry, dance, and art that are known the world over. As I said, this is an interesting place.

Beyond these basic points, however, I knew little about the island's history. My historian's curiosity was aroused by this society that seems to have taken such a different course from that of the United States. So, I signed up for a guided tour of the historic sites.

To my disappointment, our tour guide was not a native

islander, but a recent transplant from Minnesota! She began her tour by talking about the bravery and heroism of Christopher Columbus. She told us how he faced the cannibalistic Caribs—a name and description used for one of the native peoples in the region—and even lost one of his men to their attacks.

She went on to tell of pirates and warriors and captains of agriculture and trade. She noted that when slavery was abolished in 1847, "hard times" followed. She pointed out that the colonial governor who ended slavery was recalled to his native Denmark, and that although he was later "exonerated," his ending of slavery "ruined his career."

Of the island's natural history, we learned that it has a natural deepwater port, and that many of the walls are made of a native stone known as "blue bitch," because it is so hard it is really a bitch to quarry. In the words of comedian Dave Barry, "I am not making this up."

Then we visited a house museum. It was the reconstructed home of a Danish banker who came to the island about 1820. A local historical society docent—a retired New Yorker—told us the story of the house. The story was all too familiar: The banker brought his family to the island to make his fortune. They braved the hostile elements and unfamiliar culture. He was shrewd but fair. He raised a large family. He grew rich from the resources and produce of the island and the labour of its people. He became a pillar of the community.

The house (although reconstructed in the 1960s) represents the lifestyle of the merchant class of the 19th century. Some of the furniture and furnishings were imported; some made on the island. Most were collected and donated since the 1960s by historical society members, and have no provenance that connects them to this actual house. We were told that the house has high ceilings in order to catch the breeze. We learned that life was difficult, but the people were strong.

There was even an anecdote about how the Danish family suffered in the tropical climate because the clothes they brought with them from Denmark were wool! I would ask, "what is wrong with this picture?" But that would so understate the problem as almost to miss the point. The better question is, "what is this picture?" Surely it is not a very accurate or complete picture of the long, complicated, interesting history of this island in the Lesser Antilles. It sounds more like a generic script from house museum pattern book.

In connection with the death of Columbus's soldier at the hands of natives, our guide never mentioned that the European explorers and their successors killed and enslaved hundreds of thousands of native peoples in the ensuing occupation and colonization. In discussing the hard times that followed the end of slavery, she never mentioned the hard times experienced by the hundreds of thousands of enslaved Africans before slavery was abolished.

In describing how the brave governor (who ended slavery only because of an eminent revolution, it turns out), she told us his career was ruined, but she did not speculate about what happened to the careers—not to mention the lives—of the people whose actions really did end slavery, the rebellious slaves themselves. And not once did she mention the name of any of the historical figures who guided the island from colonial rule to democratic self-government. In fact, it was as if the history of this island ended about the middle of the 19th century.

The real history of the island is quite different from the version presented by our tour guide. Robert Paquette and Stanley Engerman note in the introduction to The Lesser Antilles in the Age of European Expansion that "... the transition from slave to free labour marks one of the most momentous shifts in moral sensibility in the making of the modern world." "The lesser Antilles with their diverse history of colonization provide an exceptional laboratory for the study of comparative emancipation."

Not only was the story selective and inaccurate, it was boring and predictable. By the time our tour was over, I had concluded that the "heritage" in this heritage tourism experience was, to adapt a phrase from Henry Ford, "pretty much bunk." And unfortunately this is not the only place that is true. The purveyors of heritage tourism—and this includes historical societies, museums, and government cultural agencies—all too often serve up a kind of lowest-common-denominator drivel that is designed to tell visitors what they already know.

Or at least what they think they know. Rarely does heritage tourism challenge or surprise. Heritage tourism does not present a version of history that is dirty or controversial. It does not challenge the conventional wisdom. It does not rely on the latest and best scholarship in the field. Instead, it is pabulum, based more or less (usually less) on history. And its reputation for being deadly boring is often richly deserved.

To make matters worse, there is a huge gap between the popular idea of history, and the history produced by professional historians. Americans get a great deal of their history from television, theme parks, and movies, media infamous for ignoring historical scholarship in favour of making a point. Yet they are immensely popular with the public.

In his book, History Goes to the Movies, writer Joseph Roquemore writes, "Ever since The Birth of a Nation's 1915 premiere, feature film makers have rewritten history to fashion top-dollar entertainment.... " Because of their dramatic impact, he continues, "films have extraordinary power ... to leave you with a strong sense of what is right and what is wrong, of who is bad and who is good, even though critical details presented in the movies may be slanted or false."

From The Birth of a Nation, to Walt Disney's 1950s production Davy Crockett: King of the Wild Frontier, to Mel Gibson's 2004 religious pronouncement, The Passion of the Christ, television and movies have treated historical topics and audiences have consumed them eagerly. Historians decry the lack of accuracy in the portrayal of historical people and events in these movies.

Yet people have seen them and tend to remember them as fact, in part because each one reaffirmed popular prejudices and predilections of its day. Despite readily available historical information that would permit the telling of an authentic story, the movie version is the one that enters the public consciousness.

The same is true, to a large extent with historical theme parks. Historian Mike Wallace, in his essay "Mickey Mouse History," criticizes the original Disneyland in California and its "clone" in Florida, Walt Disney World. According to Wallace, both are "... ostensibly ... grounded in historic reality ...," although they are certainly not intended to be a full and accurate retelling of history.

In fact, Wallace continues, Disney's "approach to the past was ... not to reproduce it [as Colonial Williamsburg or Greenfield Village seek to do], but to improve it." The original Disneyland alone attracts some 10 million visitors each year, ten times as many as visit Colonial Williamsburg or Mount Vernon, our most visited heritage sites.

The greatest shortcoming of these versions of history is that they oversimplify history and reduce it to a linear progression of events that lead logically and inevitably to a conclusion. All too often in popular history, the present situation is portrayed as the near-perfect culmination of centuries of human endeavor.

Missing is the improbability, the surprise, the controversy—in short the human dimension—of history. In explaining how the United States became embroiled in the Vietnam War, Frances Fitzgerald observed that "Americans ignore history.... The national myth is that of creativity and progress, of a steady climbing upward into power and prosperity, both for the individual and for the country as a whole. Americans see history as a straight line and themselves standing at the cutting edge of it as representatives for all mankind."

Most professional historians tend to view history as more complicated—and more interesting—than that. Their job is to uncover and piece together the complicated and interesting stories of the past, and to relate those stories to a contemporary audience. Yet they tend to write almost exclusively for an audience of other professional historians. There are exceptions, of course. Civil War historians Shelby Foote and James McPherson, for example, or John Adams biographer David McCullough are academic historians, whose scholarship has been accepted and consumed directly by a broad public. But mostly the people who read serious history are serious historians.

The disconnect between academic history and the broad public consciousness is nowhere clearer than in a Washington Post article about the American Historical Association's 2004 annual convention. The theme of the convention was "War and Peace." Not the novel, but the history.

The Post reporter attended the convention and reported his impressions of it. The headline on the article was "Lessons We May Be Doomed to Repeat;" the subhead was "American Historians Talk About War, But Is Anyone Listening?" The reporter's implied answer to the headline's question—not really.

Thousands of historians gathered to present their latest research on war, and to question and debate one another on one of the most obviously relevant topics their profession ever deals with. Yet the reporter described a scene of seemingly deliberate insularity and isolation. Describing one session entitled 'Thoughts on War in a Democratic Age," the reporter noted that "the scholarly papers ... had been a classic academic combination of insight and obscurity, thoughtful analysis and mind-numbing delivery, and by the time the question period finally rolled around, even the AHA's president, James McPherson, was ready to head for the door." The reporter went on to ask "if they can't even hold the attentio of their colleagues on such an innately compelling subject, how can they expect ordinary humans to absorb what they have to say?"

The reporter betrayed a degree of naivete about the nature of academic conventions, but he also put his finger on a serious problem. Academic historians talk about authenticity and historical accuracy. They complain bitterly about the incorrect depiction of historical people and events in popular culture—from Davy Crocket, to the schlocky tour of the Caribbean island I described. Yet their work is virtually inaccessible to the general public. By the time it penetrates popular culture, it has been diluted and distorted until it becomes unrecognizable.

After movies and theme parks, the third major source of historical information for the American public is what could loosely be called heritage site—museums, historic houses, monuments, roadside markers, and the like. The Travel Industry Association of America reports that about one fourth of American adults, or more than 50 million adults, travel to historic sites each year. And that does not include the millions of school children who take field trips every year. Consider the fact that only about one fifth of all Americans ever take a single history course after high school, and the importance of heritage sites as sources for historical information comes sharply into focus.

Unlike movies and theme parks, heritage sites present themselves as authentic. The information they give out is presented as fact. Obviously, they hold great potential to expose the public to the kind of history that professional historians produce. Yet, my experience is that heritage sites do surpass the movies in interpreting the best history scholarship, but aside from some of the major innovators in the field, barely so. In fact, heritage sites reinforce the popular notion of history more often than they correct it. The heritage in heritage tourism, namely the history that underlies it, is often bad. It is out of date, poorly documented, usually repeated from secondary sources.

To be sure, there is good scholarship available to heritage organizations. And the best heritage sites take full advantage of history scholarship. At Manassas National Battlefield Park, for example, a new exhibit in the visitor centre is accompanied by an interpretive film. Both are based on rigorous scholarship. Both explore the broader themes of American history which led to and resulted from the Civil War. The park superintendent, himself a Ph.D. historian, chaired a conference on "Reinterpreting the Civil War," that attracted some of the most eminent scholars in the field. Similarly, the park historian responsible for the Frederick Douglass National Historical Site organized an international conference on Frederick Douglass scholarship as part of an effort to improve the history content in that site's interpretation.

But the National Park Service is the United States' premiere federal agency that manages heritage sites. And even the National Park Service acknowledges that it has much room for improvement. At the vast majority of heritage sites the story is more akin to the Caribbean tale above.

In Maryland, for example, of more than 300 heritage sites open to the public, all but a handful are run by local government or small private organizations without the resources they think they need to bring the best scholarship to the public. Very few take advantage of the history expertise available in the state's universities. In fact, the cynical cliche "if you've seen one house museum, you've seen them all," is closer to the truth than most heritage site managers would like to admit.

Something is not right. State and local tourism bureaus promote heritage sites vigorously. Communities like heritage tourists because they spend money, and the industry is a relatively low impact form of economic development. Tens of millions of Americans visit heritage sites each year. Why, then isn't the product better? With plenty of good scholarship available, why do most heritage sites fall back on the conventional wisdom of history, often repeating stories and facts that are widely accepted, but downright wrong?

One reason might be found within the history profession. Public history—the practice of history outside the academy and with a direct popular audience in mind—has traditionally been looked down upon within the history establishment. Professional organizations have for several years recognized the importance of public history and have initiated efforts to support its practitioners. Still, the primary focus for training Ph.D.s in history is the academy.

But there is a larger reason for the paucity of current

scholarship in heritage sites. It lies with the organizations that manage these places and interpret their stories to the public. James W. Loewen's indictment of heritage sites, Lies Across America: What Our Historic Sites Get Wrong, faults the organizations and agencies that manage heritage sites, arguing that many of them start with a point to make—boosterism, hero worship, patriotism—and often miss or avoid the most interesting parts of history. They prefer to give the public a simple, predictable, safe story that reinforces preconceived ideas, even if it ignores the scholarship on the subject.

Anthropologist Dean MacCannell thinks so, too. He has lamented the sameness and lack of imagination of heritage sites. Yet he also points to the potential for telling the more complicated and authentic stories they actually represent. I been involved as a manager or board member of a wide variety of heritage sites and organizations over the past quarter century. During that time I have also visited hundreds of other heritage sites, gathering information about their presentation and interpretation, talking to managers and trustees, and forming some strong opinions about their use of history. My experience confirms Loewen's and MacCannell's observations.

Every time I visit one of these less-than-exemplary heritage sites, I wonder why I keep doing this. Why, in fact, do so many millions of people visit these sites every year? Why do we insist on trudging on with this endless pilgrimage to the Mount Rushmore and the Doctor Mudd house and the tomb of Ponce de Leon? I think I know the answer. I think we do it because real history is challenging. It is complicated and uneven. It can be risky. It can be fun, entertaining, interesting, even exciting.

History can inspire us and give meaning and relevance to our everyday lives. Obviously, heritage sites are not always fun and entertaining and interesting and exciting. They are not even usually fun and entertaining and interesting and exciting. But they can be. I think we visit them because we hope they will be. That we don't usually find fun or entertainment or excitement or inspiration is a disappointment—to visitors, to historians, and to tourism professionals. That disappointment also offers a huge opportunity for heritage tourism.

More research needs to be done, but anecdotal evidence indicates that people will visit sites that are controversial, complicated, and challenging. The U. S. Holocaust Museum gets very high visitor ratings, despite the shocking and disturbing content of its exhibits. The Maryland Historical Society's "Mining the Museum" exhibit, confronted visitors with the "... issues of curatorial choices and the role of museums as they relate to the representation of African Americans and Native Americans in traditional museum collections."

Despite the sophistication of this theme, the exhibit was one of the most visited in the museum's recent history. Visitors seek authenticity. Too often they have to settle for comfort. The challenge for heritage tourism is to become a nexus between recreation and scholarship—the place where the "public" in public history meets the "history" in public history.

Chapter 5

Third World Critique of Tourism

Third World tourism continues to expand apace. The tourism industry's promotional materials are replete with images of a "frontier" industry, new vistas of "paradise," "virgin" beaches, and "untouched", landscapes. Indeed, the imagery is that of exploration, conquest, and domination. For the people of the Third World, whose natural, human, and cultural resources provide the raw material for this industry, this is no imagery, it is reality.

The challenge of tourism to Third World people is not merely that of ecological degradation, economic exploitation or even cultural spoliation. While the expansion of Third World tourism pits the forces of modernity against those of the pre-modern, it is, in a much more fundamental way, a challenge to respond to a new political force. It is a challenge to locate, define, and articulate a livable space in changing world fragile borders, whose contours are still being mapped.

The ambitious plan of the governments of Cambodia, Laos and Thailand to build a huge golf resort in a pristine forest area where the three countries meet has elicited a heated debate about the way tourism is being developed in the region. The proposed 27-hole golf course will have nine holes in each of the three countries. Thai environmentalists strongly oppose the so-called Emerald Triangle Development Project as the Thai portion is located in a first-class watershed area in Ubon Ratchathani's Phu Chong Na Yoi National Park.

Ironically, the area is also rife with landmines, planted in the 1980s when it served as a battleground between the now defunct Khmer Rouge and the Vietnamese-backed Hun

Sen government. To make the project site safe for tourists, costly and protracted mine-clearing operations will be necessary. Yet, governmental officials argue the project is "needed at any price" because it will bring in a large amount of tourism revenue.

In response to environmental concerns, the head of Thailand's National Park Division, Vichit Pattanagosai, has said the golf resort could be defined as an "ecotourism" project and as such would co-exist well with the surrounding protected forest as golfers could watch wildlife while playing on the fairways.

This example illustrates some of the problems associated with contemporary tourism development in the Mekong River Basin area, a watershed that includes Burma, Cambodia, Laos, Thailand, Vietnam and the Yunnan province of Southern China. Thailand, with its free-market economy, had been until recently the only country in the region to have systematically developed a tourism industry, designed to boost foreign exchange earnings, investment and job creation. With the collapse of the state socialist block in the late 1980s, however, all Mekong nations decided to reform their economies and promote tourism as an engine for growth.

Since the beginning of the 1990s, Mekong countries have increasingly participated in regional economic co-operation programs. One such programme is the Greater Mekong Subregion (GM S) initiative, led by the Asian Development Bank (ADB). Established in 1992, the GMS initiative has become the prime mover of Mekong tourism. Through the ADB, the initiative has financed or co-financed over 100 infrastructure projects—including road, railway, water and air transport, electricity generation and telecommunication—aimed at developing regional tourism and trade.

The GMS tourism working group—known as the Agency for Coordinating Mekong Tourism Activities—is based at the headquarters of the Tourism Authority of Thailand, in Bangkok. It has garnered support from governments, international aid agencies, large industry associations and corporations to promote the Mekong River Basin area as a single tourism market and to remove physical, economic, organizational and legal barriers to travel that are still hampering the visitor industry in the region.

Apart from the ADB, representatives of the six Mekong countries' national tourism organizations, international tourism associations such as the World Tourism Organization, the Pacific Asia Travel Association, the Association of Southeast Asian Nations' Travel Association, as well as the UN Economic and Social Commission for Asia and the Pacffic have been involved in the programme.

In its policy documents, the GMS tourism initiative emphasizes "sustainable tourism" and "ecotourism" as worthy goals.

The Concept Plan for Tourism Development in the GreaterMekong Subregion 1999-2018, which outlines the GMS strategy for the next 20 years, forecasts that the Mekong will be "one of the world's most important ecotourism and cultural tourism destinations" by 2018. However, the list of proposed priority projects reflects a heavy emphasis on establishing large-scale transportation systems and tourism complexes.

The plan is to attract 2 to 2.5 million new international tourists per year to the Mekong area by the end of 2006 (over the current level of 14.1 million visitors in 2000). And even higher growth rates are expected in the following years after the ADB infrastructure programme is completed.

The massive GMS programme appears to be incompatible with the concept of ecotourism, which is supposed to nurture small-scale, environmentally and socially sound development. For instance, the GMS initiative envisions the creation of several "economic corridors" linking various parts of the region with advanced transportation facilities, some of which are already underway. The rapid construction of highways, ports and airports, along with hotels, resorts, casinos and other facilities, has already damaged ecosystems, disrupted community life and made local people vulnerable to exploitation by tourism and other industries.

A NEGATIVE MODEL

Thailand receives about 70 per cent of the tourists coming to the GMS and has seen the number of visitors soar over the last 20 years from one million to almost ten million annually. The country's tourism industry has often been described by academics and the local and international media as a negative model. There are countless media reports, academic studies and NGO statements on how reckless development has resulted in the environmental degradation of many places, exacerbated economic inequalities and contributed to undesirable social changes, such as the proliferation of the sex industry, AIDS, drug abuse, gambling, crime and cultural erosion.

Official and industry leaders framing Mekong tourism insist that with improved planning and management, past mistakes can be avoided in new destinations. But in reality, uncontrolled and outright destructive tourism activities have spread throughout the region over the last decade. Even officials and tourism entrepreneurs have expressed worries about the deterioration of unique cultural and natural attractions.

These include UNESCO World Heritage Sites such as Angkor Watin Cambodia, Luang Prabang in Laos, Pagan in Burma, Halong Bay in Vietnam and Lixiang in Yunnan.

Since the late 1980s, the aggressive promotion of golf tourism, first in Thailand and then in other Mekong countries, has also posed immense pressure on local communities and ecosystems. The construction of golf courses—often involving other large-scale developments such as hotels, residential houses, shopping centres, entertainment facilities, power plants, access roads and even airports—has come under heavy attack for consuming large stretches of land, replacing biodiversity-rich wilderness areas, fertile agricultural land and farming communities.

Critics have also pointed out the enormous waste of water resources and the excessive application of chemical fertilizers and pesticides for the maintenance of the courses.

More often than not, local communities have not been

properly informed about the projects and the impacts they may have, such as deforestation, contamination, disruption of community life and even forceful eviction of villagers. In Thailand, several golf course developers have been accused of illegally grabbing land and encroaching on protected areas, and it is an open secret that politicians and military officers have financial stakes in the projects. The controversial Emerald Triangle Development Project mentioned above shows that the Thai government openly supports the building of a golf resort in a pristine watershed area, even though the National Park Act prohibits such activities.

Unfortunately, Thailand has longstanding experiences with the mismanagement of forests, beaches, marine areas and other natural assets. For many years, environmentalists have campaigned to stop the Tourism Authority of Thailand and the Royal Forestry Department (RFD) from opening national parks to private tourism businesses.

Under the pretext of "ecotourism", the RFD has in recent years implemented large-scale infrastructure projects in many national parks, with funding from the World Bank and Japanese Bank for International Cooperation. These projects have involved the clearance of many park areas for the construction of roads, parking lots, visitor centres, bungalows, campsites and other facilities, despite growing public criticism and local citizens' protests.

TOP-DOWN APPROACH

A hard look at tourism development in the Mekong subregion leads to the conclusion that the policies pursued by national tourism authorities and supranational bodies such as the Agency for Coordinating Mekong Tourism Activities have been those most suitable for promoting the industry rather than for the protection of the environment and the well-being of local communities. National and regional tourism agencies have done little to develop effective mechanisms to monitor and control developments aimed at curbing environmental, social and cultural problems resulting from rapid tourism expansion. Management plans, if there are any, are often sidelined, and environmental, zoning and construction laws are not being properly enforced. Many critical tourism-related issues—such as corruption, social vices, encroachment of public lands and diversion of natural resources, displacement of local and indigenous communities, and political suppression and human rights abuses—have been typically neglected by tourism policy-makers and project managers.

Whereas the concept of "sustainable tourism" implies a high degree of public participation in the development process, Mekong tourism remains a "top-down" affair. Despite the fact that governments and international institutions have in recent years vowed to work with civil society organizations to involve all stakeholders in development initiatives, critics remain highly skeptical.

As for the ADB, for example, Walden Bello, a sociology professor from the Philippines, notes, "The ADB prides itself with being the first multilateral lending agency to have a board-approved policy statement on good governance, which it defines as governance marked by 'accountability, participation, predictability, and transparency.'" Many ADB staff members are, however, very cynical about the new policy. Says one senior person, "It's a question of practicing what you preach. There's a lot of discontent inside the Bank, precisely because it is one of the most non-accountable, non-participatory, and non-transparent institutions around."

Indeed, there is so far little, if any, evidence that civil society now has more say in shaping tourism policies at the national and regional levels. In Thailand, people can at least advance their interests to some extent through a well-established NGO community and a relatively free press. But in other Mekong countries, particularly Burma, China, Laos and Vietnam, ordinary citizens barely have an opportunity to make their voices heard due to the lack of democratic institutions.

As a result, there is no adequate public discussion on these crucial questions relating to tourism development: who owns the land and natural resources earmarked for tourism;

where and how tourism-related facilities and infrastructure should be built; how to handle the anticipated mass influx of visitors in the region; and how exactly to minimize tourism's impacts and conflicts of interests between government, industry and ordinary citizens?

The old question of who actually benefits from tourism also needs to be raised anew, particularly in the face of globalization and liberalization. As with Third World tourism in general, Mekong tourism is largely driven by foreign corporate interests, and the economic gains are often greatly overestimated. A 2001 UNCTAD study found that the economic viability of tourism in less-developed countries is threatened by levels of external financial "leakages" that can easily reach 75 per cent.

That means a high proportion of tourism revenue never reaches destination countries, or leaves as profits to foreign tourism companies or in exchange for goods and services imported to meet the demand from the tourism sector. The pressure on governments to open their travel and tourism industries is being augmented by the structural adjustment programs imposed by the International Monetary Fund in response to the 1997 Asian financial crisis—despite increasing recognition of the risks.

For instance, most of today's foreign direct investment in tourism in the region is not devoted to new job-creating projects but primarily to mergers and acquisitions. Transnational corporations are rapidly buying up domestic tourism-related companies, which results in a massive transfer of wealth to foreign corporate hands.

This situation is compounded by ongoing efforts to deregulate the travel and tourism sector under the World Trade Organization/General Agreement on Trade in Services system. There are grave concerns that progressive liberalization of the service sector further undermines the economic viability of local enterprises and countries' ability to allocate necessary resources for the preservation of natural and cultural assets and sustainable community development. In addition to the political, social and ethnic turmoil that characterizes many parts of the Mekong River Basin area, events such as the Gulf crisis in 1991, the Asian economic crisis in 1997 and the September 11 attacks in the United States have shown the highly volatile nature of the global tourism industry.

Countries that rely heavily on tourism income are most vulnerable to unexpected setbacks, with millions of people directly and indirectly involved in the industry immediately facing greater economic and social insecurity. A recent report by the United Nations' Economic Commission for Asia and the Pacific, confirms that job losses resulting from September 11 has led to "new poverty" in Asian nations with a high dependence on tourism and exports.

Given the many political and economic uncertainties in the post-September 11 era, which emphasize the issue of unpredictable demand, it is of utmost importance that Mekong countries and regional intergovernmental agencies fundamentally rethink their tourism policies. They should recognize that inflated tourism promotion and development is an unsustainable route for any country and region. Governments should seek to reduce dependency on tourism and think about alternative development strategies to bring about greater stability of national economies, secure livelihoods for local people, and social and environmental sustainability.

Rather than opening up more and more areas in the name of "ecotourism", decision makers need to be persuaded to develop and implement proper rehabilitation programs for areas already affected by inequitable and damaging tourism. Instead of relinquishing control over land and natural and cultural resources to outside tourism investors and forces of commercialization, the top priority should be to strengthen local residents' rights to self-determined development. New and bold strategies are needed to help people in tourist areas create a new identity and rebuild livable communities—in social, economic, cultural and environmental terms.

The uneven and unequal nature of development was

emphasised and it was argued that an effective analysis of tourism must acknowledge the importance of relationships of power. In this chapter we begin to consider the way in which power is reflected through tourism in more detail. We start with a consideration of concepts of power and how these can assist a critical comprehension of tourism development; ideology, discourse and hegemony will be discussed in turn. The chapter then reviews the most systematic attempt to explain the unequal nature of tourism development - the political economy of Third World tourism that seeks to emphasise the dominance and control of tourism from the First World.

The discussion moves on to trace other ways in which power has been implicated in the analysis of Third World tourism, particularly through the use of imperialism and colonialism. It is argued that these relationships of dominance have also emerged in new forms of tourism with the citation of 'neo-colonialism' and 'eco-colonialism'. This chapter also provides a review of the importance of 'authenticity' to the study of tourism. It is argued that a consideration of authenticity is a further way in which relationships of power can be traced.

While the political economy of Third World tourism is of considerable interest and applicability (and indeed remains an important framework for understanding unequal development, especially of mass tourism) it is argued that it does not provide such a penetrating critique of new forms of tourism in the Third World. Indeed, political economy approaches suggest that the dominance of the First World over the Third World can be overcome, in part, by the creation of new 'alternative' forms of tourism. We challenge this suggestion.

The final section of the chapter suggests an alternative critique through four key characteristics of much new tourism. The first emphasises that all forms of tourism are tied into the growth and expansion of capitalist relations of production. We call this characteristic 'intervention and commodification'. It builds upon the economic aspects of globalisation from the previous chapter and stresses the way in which holiday destinations are either drawn into a global system of interdependency, or are by-passed by it.

Given the context of global inequality and unevenness of development, the second characteristic stresses the 'subservience' that critics have argued characterises much tourism in the Third World, regardless of the form it takes. The final two characteristics seek to provide a more nuanced critique of new forms of tourism, referred to as 'fetishism' and 'aestheticisation', which seek to demonstrate the way in which the reality of the Third World is either hidden or is used to create a special aura of travelling in Third World regions.

Although we invariably associate tourism with pleasure and a certain playfulness, Indian academic, Nina Rao, reminds us that 'Tourism takes place in the context of great inequality of wealth and power', and power relations are central to our discussions in this book - we have already indicated in the previous chapter that power is crucial to a critical understanding of development. In pursuing this argument, we are seeking to address an identifiable weakness in much work on tourism.

On the one hand, much tourism analysis has played down relationships of power, which remain either implicit or are absent. Such studies have largely consisted of identifying structural and deterministic models of tourism. These are examined more appropriately. On the other hand, where power is invoked in a discussion of tourism it has tended to be in passing; references to ideology, discourse, colonialism, imperialism and so on, appear in a rather unstructured, even anecdotal, fashion.

Although such analysis is commendable in signalling the importance of power in the study of tourism, the treatment of power needs to be approached more thoughtfully. As Crick (1989) concludes from a wide-ranging review of social science literature, there is an inadequate representation of the complexities of tourism.

Initially, it is necessary to consider concepts of power

that may assist a critical understanding of contemporary tourism and the themes we introduced in the previous chapter (globalisation, sustainability and development). In addition, the discussion suggests how relationships of power are embodied in the 'project' of sustainability. In short, we are arguing that we require what Massey (1995b) refers to as a 'geography of power' to make sense of Third World tourism development.

IDEOLOGY

While ideology is a complex term, one profound trait stands out: namely, its concern with the 'bases and validity of our most fundamental ideas'. In using the term ideology, we will be referring not only to the sustaining of relationships of domination in the interest of a dominant political power (the USA as the only global superpower, for example) or social thought (the supposed significance of religion to 'civilisation', for example), but also to interests that are opposed to dominant power (the anti-nuclear movement, environmentalists, feminists and so on) that are themselves capable of forming ideologies in the pursuit of power.

Although, as Eagleton (1991) notes, this may signal a degree of contradiction in the meaning of ideology, it is nevertheless fundamental to the notion that ideology is about the way relationships of power are inexorably interwoven in the production and representation of meaning which serves the interests of a particular social group.

As Dobson concludes, ideologies 'map the world in different ways' (1995:7), and it is the intention of this book to map the way in which different interests are implicated in the uneven and unequal development of tourism.

Sustainability is ideological in the sense that it is largely from the First World that the consciousness and mobilisation around global environmental issues have been generated and in the sense that sustainability serves the interests of the First World. Adams (1990), for instance, refers to the ideology of sustainable development, and in the context of tourism in southern Mexico, Daltabuit and Pi-Sunyer (1990) refer to the 'ideology of environmentalism'. The power implicated through First World environmentalism has led increasingly to the 'charge' of eco-imperialism and eco-colonialism.

Implicit in these criticisms is the idea that sustainability is ostensibly ethnocentric. Reconsider for a moment the quote from Robins where he talks about the export of western valucs and priorities. Such observations can also be applied to the current debate on sustainability. For the most part, it is a discussion framed in the West and imposed on the 'Rest', and hence the acrimonious debates between First and Third World countries at the Rio Summit, Seattle trade talks and the G8 Summit in Genoa to name just a few.

DISCOURSE

The second key concept, discourse, is closely related to ideology. Ideology is perhaps best thought of as a discriminator between power struggles which are central to a 'whole form of social life' (socialism, feminism, ecologism perhaps) and those which are, for whatever reason, relatively less holistic. Prioritising the most important forms of struggle may be an exercise of power itself, but it is important to signal which struggles are ideological and which are not.

Discourse can be considered as complementary to ideology. Indeed ideology is a matter of 'discourse', a 'question of who is saying what to whom for what purposes'. But discourse can also be non-ideological; in other words, it is not reducible to ideology.

The French philosopher, Michel Foucault (1980) suggests that discourse expresses how 'facts' can be conveyed in different ways and how the language used to convey these facts can interfere with our ability to decide what is true and what is false. Discourse, Foucault argues, is so much more than 'mere' words; words are not 'wind, an external whisper, a beating of wings that one has difficulty in hearing in the serious matter of history'; words as a discourse provide the conditions, practice, rules and regulations on thought.

As such, 'development' and 'sustainability' are powerful discourses as our earlier discussion suggested. For example, the term 'carrying capacity' (an important tool in the study of sustainability) can be subdivided into different types: ecological, social, economic, physical, real, effective, aesthetic; and all of these can be interpreted and measured in different ways by different people at different times and in different circumstances. But carrying capacity is often treated as if it were a 'neutral' ecological term. Zaba and Scoones challenge this neutrality: 'most of us have no problems with the notion of the carrying capacity of Botswana (pop. 1.3 m, area 567,000 sq km), but would be incredulous at the idea of calculating the carrying capacity of Birmingham (pop. 1.1 m, area 300 sq km)' (1994:197).

Not only does the notion of ecological sustainability bring some kind of scientific validity with it, but it also suggests that some places (in this case Third World environments) are more suited to its application than others. In this way, carrying capacity as discourse transmits and translates power.

There is no agreement over the exact nature, content and meaning of sustainability. It is a contested concept in all senses of the word. Different interests - supranational and transnational organisations, INGOs, socio-environmental organisations, social classes and so on - have adopted and defend their own language (discourse) of sustainability. The new socio-environmental organisations mobilised around issues of environment, for example, are not in power, and yet their ability to influence the meaning of sustainability for our everyday lives has been marked.

Similarly, consider the power to interpret and represent the Third World through travel books and brochures. On the one hand, we have the highbrow, intellectual accounts of best-selling travel writers such as Paul Theroux and Eric Newby, authors noted for the 'authoritativeness of their vision', and the serious travel pages of broadsheet newspapers.

On the other hand, we have glossy high street tourist brochures selling destinations from the Caribbean to Thailand, and which are the subject of much highbrow, intellectual criticism. These are simply different ways of outsiders representing and interpreting the Third World to their audience, each claiming authenticity and truth, albeit in very different ways.

Foucault's ideas may lead to the conclusion that knowledge in tourism is produced by competing discourses. Discourse, therefore, is a useful concept in emphasising how a certain subject or topic is talked and thought about and how it is represented to others. Most importantly, discourses are 'part of the way power circulates and is contested' (Hall, 1992b: 295).

HEGEMONY

Discourse is also an essential property of hegemony, our last concept, in the power jigsaw. Hegemony was a concept developed by the Italian marxist, Antonio Gramsci, to emphasise the ability of dominant classes to convince the majority of subordinate classes to adopt certain political, cultural or moral values; a more efficient strategy than coercing subordinate social groups into conformity.

Hegemony, therefore, is essentially about the power of persuasion and is immediately differentiated from ideology, which by contrast may be imposed forcibly (Eagleton, 1991), as in the former apartheid system in South Africa or through the imposition of IMF structural adjustment policies. The best way to conceive of hegemony is as a 'broader category than ideology' which '*includes* ideology, but is not reducible to it'.

The real innovativeness of Gramsci's thinking is the conclusion that hegemony is never fully realised in capitalist societies - that it is continually contested. As Williams concludes, hegemony must be 'renewed, recreated, defended, and modified' and is 'inseparable from overtones of struggle'; a relationship that does not necessarily hold true for ideology.

The concepts of the Third World, development, sustainability and tourism are examples of hegemony in practice. Tourism, as we shall see in later chapters, is replete with examples of hegemonic strategies ranging from tourism codes of conduct to the advocacy of more responsible, appropriate or sustainable forms of tourism.

It is also evident in the way in which tourism is contested between different social groups (traveller versus tourist, for example) and between different places (Thailand versus Chile, for example). Hegemony is especially useful for its dynamism and practical usage encompassing and focusing attention on a wide range of practical strategies that are adopted by a variety of interests.

Such characteristics place notions of struggle and contest at the centre of the enquiry. A useful example is provided by Hutnyk's critique of travellers-cum-volunteers in Kolkata (India). Considering questions of cultural hegemony, Hutnyk argues that travellers' ability to engage in and promote the complexities of Kolkata are compromised by:

- The insularity of traveller culture and traveller style;
- The cultural and class background of western travellers;
- The hegemony of western versions of Calcutta in "traveller lore"; and
- The hegemonic effects of the traveller "gaze"' (1996:44).

The advocacy by environmentalists of the need to act globally, for example, is an interesting aspect of the persuasiveness of sustainability and how it ties in both the global and local dimensions and stresses the interdependency of places. Residents of distant places are asked to 'consider' other places; in the dictum of Friends of the Earth, 'think globally, act locally'.

Conservation measures in southern Africa and rainforest preservation in Central America can be lobbied for and financed from the First World; and a degree of control and influence over Third World affairs is exercised through First World conscience-prodding. Sachs refers to this as the 'hegemony of globalism':

Until the 1980s, environmentalists were usually concerned with the local or national space ... But in subsequent years, they began to look at things from a much more elevated vantage point: they adopted the astronaut's view, taking in the entire globe at one glance. Today's ecology is in the business of saving nothing less than the planet. Testimony to the hegemonic properties of sustainability, perhaps, is the rapidity with which the word has entered public usage on a seemingly global level since its use by Brundtland in 1987 (World Commission on Environment and Development, 1987), along with the large number of texts that are devoted to dissecting, interpreting, defending or reclaiming the idea of sustainability. For some it is a means of sustaining much more than just environment. It is about 'sustainable development' and incorporates indicators such as income, employment, health, housing, human welfare indicators that are concerned with a 'more rounded policy goal than "economic growth"'.

For others sustainability is to be reclaimed within a far more radical agenda of political ecology where ecological issues and questions of social justice are paramount. Characteristic of hegemonic positions, sustainability is contested within a continuum of viewpoints ranging from 'reformism' (often referred to as light green, conservationist or environmentalist) to 'radicalism' (referred to variously as dark green, deep ecology or, in Dobson's (1995) phraseology, ecologism).

Similarly, sustainability and its application to tourism should not be considered a once-and-for-all position - a neutral, scientific term to which techniques can be applied and upon which policies and programmes can be implemented and evaluated and blueprints, ideal types and models catalogued and advocated.

Rather, it constantly changes as the broader influences and interests change, reflecting a dynamic situation and concept. In the next section we turn to the most concentrated analysis of power in tourism: that offered by the approach known as political economy which is derivative of the neo-Marxist dependency theory discussed in the previous chapter.

THE POLITICAL ECONOMY OF THIRD WORLD TOURISM

By the early to mid-1970s it was already acknowledged

that tourism did not necessarily offer a panacea to Third World countries struggling for economic growth. A number of highly critical studies focusing, in particular, on the fate of the small island economies in the Caribbean began to highlight the unequal economic and social impacts associated with tourism. Of special importance was the observation that Third World economies drawn to tourism as a way of earning foreign exchange witnessed the leaking of much of the money made, straight back out of their national economies. This leakage, as it is now commonly known, was seen to arise primarily as a result of the First World ownership and control of the tourism industry in the Third World: from hotels to tour operators and airlines.

These early studies also began to hint at the relationship between tourism and 'underdevelopment'. It was not until Stephen Britton's analysis of Fiji, however, that a more thorough attempt was made in applying dependency theory to the study of tourism. The importance of Britton's analysis is that he stresses the need 'to place tourism firmly within the dialogue on development' (1982:332) and investigate why tourism so often perpetuates uneven and unequal relationships between the First and Third Worlds.

The theory of dependency is best understood as a riposte to the *laissez-faire* (free market economics) approach to economic development and international trade. The global expansion of capitalism has drawn the Third World into increasingly tight economic relationships with the First World, and tourism, now the largest global industry, has been a significant component in this process. Dependency theory has sought to demonstrate how and why these tightening relationships are highly unequal.

Dependency theory argues that western capitalist countries have grown as a result of the expropriation of surpluses from the Third World, especially because of the reliance of Third World countries on export-oriented industries (coffee, bananas, bauxite and so on) which are notoriously precarious in terms of world market prices. The theory uses the notion of centre-periphery (or core-periphery) relationships to highlight this unequal relationship, where the core is the locus of economic power within a global economy.

The most widely cited of the dependency theorists, André Gunder Frank, takes matters one step further in his notion of the 'development of underdevelopment' which stresses that it is the underdevelopment of the structures in Third World countries created by First World capitalist development that creates dependency.

Above all else, theories of dependency are in general agreement that the interdependence resulting from global economic expansion and the inability for autonomous growth results in unequal and uneven development. Britton applies this body of theory to tourism.

Centrally, he argues, dependency involves the 'subordination of national economic autonomy' (1982:334) as a direct result of the unequal relationships inherent in the world economy and that within the present structure of international tourism, Third World countries can assume only a passive role (1981a). Britton summarises his approach as follows:

Underdeveloped countries promote tourism as a means of generating foreign exchange, increasing employment opportunities, attracting development capital, and enhancing economic independence.

The structural characteristics of Third World economies, however, can detract from achieving several of these goals. But equally problematic is the organisation of the international tourist industry itself. But Britton's research and narrative are very much part of the analysis of the mainstream - mass - tourism industry.

As such, he argues that tourism in Third World economies is best conceptualised as an enclave industry as the 'golden ghettos' and by Krippendorf (1987) as 'holidays in the ghetto') where tourists only occasionally venture beyond the bounds of their hotel compounds (referred to as an 'environmental bubble'). While Britton's critique is widely cited and provides valuable insights into the unequal structure of Third World tourism, we must ask how useful his analysis is for a critical understanding of new forms of Third World tourism that seek to escape the 'ghettos'. We return to this consideration a little later.

TOURISM AS DOMINATION

Given the arguments advanced by an increasing number of tourism commentators that the Third World is structurally dependent on the First World, there is little surprise in finding a wide range of references to the principal forms of global domination: colonialism and imperialism. While these terms are often used loosely and interchangeably, colonialism is best conceived as a special form of imperialism (that is, the imposition of power by one state over another) involving the occupation of territories. The following sections begin to build up a picture of how these relationships of power are reflected in the analysis of tourism.

The significance of colonialism and imperialism to theories of underdevelopment and dependency has a special appeal to writers on tourism. Both the characteristic First World ownership of much Third World tourism infrastructure and the origin of tourists from the First World have for many become an irresistible analogy of colonial and imperial domination.

Indeed, the distinction drawn in dependency theory between a First World core and Third World periphery is part of a more general theory of imperialism. Nash argues that tourism only exists in so much as the metropolitan core generates the demand for tourism and the tourists themselves. He concludes 'it is this power over touristic and related developments abroad that makes a metropolitan centre imperialistic and tourism a form of imperialism' (1989:35).

Similarly, van den Abbeele (1980) laments tourism as doubly imperialistic both in turning Third World cultures into a commodity and providing hedonistic practices for wealthy First World tourists.

Clearly, this is more than just an academic concern or critique. Take, for example, Box 3.1 which provides the background to Survival's campaign on tourism and tribal peoples.

For Third World critics in particular, as Gonsalves observes, it is the very presence of tourists that leads to the 'view that modern tourism is an extension of colonialism (with all the attributes of a master-servant relationship)' (1993:11). It is an increasingly widely shared opinion within the Third World.

Chung Hyung Kyung's observations are illustrative of the passion and conviction with which these are expressed: 'Colonialism has many faces. Third World tourism, an advanced form of "post-colonialism", is a disease which destroys people's bodies and souls ... Third World tourism carries a major symptom of colonialism: "Domination and Subjugation"'.

It is this notion that tourism is implicated in the maintenance of neo-colonial states that is so important here. Perez (1974), for example, argues that 'Travel from metropolitan centres to the West Indies has served historically to underwrite colonialism in the Caribbean' (1974:473). And Bruner insists that, however much we attempt to deny or evade the relationship, 'colonialism ... and tourism ... were born together and are relatives' (1989:439).

They are, Bruner contends, driven by the same social processes involving the occupying of space (by tourist infrastructure and ultimately by tourists) opened through the expansion of power.

It is not just academics that are drawing parallels between tourism and colonialism. Srisang, a former Executive of the Ecumenical Coalition on Third World Tourism (ECTWT), the world's largest NGO on tourism, suggests that:

tourism, especially Third World tourism, as it is practised today, does not benefit the majority of people. Instead it exploits them, pollutes the environment, destroys the ecosystem, bastardises the culture, robs people of their traditional values and ways of life and subjugates women and children in the abject slavery of prostitution. In other words, tourism epitomises the present unjust world economic order where the few who control wealth and power dictate the terms. As such, tourism is little different from colonialism.

The ECTWT itself is equally outspoken, referring to the majority of Third World tourism as 'an expression of neo-colonialism contributing to racism, erosion of moral values, economic impoverishment and cultural degradation' (ECTWT leaflet, undated).

For other writers, however, the relationship between colonialism and tourism to which they allude amounts to little more than a casual or anecdotal observation, often on the tourists themselves.

Hence, the analogies between the affluent middle classes and 'scavengers', the 'easy-going tourist' and the 'conqueror and colonialist', the suggestion that 'for many tourists, aggressive - almost colonialist - behaviour becomes a norm while on holiday', and the charge that tourists are the 'terrorists of cultural expansion'. As Krippendorf concludes, in the absence of changes, tourism will remain for the host 'a special form of subservience'.

While such observations are understandable, even justified in the way in which tourism seems to reawaken memories of a colonial past, they represent a reaction to tourism based more upon an emotional response. In this vein, as Allen and Hamnett conclude, it 'can be argued ... just as some "Third World" countries have thrown off the yoke of colonialism, they have taken up the yoke of tourism'.

Two observations arise from this review. First, is the rather ambiguous fashion in which the charge of imperialism and colonialism is often made. Because tourism is a conduit for relationships of power, it has been easy for authors to use terms for these forms of domination to describe a vast array of relationships involved; from multinational hotel chains to a waiter-diner exchange.

It has, therefore, become an attractive comparison to make, with the words imperialism and colonialism immediately invoking certain images and responses in our minds. Second, as we observed with Britton, a good deal of the critique arises from observations of the mainstream mass tourism industry. It is somewhat blunt or crude in dealing with new forms of tourism whose claim is to escape these very relationships of domination.

In the section 'Alternative critiques for alternative tourism?', therefore, we attempt to analyse (or disaggregate) these forms of power. This provides a clearer picture of how relationships of domination are manifest and suggests how these observations might be applied to new forms of tourism.

One way in which the discussion can be reframed, is through the reference to 'neocolonialism'. As Thomas argues, although colonialism as a pervasive moment in history has all but gone, 'the persistence of neo-colonial domination in international and inter-ethnic relations is undeniable' (1994:1). In the context of tourism, the charge of neo-colonialism has already emerged as a principal way of describing the retention of former colonies in a state of perpetual subordination to the First World, in spite of formal political independence, a view reflected in de Rivero's analysis of non-viable national economies (2001).

Hence, Britton (1981c) refers to Fiji as a neo-colonial economy and seeks to demonstrate why tourism reinforces the pattern of spatial organisation which evolved during colonialism. The tourist industry he argues is a 'neo-colonial extension of economic forms present in pre-independent Fiji'. Similarly, Shivji argues of Tanzania, 'Since the success of tourism depends primarily on our being accepted in the metropolitan countries, it is one of those appendage industries which give rise to a neo-colonialist relationship and cause underdevelopment'.

While such analysis is clearly significant in constructing a broader critique of Third World tourism, the discussion has too often been restricted to a consideration of economic impacts. So, for example, the complexities of class and race have been largely neglected and the spectre of neo-colonialism engendering a subtle, but pervasive racism, has remained largely unexplored.

Again, we will return to such considerations below. Most notably then, a discussion of neo-colonialism allows us to think in terms of the existence of discourses of 'colonialisms' (Thomas, 1994), and explore the many different ways in which power is spatially and socially expressed in a so-called post-colonial world.

One way in which we can immediately see the relevance of thinking in terms of different forms of neo-colonialism is its application to sustainability and environmentalism, and ultimately to development. On the one hand, there are emerging critiques of environmental organisations themselves, not far removed from the critical attacks launched on other supranational agencies such as the World Bank and IMF. Phillipson, an internal auditor of the WWF, for example, accuses them of 'egocentricity and neo-colonialism'.

Central to these criticisms is the way in which organisations seek to impose policies and programmes on Third World countries. On the other hand, a more thorough critique of environmentalism and ecologism as a movement has begun to emerge. Such criticisms have tended to focus on the morality vested in the 'environment' (an entity that must be protected and saved) and the crusade-like fashion with which environmental issues are pursued.

To advance the analogy, there is a sense in which an army of eco-missionaries, or as some would argue, eco-fundamentalists, have fanned out across the Third World to green the Earth's poor.

As noted earlier, the moral basis for environmentalists' claims has emanated from the symbol of interdependence and 'oneness' of the Earth which is founded upon the notion of a global ecosystem. Wolfgang Sachs neatly draws out the relationships of power and domination from this 'systems language' that is committed to 'regulation and control' (1992a: 22), arguing the 'terms "ecosystem" or "global system" cannot shake off the legacy of engineering', and the 'concept ecosystem that gave to the ecology movement a quasi-spiritual dimension and scientific credibility at the same time' (1992b: 31).

Sachs concludes that for many environmentalists 'ecology seems to reveal the moral order of being ... it suggests not only the truth, but also a moral imperative and ... aesthetic perfection' (1992b: 32). Central to Sachs's concern is the way in which the universalistic discourses on development, or the 'hegemony of globalism' as he refers to it, have imposed a system of global resource management that undermines nature and undercuts local autonomy, difference and diversity. Sachs concludes:

In the face of the overriding imperative to 'secure the survival of the planet', autonomy easily becomes an anti-social value, and diversity turns into an obstacle to collective action. Can one imagine a more powerful motive for forcing the world into line than that of saving the planet? Eco-colonialism constitutes a new danger for the tapestry of cultures on the globe.

From Sachs's (and others') writings, we are quickly led to question the intention and outcome of much environmentalism and the way it is advanced through notions of sustainability. As the environmental critic, Vandana Shiva, asks rhetorically: 'Global environment or green imperialism?' The importance, once again, is the way in which such discussion reflects back on the global changes considered. Globalisation drives us towards the logical conclusion that there is only one world: a global economy, a global culture, a global environment. It is the violent imposition of this idea from the First World, an imposition clearly reflected in the Rio Summit, which creates the 'moral base for green imperialism'.

These critiques of environment and ecology have clear and wide-ranging ramifications for the study of tourism too. It is the power invested in the concepts such as sustainable tourism and environmental tourism that have been central to critical responses. Reflecting the discussion of discourse, Herman argues 'sustainable tourism is rooted in much "double-speak"'.

This double-speak needs to be recognised as 'The misuse of words by implicit re-definition, selective application of ... words, and other forms of verbal manipulation'. Similarly, writing of tourism development in Quintana Roo, southern

Mexico, Daltabuit and Pi-Sunyer refer to environmentalism as a 'powerful rhetoric' (1990:10).

A CALL TO SOLIDARITY

The debate on tourism, in the Third World, now nearly three decades old, was long dominated by voices from First World sending countries. However, during the past decade an indigenous Third World critique has been articulated, initially by and through the Ecumenical Coalition on Third World Tourism and its, global networks, and more recently, by NGOs, church's, tourism activists, evironmentalists and women, in destination areas, who have chosen to react directly to the issue, as well as indirectly through the communications media.

Acting on behalf of the "host" community, Third World tourism activists (particularly those in Asia) have souity with concerned people in sending nations. They have successfully conducted campaigns against five-star tourism (especially hotels and resorts set up by multinational corporations) with active collaboration of network partners in the West.

The action of the Goa-based Jagrut Goenkaranchi Fauz (JGF) against the Kempinski hotel conglomerate, in tandem with German-speaking members of Tourismus mit Einsicht (TmE), is perhaps the best known example of international solidarity on Third World tourism. Of late, the campaign to End Child Prostitution in Asian Tourism (ECPAT) has sought to create its own model of global collaboration on one very, specific tourism-related issue, child prostitution.

Although the primary focus of tourism activists in the Third World is on building up local awareness and resistance, worldwide solidarity is an important aspect of the struggle against an industry that has a web of international links. For Third World tourism activists, the solidarity they seek is interms of a response to their local struggles. No less, no more.

TOURISM AND THE NEW DEVELOPMENT DEBATE

The ideological roots of Third World tourism activism lie in the post-World War II decolonization process and the resulting debates on socio-economic strategies to be followed in the "developing world." Central to the development debate were issues of class and state formation in these countries, as well as the nature and extent of capitalist development that had already taken place.

In the terms of this discourse, the tourism industry was once characterized by Frantz Fanon as a "European hedonocracy," where "the national middle class [in the host country] will have nothing better to do than to take on the role of manager for western enterprise and... will in practice set up its country as the brothel of Europe."

Three decades later, another war has ended, and the debate on nation-states and national identity has started afresh. While most visible in the former Eastern bloc (and countries such as unified Germany), its current is sweeping through much of the Third World as well.

No longer underscored by the economic and military might of the erstwhile Soviet Union, socialist countries such as Vietnam and Cuba are forced to embrace the gospel of global capitalism, in a desperate bid for survival. Even India and Brazil, with more resilient economies, have begun to restructure along lines suggested by multinational capital and its lending agencies, the World Bank and the International Monetary Fund (IMF).

Inevitably, the Third World development critique has come under pressure. It is being asked to reexamine its fundamental premise that the world is an unequal one, and to accept that, since development strategies followed so farhave "failed," a renewed attempt should be made to "uplift" the impoverished masses, with fresh doses of bilateral aid and private capital.

A decade into the struggle, tourism activists are being told that tourism is here to stay, and therefore, action towards a new form of tourism—humane, acceptable, eco-friendly—could win them new friends and influence more people They are being asked to participate' in tourism decision-making, in spite of the fact that they have already made a decision against' tourism.

RADICALISM OR ALTERNATIVE ACTION

In order to establish the kind of alternative tourism we would want to establish we would need a high degree of independerice from existing structures. Tourism activist Peter Holden notes that "this probably means we would need to own and operate out own airline, control vast amounts of capital, and operate a giant bureaucracy. Perhaps it's just as well that this is beyond our immediate grasp," Holden says, "and we are free of some of its pitfalls."

The idea (or hope, for some) that tourism activists would participate, in shaping tourism policy has been around for quite a while. As long ago as 1977, Harry Matthew was saying, "Whether or not future tourism policies...reflect constructively the radical critique will depend immensely upon the ability of the radical critics to put their point across to political leaders. How much political clout do critics of tourism have? In developing countries where tourism has not yet become a pervading sector of the economy, there may yet be time for radicals (who will no longer be radicals) to help shape tourism policy."

For the Third World activist, involvement in "alternative tourism" meant something quite different, however. Chayant Pholpoke, an early practitioner, described his work thus in 1984: "Alternative tourism, as I perceive it, can play a supportive role in building solidarity among people all over the world who want to build a more just society."

At about the same time, German churches, who were supportive of tourism concerns, evolved a set of "criteria for the promotion of study tours into countries of the Third World and for their reverse programs (return visits)." The aims clearly stated such study tours "must be in line with the ecumenical principles of development which means that they have to be part of processes that strengthen liberating and just structures."

The message that Pholpoke and others were tying to convey was one that was picked up quickly, too quickly perhaps. While they saw their efforts as having an essential political basis, their "followers" saw a market for a new tourism. Literature aimed at the "concerned" tourist flooded Europe, the German-language *Sympathie* magazines setting a trend of sorts. Ludmilla Tuting and Kunda Dixit's *Bikas-Binas:Development-Destruction*, a collection of material on environmental issues in Nepal and the Himalaya, is a "handbook" that was published in 1986 for the new breed of "ecc-tourists."

Commercial publications such as the Rough Guides and Lonely Planet handbooks reach out to the individual traveller rather than the mass (charter/package) tourism market. Alternative tourism, in the wake of the Vietnam War, became a collage of red and green, reflecting the pro-left and (early) ecological agendas of the peace movement.

Uncomfortable with this rendition of alternative tourism, Chayant Pholpoke, wrote in 1985: "Our friends in the West still do not get the message we are trying to get across. And it seems that the word 'alternative' has confused them more than enlightening them on the negative aspect of mass conventional tourism. Indeed, the word 'alternative' has many alternative meanings. We may not have that many alternatives left but to build up more awareness."

Peter Holden joined the debate in 1988, writing: "I hope that: the 'red herring' of alternativelourism can be seen for what it is....I do not believe that alternative tourism is the agenda of the Third World, but rather the agenda of some elite people in the 'First World' who want to travel in an alternative way....Our business is to change the shape of tourism."

The view that modern tourism is an extension of colonialism (with all the attributes's of a "master-servant' relationship) is widely held by Third World' critics of tourism. It is hardly surprising, therefore, that the critique 'opposes any form of its expansion, and refuses to be drawn into a discussion of so-called "alternative," "responsible," or "acceptable" tourism. To a Third World critic, such proposals would resemble those on "acceptable" colonialism or "acceptable" nuclear power.

The following exchange between a Third World radical

and a Western industry specialist illustrates the width of the divide that separates the two sides in debates about native participation in tourism promotion.

First, from activist Haunani Kay-Trask: "I don't agree with the fact that we have to accept tourism. I don't want tourists....I'm tired of people saying, 'Well, you know, you need tourism.' We don't need tourism. We lived for 2,000 years without tourism. There is no such thing as an innocent tourist. Everyone is culpable, and the violence that has been done against us and my people, against my culture and my sacred land, will be returned in kind."

In response to Haunani Kay-Trask's statement at the 1985 Bad Boll meeting on Third World People and Tourism, industry specialist Leo Theuns writes: "The church multinational (World Council of Churches) moves in strange company opposing multinationals in the travel industry. Not only in the sense that 'anti-imperialist forces' were brought together at the Bad Boll meeting under church aegis but, more than that, a revolutionary was given an opportunity to bring her message about the inevitable violence that she hopes will soon occur on the island of Hawaii."

Whether or not tourism is here to stay, many of its critics in the Third World will continue to oppose it, on the grounds that the tourism industry is a means of the continued expansion of Western domination in socio-cultural, economic and political terms. That tourism has the support of many Third World governments and national leaders does little to allay the doubts of critics.

As Satinath Sarangi says: "To demand 'people's participation' in planning such schemes is particularly illogical. It implies that a development process which goes fundamentally against the interests of the people can become acceptable if people participate in it."

THIRD WORLD POLITICAL ECONOMY OF TOURISM

Many—if not all—of the underlying factors that motivated Third World people in the first place to act on tourism (and a variety of other related issues) continue to exist and grow, and the development gap is widening. It is imperative to take stock, not just of the issues of tourism, but also of the perspectives Third World people have, particularly on the political and economic agendas of tourism.

This is not to say that a clear Third World political economy. of tourism exists. In the past decade, we have listened to a variety of Third World voices and arguments against tourism. These have ranged across a wide spectrum of philosophical and ideological lines: anarchist, nationalist, conservative, liberal, progovernment, feminist, nostalgic conservationist, radical ecologist, Marxist, religious, atheist, and just plain moralist.

The response of concerned people elsewhere has been largely to the issues raised (the text), with little attention paid to the varied ideological underpinnings (sub-text). As a result, we have failed in the effort to articulate and incorporate a comprehensive Third World critique of tourism. What dominates is a critique of tourism developed and articulated from a Northern, sending-country perspective.

A similar fragmentation exists in academic discussions on tourism and for much the same reasons. To quote Nina Rao: "Is there a forum for Third World narratives in international tourism discourse? Can Indian narratives like exploitation of gender, class, caste, poverty, [or] terrorism ever enter the tourism discourse?

Can one really describe the encounter between the tourist Self and the Other in the so-called voluntary relation of guest and host? Such: a relation is again dictated by the tourism discourse which seeks to sweep away the basic commercial nature of the encounter. What causes concern in the Third World narrative (the subversive narrative) is the effect on the Other."

Conflicting perspectives and expectations within the international networks concerned with Third World tourism have inevitably led to doubts, on the part of several Third World activists, regarding the reliability and motivation of their Western partners, on whom they depend for solidarity action. First raised by the JGF at the 1991 global meeting of tourism activists at Cyprus, these doubts have been more comprehensively expressed in Anita Pleumarom's paper "Understanding the Crisis in the Third World Tourism Debate."

Third World activists have a point. A sea-change is needed in the kind of solidarity that we have today, one that is shaped by contemporary realities. But we must realise, at the same time, that part of the responsibility for shaping the critique of tourism lies within the Third World itself. Too often we have depicted a romantic past that has been defiled by tourism and other evils of "modernity." Rarely do we acknowledge that our own histories are tainted, and not just by former colonial powers. As Sophie Dick writes:

This longing for what [E.] San Juan [Jr.] calls an "antediluvian paradisical origin before the Fall," which neatly tucks sexual politics into nationalism, makes it possible to replay every invasion of the Philippines in the rape of every Filipino child...minimizing continuities, ignoring moments of cultural change, and missing questions about family structure and sexual politics that have been monopolized by the right. As Michael Tan says, "a fascist solution is to repress sexual attitudes without solving the problem of poverty which nurtures sex tourism.

What the fascists want is to drive the women back to the kitchen and the bedroom, and not to display themselves 'indecently' in bars. So long as some nationalists also subscribe to a belief in mythical 'good old days' when women didn't have to be exploited in bars and brothels and never mind if they got beaten up at home, pushed into the funeral pyre, we (the nationalists) may well become willing accomplices to the fascists."

WESTERN SOLIDARITY

Recessions and economic slowdowns in the North have prompted many industries to relocate their manufacturing facilities in Southern nations in a search for cheap labour. Other "favorable' conditions offered by host countries in the

South include less stringent quality standards, legal loopholes that permit companies to operate in ways that would not be possible in their own countries, a lack of environmental safeguards, corrupt bureaucrats and politicians, and so on.Northern economic agendas have also dominated discussions about intellectual property rights, GATT, and international aid issues.

These discussions ensure that multinational investments are not merely protected, but are guaranteed artificial profitability, all in the name of "fair" trade and the "free movement of capital."Third World tourism figures prominently in these debates. It is not by chance that a recent annual theme of the World Tourism Organization promoted the "free movement of tourists." The plain fact is that tourism in the Third World is far cheaper than a holiday at home. Everybody profits from it: the industry, the tourists and the economies of the countries they come from. There is laughter all the way to the bank.

Solidarity on Third World tourism issues needs a clear recognition of this reality. The Third World is not a cesspool for the poverty of the West. International networks concerned with Third World tourism have failed to capitalize on opportunities to influence mainstream development debates at forums such as the Earth Sumniit and the World Human Rights Conference We must take better advantage of the opportunities that will certainly arise in the future.

The choicess are clear: either we find new ways of understanding our communicating our concerns, and thereby polilticizing the debate in the widest international arenas or we will remain at our present levels of functioning and interaction. If we choose the first, we must also be willing to accept and work with the consequences of radical change.

Chapter 6

State-Civil Society Relations and Tourism

At the height of the outbreak of the Severe Acute Respiratory Syndrome (SARS) in Singapore in 2003, Singapore Airlines (SIA) pilots belonging to the Air Line Pilots Association of Singapore (Alpa-S) criticized their union's leaders for giving in too easily to management on wage cuts and lay-offs. When the leaders were eventually ousted, then Deputy Prime Minister Lee Hsien Loong (current Prime Minister), stated his support for the ousted Alpa-S leaders and issued this challenge: "the [new] leaders of this group have to think very carefully, do they really want to take on the Government?" ("Govt Will Not Let Pilots 'Do Singapore In': DPM", 29 November 2003).

He echoed what his father—the then Prime Minister (now Minister Mentor) Lee Kuan Yew—said in a similar dispute in 1980: "I don't want to do you in, but I won't let anybody do Singapore in" (ibid.). Lee Hsien Loong's support for the ousted union leaders reflected government concerns that industrial unrest would threaten Singapore's position as an international air hub.

The government warned that it would not tolerate a rebellious pilots' union ("Govt: We Cannot Afford Such Acrimony", 1 December 2003), and subsequently changed legislations to make it unnecessary for union leaders to seek approval from members on agreements ("SIA Pilots: Law to Be Tightened", 1 December 2003). The industrial dispute was resolved amicably between the new union leaders and the senior Lee ("SIA Pilots Pledge Amicable Solution", 24 February 2004). Minister Mentor Lee Kuan Yew said the fact that the pilots agreed to lower wages shows that the country could do what many other countries could not because Singaporeans understand "we got here because we work on special rules" ("Staying Ahead: It's All in Teamwork, Says MM", 14 October 2004).

This example is important because it points to the central role that tourism plays in the Singapore economy. The SARS outbreak and the SIA pilot's dispute threatened the tourism industry. The actions by the Singapore government clearly demonstrate its willingness to intervene for the sake of the industry. Despite the significance of these events and the central importance of tourism in Singapore's economy, tourism is under-examined in research on state-civil society relations in Singapore.

To address this gap, this chapter explores state—civil society relationships in Singapore, paying careful attention to three recent issues that have affected the tourism industry—the re-branding of Singapore, the casino debate, and the introduction of health and medical tourism. In the business of governing Singapore, the People's Action Party (PAP) government has been able to close, absorb, re-define, and open up civil spaces, as a result of which the line separating state and civil society in Singapore is blurred.

Tourism has opened up important civil and social spaces that were once closed. At the same time, the tourism industry has played a central role in shaping Singaporeans' own understanding of their national and ethnic identities.

This chapter is divided into two sections. In the first section I briefly review the body of knowledge on state-civil society relations and tourism.

The short review provides a framework for understanding the situation in Singapore. In the second section, three examples—the re-branding of Singapore, the casino debate, and the introduction of health and medical tourism—illustrate how state-sponsored tourism development and civil society in Singapore are intertwined.

The role of the Singapore Tourism Board (STB) in the Singapore society will also be discussed.

TOURISM AND POLITICS

To many people, tourism is about having fun. For many governments, however, it is an important source of foreign revenue. It provides employment in restaurants, airlines, airports, hotels, and tourism attractions. In addition to their economic impact, tourists can also influence the host country's cultural and social environment.

The tourism industry impacts on civil society in a number of ways: it can lead to social and political activism seeking to balance the positive and negative impacts of tourism; local residents and foreign tourists may be politically socialized through tourism, and that process inevitably re-defines local identities and civil spaces; and the influx of tourists can lend support to the political regime in the destination country, such that tourists may eventually be treated by the government as if they are part of its constituency. These issues are explored in further detail below.

MANAGING THE IMPACT OF TOURISM

Besides the economic benefits of tourism, there are other ways that the industry affects the host society. Problems related to traffic and parking, pollution, wear-and-tear of heritage sites and price inflation may irritate and infuriate the local population. Aspects of the host society may also be commodified and touristified; mass trinketization, for instance, debases the value of local handicrafts. The social impact of tourism, however, is not necessarily negative. Attempts to create a balance between the positive and negative impacts are often underpinned by ideological and political considerations. While tourism businesses and researchers agree that a balanced approach is needed, there is still no specific agreement as to what constitutes a balanced strategy.

Attempts to balance these impacts emerge from negotiations amongst tourism stakeholders—residents, industry, cultural institutions, tourism attractions, tourists, politicians, and others—resulting in different destinations coming up with their own version of "balanced" tourism development. Civil society may emerge to challenge state-sponsored tourism plans and be engaged in the negotiation process but the amount of space that civil society has differs across host societies.

POLITICAL SOCIALIZATION AND RESPONSES FROM CIVIL SOCIETY

Tourism offers avenues and resources for the authorities to politically socialize local residents and foreign tourists through a process of "branding". Such exercises reify particular identities for locals to imagine themselves and their identities. In this process, tourism also becomes a vehicle for destinations to selectively market their crafts, their own philosophies, and their cultural identities.

Routing and zoning provides a framework for reorganizing space, while events and revising history in tourism settings transform the cultural and historical life of communities. State authorities may package and redefine customs and cultures, and reframe relationships between cultural groups in society through tourism.

While local residents may internalize officially promoted versions of political reality, the engineered reality may lead to the emergence of civil society organized along social cultural lines that the authorities have fashioned. The relationships between state and civil society are always open and responsive; this too can be observed in tourism.

POLITICAL SUPPORT

Tourist consumption of local politics is often implicit, rather than explicit. Tourists, despite their relatively short trips, are subjected to many of the same conditions as local inhabitants. Countries perceived as unstable and unsafe do not receive many tourists. Their governments are often portrayed as being out of control, corrupt, or incompetent. Therefore, when countries draw tourists, it implies that the tourists trust the host environment and system enough to come. And in effect, tourists indirectly give a vote of confidence to the political regimes in the places they choose to visit. Some governments justify political control of their own citizenry through reference to its tourism policy. For instance, the former Marcos government of the Philippines used tourism to endorse martial law.

Under martial law, the imposed stability was said to have allayed the security concerns of tourists, leading to more tourists visiting the country. Therefore, tourism is important not only for economic development, but also for governments when they want to claim international support for their policies. While foreign tourists cannot vote for politicians, tourists' interests are often taken into account by the state.

Tourists may not organize themselves like voters in local civil society but they are able to act through their economic might. (The influence of external force on the Singapore civil society landscape is examined separately by others in this volume, namely, James Gomez ["International NGOs"], Kersty Hobson ["Considering 'Green' Practices"], and Lenore Lyons ["Transient Workers Count Too?"]). To gain political mileage, politicians and the state often address the interests of tourists, similar to them championing and appropriating interests of local civil groups. Tourists in effect have become a political constituency in the host country.

STATE-SOCIETY RELATIONS AND TOURISM IN SINGAPORE

This short discussion of various streams of research on tourism and state-civil society relationship helps frame the case of Singapore. As other papers in this special collection demonstrate, the line demarcating the state and civil society in Singapore is unclear. By focusing on three aspects of tourism development policy in Singapore I show how the Singapore government is able to absorb civil spaces, redefine cultural spaces and identities, and in some instances, let social spaces open up for reasons of tourism. These three examples deal with different aspects of tourism and their impact on the Singapore society. The re-branding of Singapore is the STB's conceptuatization of Singapore and how that imagination is distributed to and then embedded in the local psyche.

The decision on the casino raises moral issues and the decision was highly controversial, requiring the government to assert leadership and appease various civil groups. Education and medical tourism deals with professional services, and we shall see how this new form of tourism can affect the home economy.

All three examples point to various strategies used by the PAP government to manage both the tourism industry and the Singapore society. To appreciate the impact of these strategies on Singapore, it is important to understand the role of the STB.

THE STB AND TOURISM IN SINGAPORE

Tourism development requires the cooperation of various agencies. Tourism authorities, local government, land control authorities, cultural management agencies, civil groups, and others have to cooperate to develop the industry. How the various agencies and political institutions within a country organize themselves to promote, plan, and develop itself as a tourist destination affects the speed, scope, and effectiveness in realizing its tourism development plan. Each agency has its own interests and agendas.

Official tourism promotion authorities often need to mobilize resources and take on a leadership role in the industry, and harness cooperation amongst various agencies through coercion and persuasion.

The STB is a statutory board it is a public body financially supported by the government, including through the 1 per cent cess collected from customers in restaurants and hotels in Singapore. The STB has the task of promoting the tourism industry in the island-state. It has cultivated close relationships with the private tourism sector, other state agencies, and local society. In 2004, Singapore attracted 8.3 million visitors and generated S$9.6 million in tourism receipts (STB 20 January 2005). The industry is estimated to be contributing 5 per cent of Singapore's GDP, and the STB has a target to triple tourism receipt to S$30 billion, increase visitor numbers to 17 million, and generate another 100,000 jobs by the year 2015 (STB 20 January 2005). The STB receives strong financial support; the government has allocated S$2 billion to achieve the 2015 goals (STB 11 January 2005). The STB plays not only a central financial role but also a social and cultural one; it is at the centre of the web of relationships in the tourism industry.

The STB works closely with other state agencies such as the National Heritage Board, Urban Renewal Authority, Ministry of Defence, the National Arts Council, and other agencies. For instance, in 1995 the STB and the Ministry of Information and the Arts (MITA) released a blueprint to make Singapore a "Global City for the Arts". According to the blueprint, there will be three national museums—the Asian Civilisations Museum, the Singapore Art Museum, and the Singapore History Museum. As in the plan, these museums help the tourism industry assert the city-state's unique Asian heritage and identity.

Just as importantly, the museums work with various state agencies to send out certain (social engineering) messages. For instance, the Singapore History Museum exhibits complement the Ministry of Education's history curriculum in the schools. In addition, the STB uses a carrot-and-stick approach to incorporate private tourism businesses into its vision.

The STB issues licences to tour guides and travel agencies, thus giving the authorities control over the products and messages that guides and travel agencies send out (STB 1998). The STB subsidizes the printing of promotional materials by travel agents if they support the STB's marketing and product policies. It engages consultants and actively helps in-bound travel agents to develop new products.

For the new "Uniquely Singapore" branding campaign, the STB has, for instance, created new tour packages for tour agencies (STB 12 May 2004). Other private businesses in

Singapore are also encouraged to take the initiative to promote tourism activities. For example, the STB has initiated and continued to support various business groupings such as the Orchard Road Business Association, which has not only assumed the responsibility to light up Singapore's main shopping street for Christmas, but has also taken the initiative to organize the Singapore Street Festival.

The STB also attempts to shape local life, as the re-branding of Singapore will show. The STB is the central coordinating body for the Singapore tourism industry, endowed with the financial and political resources to make itself relevant and important in the sector. The details follow.

RE-BRANDING SINGAPORE: FORGING SINGAPOREAN IDENTITIES

In March 2004 the STB began to use the phrase "Uniquely Singapore" in its promotional material. This slogan replaces the former tag line "New Asia" (Ooi 2004a). New programmes have been launched to generate a sense of brand ownership in the local tourism industry and among local residents. Uniquely Singapore products are being created and Singaporeans are encouraged to search for things that make their country special.

Uniquely Singapore—Unique is the word that best captures Singapore, a dynamic city rich in contrast and colour where you'll find a harmonious blend of culture, cuisine, arts and architecture. A bridge between the East and the West for centuries, Singapore, located in the heart of fascinating Southeast Asia, continues to embrace tradition and modernity today. Brimming with unbridled energy and bursting with exciting events, the city offers countless unique, memorable experiences waiting to be discovered.

As in the previous branding, "Uniquely Singapore" is a response to the manifestation of modernity and Westernization in Singapore. "Uniquely Singapore" self-orientalizes Singapore and accentuates the Asianness in the country by pointing out Asian practices, such as modern buildings arranged according to Chinese geomancy and

Western dishes cooked with Asian spices and flavours. For instance, in creating a world-class museum to showcase the glorious ancient material cultures of Asia in the Asian Civilisations Museum, the story of Asia is presented within the framework of Singapore's Chinese, Malay, Indian, and Other (CMIO) ethnic model. All Singaporeans are ethnically classified into these categories despite diverse differences within these communities.

The Asianness that the STB is promoting is built along the state's ethnic engineering framework. "Uniquely Singapore" messages and stories are also sent out to local residents. Some Singaporeans have internalized these messages. For example, schoolteacher Miss Anjali Raguraman took her pupils to visit the STB. After the trip, she wrote a letter to the Straits Times ("Know What Singapore Has to Offer and Be Its Envoy", 28 April 2005). She cited the example that I have heard frequently from my respondents in the STB: Singapore is unique. Let me illustrate with an example that the speaker, Mr Dominic Raymond Chew cited. Think of the void decks underneath the blocks of flats all over Singapore. The phrase "void deck" is an oxymoron! But in that one place, we see a funeral taking place one day, and a wedding the next. There is beauty and uniqueness in that itself. (Ibid.)

As a voice from the "grassroots", Miss Raguraman further suggested "that the STB organize such talks for ordinary Singaporeans to make us that much more competent in promoting our motherland". The STB used to be involved only in the marketing of Singapore. In the 1980s, however, it became actively involved in product development and the shaping of local life. As Mrs Pamelia Lee, who headed tourism product development in the STB then, lamented:

Like other developing nations, we also watched the charm of our old city disappear and diminish, bit by bit.... In recent years, we have often been described as a city without a soul; modern, efficient and hygienic, but lacking in grace, refinement and charm.

With this realization, the STB "started to enhance areas in Singapore that did not come under the STB's purview.

The festive light up of Chinatown, Little India and Kampong Glam were introduced". Essentially, private celebrations of these festivals in Singapore have become public spectacles, so that tourists can also celebrate with Singaporeans. As many of the streets of newly refurbished conservation sites became lifeless, Mrs Pamelia Lee pointed out that "through software organized by the STB and the stakeholders, we can bring back life so that tourists are not disappointed and to give market forces more time to settle".

This is a proud claim of not only how the STB has shaped the physical landscape but also how it is deliberately shaping human activities in Singapore. Effectively and rather pragmatically, the Singaporean government has married the interests of their social engineering programmes and tourism. The tourism authorities have claimed, asserted, and established a symbiotic relationship between local and tourist needs.

It is believed that attractions that are meant for tourists are also appreciated by local residents (National Tourism Promotion Committees 1996). Not only is that, messages meant for locals packaged for tourists and vice versa. In a pragmatic manner, tourism products are consumed and messages are sent out simultaneously to both residents and tourists. In the process, both groups are jointly engineered towards the PAP's vision of Singapore.

THE CASINO DEBATE

In 2009, Singapore will have two Las Vegas style "integrated resorts", hosting hotels, restaurants, theatres, museums, amusement centres, and casinos. The issue on the two casinos in Singapore was highly controversial. The cabinet itself was not unanimous on the decision, and it generated one of the most heated public discussions in Singapore ever.

There had been occasional proposals for a casino in Singapore since the 1970s ("Timeline", 16 April 2005). But the suggestions were never taken up because of moral and social issues. However, in March 2004, the then Minister for

Trade and Industry, George Yeo, mooted the idea again. Many religious groups voiced strong objections to having a casino in the city-state. Civil groups against any casino in Singapore emerged. For instance, a conservative Christian group started "Families Against the Casino Threat in Singapore" or "FACTS".

FACTS was created to rally all Singaporeans against Singapore hosting any casino; as reported on its website, it managed to collect close to 20,000 signatures through an Internet petition, which was eventually sent to the Singapore President. The casino discussion was a lively money-versus-values debate.

An STB officer, voicing his own view, was exasperated and complained to me about those members of the public who were against the casino. Not only has a tourism project become a focal point for criticism; he was alarmed that naysayers like FACTS are ignoring the reality that Singapore is losing foreign exchange—Singaporeans have been travelling overseas and taking cruises just to gamble.

At one stage, the minister leading the decision-making process, Dr Vivian Balakrishnan, framed the discussion into a freedom of choice debate. He said in parliament:

So I want to set this debate in perspective. I think the real question which we need to confront is what type of society we are or, to be more accurate, are we now a more mature society than, say, decades ago, meaning can we trust the vast majority of Singaporeans to act responsibly, to exercise common sense and to make their own choices as to how they wish to spend their disposable income, how they wish to entertain themselves? ("Casino Here Is Not a Matter of Money versus Values", 17 November 2004)

Effectively, the minister invoked the argument that Singaporeans should have the freedom of choice. It is an indirect reference to whether Singapore should continue as a nanny state or a more open society.

Prime Minister Lee Hsien Loong reminded religious groups that his government takes a secular and pragmatic approach, based on the long-term interests of the country:

"the government cannot enforce the choices of one group on others, or make these private choices the basis of national policy" ("Casino: Not Fruitful to Keep Arguing, Says PM", 27 April 2005).

While Singaporean civil society became active during the casino decision-making process, civil groups against the casinos were ironically campaigning against giving choices to Singaporeans. Even after the decision was taken in April 2005, members of parliament and the public continued to criticize the decision. Prime Minister Lee responded at the "Glassroots Club":

Beyond a point, this [debate] can be counter-productive because the risk is we may harden views for and against, and polarize our multiracial, multi-religious society. And that is something which I think we should avoid at all costs. (Ibid.)

As part of the process to shape public opinion and appease civil society, the Ministry of Information, Communications and the Arts (MICA) issued a brochure—Why Integrated Resorts?—to convince the general public of the decision (MICA 2005).

The decision was basically presented as a pragmatic one—Singapore tourism, while still healthy, is losing market share; Singapore is facing strong tourism competition in the region; the casinos will give a S$1.5 billion boost to the economy and create 35,000 jobs.

Religious parties who are opposed to the casinos were reported to have expressed a willingness to help the government control the social problems that may arise from the casinos ("They Are Anti-Casino, but Ready to Help", 22 April 2005). The Straits Times reported that some Singaporeans felt that the whole discussion was merely a public relations exercise, through which pragmatism again rules. Others felt that it was an important consultation process ("Worthwhile Debate or Not? It's a Toss Up", 23 April 2005). Regardless, through tourism, the PAP government has invoked a freedom of choice argument. And civil groups have been roped in to handle future social problems that would arise from the casinos.

NEW TOURISM SPACES

Singapore has established itself as a modern destination with world-class services. Singapore is not only attracting tourists to spend time and money in a safe and secure destination but also drawing foreigners to use the country's educational and medical services. The STB has taken on the responsibility to market these services to the world. Visitors' stays can be relatively short (a few hours) to a few years. While it is debatable whether visitors staying in Singapore for a few months or even years can still be considered "tourists", what is remarkable is that the STB has assumed responsibility for wooing them to the city-state to spend money.

As part of the promotion of Singapore's educational services, the STB, together with the Economic Development Board (EDB), is promoting basic and tertiary education programmes, as well as professional and enrichment courses to the world. Education tourism was first promoted in 1993 when the authorities found that many Thai students visited Singapore to learn English. And in August 2003, "Singapore Education" was launched. Under this scheme, the authorities aim to attract 200,000 full-fee paying students to Singapore for tertiary and professional education by 2012.

Most of the educational services consumed by tourists are provided by commercial schools, which are less regulated than the public education sector. There has been an increasing number of complaints against private schools, including complaints from those foreigners whom the STB wants to attract. In normal circumstances, active groups within a civil society can intensify public scrutiny of the actions of businesses.

Such an option of getting organized, however, is not available to tourists on short stays. The complaints against private schools in Singapore threaten the Singapore Education brand. To maintain the integrity of its brand, the EDB has announced schemes to preserve Singapore as a reputable education hub. Instead of allowing the industry to regulate, the EDB has intervened to improve consumer protection and academic standards. The swift action taken by the authorities to protect the interests of "education tourists" indicate not only the efficiency and effectiveness of the PAP government but also the willingness of the government to act as de facto activists for education tourists. This intervention is not unique; the Singaporean government has shown its ability to absorb and appropriate the interests of emerging civil spaces, so as to neutralize political activism.

The EDB managing director said, "When we add to this the high standard in student protection and welfare, organization practices and academic quality ... we will set Singapore further apart from the competition and make us an even more compelling hub for education" ("Three Plans to Ensure Reputation of Private Schools", 10 September 2004). Consumers welcome the state's intervention; the PAP government has literally absorbed their interests and reflected them in its policies.

Singapore is also promoting itself as a medical hub—Singapore Medicine. To facilitate this strategy, medical centres and doctors are now allowed to advertise. The government is also considering removing restrictions imposed on local doctors that maintain a clear separation between medical and non-medical treatments. These restrictions are meant to protect unsuspecting patients from predatory doctors, who may drum up business for profits rather than cater to the needs of patients ("A Facelift for Singapore's Health Tourism", 15 October 2004). For example, the government is now reviewing legislation to see whether spas could offer dental treatment.

As Singapore faces competition from Thailand and Malaysia in the region, the government is willing to be flexible and change legislation to boost the fledgling medical tourism sector. In contrast to the Singapore Education scheme where standards are being raised, the Singapore Medicine scheme has loosened control on the medical profession by allowing services such as spas and cosmetic treatment to become part of the medical industry.

While many doctors frown on such services, the

Singapore government wants to cater to the demands of tourists. But it is debatable if the loosening up of the medical industry will better serve the needs of both local and foreign consumers.

Undoubtedly, the educational and medical health industries in Singapore welcome assistance from the authorities to promote their services overseas. The government has changed regulations for the private educational and medical sectors, so as to assure an increased number of foreign consumers.

While tourists cannot organize themselves against lousy educational services in Singapore, the Singapore government acts on their behalf. Such state-sponsored activism benefits local residents too. However, it is questionable if it will help consumers when the medical industry is loosened up to include more services. In both cases, the policies will enrich Singapore's economy.

TOURISM AND SINGAPOREAN SOCIETY

The PAP government has constantly invoked the concepts of "survival" and "pragmatism" in the ideological and institutional entrenchment of public policies and popular consciousness. The term "Singapore Inc." is frequently used by researchers to describe how Singapore is ruled and run by the PAP; economic development takes precedence in most policy decisions in Singapore.

The ruling elite claims that public institutions, social life, and private businesses need to be engineered towards Singapore's economic development or else the country will not survive. The industrial relations dispute between SIA and one of its independent-minded pilot unions which I used by way of example at the beginning of this chapter is indicative of this view.

The extent to which the Singapore government is able to push through its tourism agenda on the grounds of economic growth shows that Singaporeans have generally accepted the pragmatic arguments. Such acceptance comes with coercion and persuasion of various tourism stakeholders, including local civil society actors. The three tourism-related examples used in this chapter provide a number of important insights into the particular nature of state-civil society relations in Singapore.

First, considering that Singapore had more than 8 million visitors in 2004, and a population of only 4 million people (STB 20 January 2005), tourists have become a feature in local life. While individual tourists may come and go, as a group they form a permanent, albeit fluid, constituency. As non-citizens, however, tourists cannot organize themselves in the Singapore civil society. Instead, their interests have been absorbed by the Singapore state.

Parliamentarians regularly raise the interests of tourists in parliament. For instance, PAP MP Mr Ang Mong Seng said that Singapore needs to attract more tourists from China. In order to do so, he suggested that Singapore should increase the use of Chinese signage: "in order to attract the Chinese tourists, we have to use their language so that they could feel at home when they are in Singapore" (Singapore Parliament Hansard, 13 March 2004). Opposition MP Mr Low Thia Khiang agreed.

The then Minister of State for Trade and Industry, Dr Vivian Balakrishnan, replied that the Chinese market is important for Singapore tourism, and efforts are being undertaken to attract them, including extending the period of visa validity for Chinese tourists, making it easier for the Chinese to apply for visas, stepping up marketing, and getting the relevant authorities to install Chinese signage (Singapore Parliament Hansard, 13 March 2004). In other words, tourists are effectively being represented in Singapore's parliament through the seduction of their economic might.

Second, it is difficult to imagine a "pristine" and "untouched" Singapore that is different from a socially engineered and touristified Singapore. In fact, many products initiated for tourism have become part of local life. For instance, in 1984 the STB introduced festive illuminations along Singapore's main shopping belt—Orchard Road—for

Christmas. Subsequently, from 1985, Chinatown is now lit for Chinese New Year, Little India for Deepavali (Hindu festival), and Geylang Serai for Hari Raya Puasa and Hari Raya Haji (Muslim festivals).

While these illuminations attract locals and concentrate festive shopping activities in the respective areas, they allow tourists to experience the festivals. Today, Singaporeans wait in anticipation for these illuminations; the STB has not only helped Singaporeans celebrate their ethnic identities, it has entrenched the Singaporean ethnic model and allowed tourists to experience aspects of Singapore's ethnic festivals. Local identities are constructed, asserted, and reified through tourism; tourism agendas are embedded in Singaporean culture and society.

Third, and closely related to the second point, socially engineered categories may generate civil energies. For instance, the STB is heavily involved in the re-invention of Chinatown. Some Chinese Singaporeans, however, disagree with the tourism-inspired vision for the area. An STB officer revealed to me that many Chinese Singaporeans, including those in the independent Heritage Society, took offence to the original plan to theme Chinatown into the five elements—water, fire, earth, metal, and wood—as entrenched in a traditional Chinese worldview.

While the authorities wanted to introduce more Chinese elements into the district, many Singaporean Chinese wanted to return Chinatown to what it was in the past without the new elements. While such protests were healthy and the STB eventually withdrew the five-element theme, the master plan remains. The lesson learned, according to my STB respondent, is that "it is important to consult local residents". In this instance, the socially engineered ethnic category "Chinese" had been taken seriously by Singaporeans, and grassroots energies were being generated within Singapore's CMIO ethnic framework.

Fourth, on the grounds of being economically pragmatic, the PAP government has opened up civil and social spaces that were once closed. The PAP government advocates that individuals in Singapore should make choices and be given more responsibility for their actions. This is a move away from the nanny-state mentality. The government wants to replace the strait-laced image of Singapore with an image of a more tolerant and open city.

This move has been partly motivated by the demands of tourism. Sanctioning gambling to attract tourists is just one example. Another example relates to attitudes towards sexuality. During a parliamentary sitting on 13 March 2004, a few MPs voiced their concerns about changes in sexual attitudes. PAP MP Mr Ahmad Khalis bin Abdul Ghani said:

> We have seen discernible moves towards greater easing up of our social scene. The main reason for this easing up is to present Singapore as a more happening place to woo tourists and foreigners. [... Some people] are concerned that such moves promote the idea that sexual promiscuity is acceptable, and therefore, this may undermine our family values. [... I believe...] we do not quite need bar-top dancing or such other types of items to woo more tourists and foreigners. (Singapore Parliamentary Hansard, 13 March 2004)

The then Minister of State for Trade and Industry, Dr Vivian Balakrishnan, replied that he agrees that Singaporeans "must not lose our values, and we must not lose our compass" and he continued:

> There was an article that Professor Richard Florida wrote, entitled "The Rise of the Creative Class".... His research found that cities, which are able to embrace diversity, are able to attract and foster a bigger creative class. These are key drivers in a knowledge-based economy. The larger lesson for us in Singapore is that we need to shift our mindset so that we can be more tolerant of diversity.
>
> To achieve this, we have begun to take small but important steps to signal that we need a new respect for diversity and openness to ideas. So these examples that the Members cited, e.g., night spots to open 24 hours, bar-top dancing, and bungee jumping, are just part of that signalling process. (Singapore Parliamentary Hansard, 13 March 2004)

Thanks to tourism, the PAP government is loosening social controls and giving people opportunities to choose and take responsibility for their own social and personal actions. It remains questionable to what extent this will translate into a more active civil society.

The PAP government has invoked the freedom of choice argument, and future civil society arguments can tap into this precedence.

The government has also invited civil groups to help manage any negatives that may arise of the two casinos in Singapore, for instance—social and civil spaces are undoubtedly being sanctioned and created. (Gomez, "International NGOs", in this volume, and Hobson, "Considering 'Green' Practices", in this volume, however, show that there are still many limits to the ability of government-sanctioned civil spaces to contribute to the growth and development of Singapore civil society.)

Fifth, while the Singapore government is protecting the needs of tourists, it is also supporting many local businesses, such as those in the education and medical industries. The STB is able to provide incentives for private companies to follow their lead.

The various STB strategies are efficient and are able to boost the local economy but such state-sponsored initiatives may stifle private initiatives. (2) The Singapore approach is not only pragmatic; it is efficient in providing seamless tourism experiences; the negative aspect seems to be that the private sector has more incentive to follow than to lead, a complaint I heard from two STB officers.

In using Giddens' "Third Way", Burns (2004) paints a bipolar view of tourism planning. The first view—"leftist development first"—focuses "on sustainable human development goals as defined by local people and local knowledge. The key question driving development is 'What can tourism give us without harming us?'" The second view—"rightist tourism first"—aims to "maximize market spread through familiarity of the product.

Undifferentiated, homogenized product depends on a

core with a focus on tourism goals set by outside planners and the international tourism industry" (ibid.). In trying to bring different interests together, and to manufacture consensus, the Third Way conceptually bridges the two poles, although in practice, how this works out remains to be seen and tested. But as this chapter shows, Singapore has its own Third Way in tourism planning.

The PAP government has created a bureaucratic state structure that makes different government agencies work together.

It has empowered the STB to develop tourism products and realise a vision that not only serves tourists but also the locals. From the consideration of efficiency and effectiveness, the Singaporean system is able to draw cooperation amongst different parties.

Private sector cooperation is garnered through incentive schemes, such as financial support for products that reflect the STB's goals. The leadership and visions of the STB are supported by other state institutions. This means that the STB has become a powerful organization that has the ability to distribute resources.

To make Singapore an attractive tourism destination, tourists have become a de facto constituent in Singapore, as their interests are absorbed and represented in parliament. Many tourism products in Singapore match various social engineering programmes in the country; locals and tourists are subjected to the same messages and experiences.

Consequently, some civil groups that challenge STB's initiatives are organized along Singapore's social engineered categories (for example, being Chinese in the CMIO ethnic model).

Regardless, social and civil spaces are being opened up for the sake of tourism. In sum, tourists are being Singaporeanized and Singapore touristified.

This chapter is the product of ongoing investigation of the Singapore tourism industry since 1996. Primary and secondary data were collected for this study.

Besides documented materials from the STB, the mass

media, and the Singapore Parliament Hansard in-depth interviews and discussions were conducted with officers of the STB, operators of tourism attractions, and tour agents. Since some of the issues raised can be construed as sensitive, my respondents have requested that their identities be kept anonymous.

Chapter 7

The Rise of Indigenous Cultural Tourism

The nineteenth century Aboriginal corroboree performed for non-Indigenous settler audiences was Australia's pre-eminent prototypical Indigenous cultural tourism product. Options for the development of this product by both Aborigines and settlers were fashioned by competing and complementary strategies of various colonial interest groups. The implementation of these strategies acted directly to restrict supply of traditional corroboree performances and access to markets. Producers had to find new socially acceptable genres, such as minstrelsy and temperance entertainments in order to reproduce their product.

This necessarily resulted in product transformation, but enabled continuity of a performance tradition to the present day. The Tjapukai Aboriginal Dance Theatre and the Bangarra Dance Theatre are but two modern inheritors of this tradition.

Come Share Our Culture, the title of the Northern Territory Tourism Commission's first Indigenous tourism information brochure (NTTC 1993), sums up the core invitation extended by Australian Indigenous cultural tourism to consumers. However, there are different types of Indigenous cultural tourism enterprises, each allowing a different kind of interaction between host and guest, and, in consequence, a different kind of 'sharing experience'.

These types of Indigenous cultural tourism can be characterised in terms of degrees of intimacy. Within ranges along this continuum, various types of tourism enterprises, defined by their core business, may be distinguished in terms of exhibiting low, medium and high levels of intimacy.

The lowest level of intimacy is provided by forms of indirect tourism, where no face-to-face encounter takes place, and where the cultural experience is entirely brokered. One example is the provision of themed tourist accommodation, in which an Indigenous group may simply hold equity.

But in Australia the major example of Indigenous indirect cultural tourism is in the purchase of Aboriginal and Torres Strait Islander art and craft from non-Indigenous retailers in capital cities. In Australia, the overwhelming majority of Indigenous peoples in remote areas involved in the tourism industry are represented by this area of indirect tourism: the distant sale of art and craft products, and the licensing of reproduction rights.

The typical Indigenous cultural tourism enterprise exhibiting a medium level of intimacy is the Indigenous-owned art and craft retail outlet. There is a face-to-face encounter between the Indigenous salesperson and the customer, but it is necessarily restricted in scope, being framed by an arena of commercial transactions. The explicit focus of the encounter is upon the prospective sale/purchase, rather than on imparting a cultural experience and the sharing of cultural knowledge.

Indigenous cultural tourism enterprises displaying high levels of intimacy are typically those that bring or invite tourists into their communities or onto their traditional lands. They include, for example, interpretive guided tours of sites by traditional owners, and the equivalent of 'farm-stay tourism' experiences in Indigenous communities or homelands.

While the overall encounter between host and guest is structured by these enterprises' commitment to delivering the attractions and highlights promised in their brochures with continuous face-to-face encounters, there are generally more opportunities for unstructured interaction and free-flowing questioning and discussion between host and guest, opportunities that obviously increase with the extension of the time frame.

As these categories relate to core business activities, they may not necessarily be exclusive to a particular enterprise. A retail art and craft store or space may offer a higher level of intimacy between host and guest groups than that normally offered by retail transactions through fostering highly interactive encounters between their clientele and performing artists and musicians. The framing offered by the retail space tends to make such encounters, however, relatively brief. A guided tour of a jointly-managed national park may also, as part of the tour package, offer occasions for lower levels of intimacy in the provision of hotel accommodation, souvenir sales, formal lectures, and staged dance performances.

Generally, in moving from low intimacy level to high intimacy level ventures two important shifts may be observed. Firstly, there is the shift in emphasis from product to person; from 'making a sale', and 'putting on a show' to 'being on show' oneself. Depending on the degree of Indigenous control of the process, 'being on show' may oscillate from 'being exhibited' to 'exhibiting one's being'; choosing to communicate one's way of 'being-in-the-world'.

Secondly, there is the shift along a continuum, from presenting culture as object or, in Bourdieu's terms (1986:243), cultural capital in its 'objectified state', to culture as subject, expressed by cultural capital in its 'embodied state'. The history of the presentation of Indigenous Australian cultures in its objectified state can be traced through studying changes in the actual objects, which document in themselves processes of tradition and transformation.

The history of the presentation of Indigenous cultures in its embodied state, as exemplified in dance performances, is not so easily traced, and therefore must be constructed out of the overall historical record of host-guest interaction.

In the tourism marketplace references to 'Indigenous cultural tourism' often refer to tour operations conducted by Indigenous persons offering medium to high levels of intimacy, as their core tourism product is the sharing of Indigenous cultural knowledge and practice. Such ventures invite visitors to experience aspects of a different way of life, and a different way of seeing this different way of life. The embodiment of this culture, and of this difference, is the people themselves. What is said and what is done by the host group is, for the guest group, mediated by whom they perceive the host to be, and historically determined by where they perceive the host to live.

Indigenous cultural tourism can be seen as a modern 'touriculture', the cultivation of the symbolic landscape for a non-traditional market. For Australian Indigenous peoples, this landscape acts as the foundation and 'anchorage' of all myth that underpins cultural production.

As the berndts state in the speaking Land:

... it is, then, the land which is really speaking—offering,to those who can understand its language, an explanative discourse about how it came to be as it is now, which beings were responsible for its becoming like that, and who is or should be responsible for it now. The Speaking Land must be heard. But what it says may be understood only if we know its language.

This language is a semiotic system. 'The whole land is full of signs: a land humanised so that it could be used and read by Aborigines who were/are intimately familiar with it, and read as clearly as if it were bristling with notice-boards'. The source of traditional meaning for Indigenous Australian cultural tourism products has been the symbolic landscape, and ultimately the land itself. Notably, as a consequence, without access to this source and the knowledge it allows to be transmitted, reproduction of the traditional forms of these meanings becomes difficult.

In Australia, as the actions of British colonisation proceeded, Indigenous cultural tourism increasingly acted to express covert control by Indigenous individuals over their domains. The framing of the supply of cultural tourism performance became the struggle for physical and cultural survival given rapid depopulation, separation of families and denial of access to traditional lands, goods and services. The nature of the historical demand for such products was to be uneven and contested in non-Indigenous society, ranging from promotion to appropriation to restriction through the application of policies of social control; consequently their supply was to be similarly uneven.

The current interest in Indigenous cultural tourism has masked this fact, that it is an industry with a long history; a knowable past.

While in the late twentieth century it developed as an out-working of the decolonising process of returning some Indigenous land, it was initially shaped in response to demands from a colonial market as a re-working of an Indigenous pre-colonial trade in art, song and dance.

Prior to European contact, there was an extensive traditional market for all forms of artworks, weapons and utensils, one that came to be consumed by an evolving non-traditional tourist market. The traditional marketplace consisted of a trade in ritual, songs and dances between groups and within groups.

Butlin has commented on the latter, in particular the importance of 'intergenerational transfers of knowledge' as a dynamic element in the Indigenous economy. Traditionally, these transfers were accompanied by payment by younger to older men, for example. Butlin sees them as encompassing 'more than just the productive activities of hunting and gathering or even resource management. The intergenerational transfer of ritual and myth, both lore and law, is vital.

As education for life, such transfers go beyond the realm of the secret-sacred, and include what non-Indigenous observers may regard as meaningless 'leisure time activities' in which older men schooled the young in games and sports. 'Entertainment' and 'sport' have been nominated by Sutton as examples of 'domains of relative autonomy' of Aborigines that 'tend to be concentrated in areas conceived of by outside interests largely as private affairs, not as part of the public domain'.

One of the main attractions for Indigenous peoples in meeting guests' demand for cultural performances and survival skills was because in their domain these were not trivial, but related directly to 'focal and basic stages on which the Aboriginal public, political, and economic life is lived out ... not a side-show ... [but] core activities for people and core activities for whole communities'. Nineteenth century settler-defined domains of 'entertainment' and 'sport' provided a space for the growth of the 'corroboree', the first, and still one of the major, forms of organised Indigenous cultural tourism in Australia. Encouraged by some parts of settler society and contested by others, this performance event heralded latter-day commercial Indigenous Australian cultural tourism ventures.

SEEING CORROBOREES

Corroborees were primarily dance accompaniment to songs; that is, the verbal content was at least as important as the morphology, the form of the corroboree. The multiplicity of Indigenous languages, and settler ignorance of even local languages shifted this balance; with the tourist corroboree, the form became all-important. This was not necessarily disadvantageous. If the spectators were unable to know the meaning of the words, they could all the more easily impute a significance of choice to the overall performance.

Settler corroboree-audiences were well aware that there was an Indigenous significance, which was hidden from them, in what they were seeing and hearing.

'It is not clear what a corroboree is intended to signify', wrote J.D. Woods in his A Narrative of the Visit of HRH The Duke of Edinburgh KG to South Australia (1868:87). 'Some think it is a war dance—others that it is a representation of their hunting expeditions—others again, that it is a religious, or pagan observance, but on this even the blacks themselves could or would give no information'.

Few translations of corroboree songs in South Australia and Victoria appeared in the first half of the nineteenth century. Where corroboree songs were faithfully translated, they often appeared, wrote W.A. Cawthorne in 1844, to be 'taken from some of the most trivial circumstances. To a European they would appear quite nonsensical'. Cawthorne's confidant, George French Angas, noted 'the frequent repetition of a few words, such as, "Water, water, where is water? There is water, welling out of the ground;" but this, of course, is sung in their own dialect'.

Strehlow, however, writing of the Arrernte of Central Australia, has argued that their Ltata songs, 'the true "corroboree" songs done for pleasure and amusement', were not entirely unrelated to sacred dances. The connection was in the allusive meaning of the words of the songs. The degree of coded meaning in the allusions meant that the meaning was often only 'intelligible to the singers who know the sacred myth'.

In this way, as the Berndts have noted, the existence of 'inside' and 'outside' words could hide the 'true' meaning of songs from some who apparently understood the language of the song. Even the 'pantomime' style of corroboree, a major source of commenting upon and critiquing the new settler society, could encode hidden meanings. Corroboree performers, declared Massola (1971:64), often 'mimicked, with veiled allusions, the activities of certain of their tribesmen'. They could do this even when they 'imitated the movements and calls of different animals', because of the totemic associations between animals and a people. As Strehlow has shown, some of these associations required ritual knowledge.

Assuming the encoding of hidden meanings in at least some tourist corroboree performances, it is possible that these performances may have served to maintain ritual knowledge and traditions. These meanings, even where offered by the hosts, were not generally assimilated by the guests. Primarily this was a language difficulty, of course.

Given that most settler audiences lacked Indigenous language skills, choreography rather than song content was the most accessible feature of corroborees. Second, it was a cultural difficulty: the guests were unable to access the coded meanings. Therefore morphology became the primary determiner of meaning, often guided by the established articulation of a people with place.

For nineteenth century corroboree audiences in both newly established and well-established locations, tourist corroborees evolved as a joint invention by Indigenous and non-Indigenous settlers that articulated a sense of place. This articulation of a sense of place oscillated between two poles: experienced initially as new colony and home country, and later as bush frontier and settled metropolis.

This articulation was to mesh with the peripheral place occupied by the 'Primitive' in European thought, and the historical distinction made by modern tourism between places visited by the 'tourist' and the 'traveller' (Buzard 1993: passim). The logical consequence of this articulation for its practitioners was the manifest determination of the Primitive's authenticity.

The new Australian colonists inhabited the socially insecure world that was the Indigenous peoples' domain. They experienced displacement from the old country and interpreted the corroboree in terms of the society they had lost. In this milieu, settlers perceived the domain in which they found themselves as Indigenous, not-yet-settled and thus not-yet-civilised, and their corroboree performances were perceived as authentic, despite the European trappings that may have been adopted.

There was, however, a further factor. New settlers' displacement was accentuated by the Antipodean inversions of their new surroundings. Added to this strange confusion and confutation of the known and normal was the apparent disorganisation of Indigenous Australian society—its lack of centralised authority and common language. Perceived incoherence of the new environment was thus experienced simultaneously with social and psychological ramifications of physical displacement.

In this unpredictable, unknown world, settlers could take some comfort in the fact that, to them at least, Aborigines all danced the same. The "'corrobory', their universal and highly original dance ... [was] from its uniformity on every shore, a very striking feature in their character", commented the explorer Thomas Mitchell (1834:4-6). In particular, the 'shake-a-leg' action of male corroboree performers was reported from Sydney in the eighteenth century to virtually everywhere explorers were to penetrate in the nineteenth century. It was even observed underwater: ... the dance consisted chiefly of the performers leaping two or three times successively out of the sea, and then violently moving their legs so as to agitate the water into a foam for some distance around them'.

This 'universal accompaniment' meant that Aboriginal dance for visitors could be read as undifferentiated across the continent by colonists as 'the corroboree'. The 'corroboree', as performed for colonial audiences, demonstrated that here was one people in one country. It became a familiar, and thus reassuring and welcome aspect of the social landscape.

Later, the 'civilisation' of this domain, with the consequent removals of Indigenous peoples, led to these performances often being seen as 'inauthentic' in published reviews. In this manner, colonial perceptions of a corroboree's 'authenticity' emerged as a response to a sense of place, in terms of a projection of the viewer's own sense of displacement from home. 'Inauthenticity' correlated with the colonial transformation of nature into property consequent upon Indigenous removal, and subsequent social marginalisation. Imagining the corroboree as opera and ballet

Massola has characterised southeastern Australian corroborees as having been 'an artistic and aesthetic expression in no way different to our own theatrical performances', in some cases 'a type of ballet'.

In the late 1820s, Mitchell watched a corroboree at Bathurst in which 'the Aborigines imitated various animals, such as dingoes and the way in which they would catch and kill kangaroos'. As a finale they even imitated the wind by humming while waving a bough of a tree. To Mitchell it 'was a greater treat than any ballet he had ever seen on the stage at Covent Garden'.

Similarly, during her visit to Port Phillip in 1839, Lady Jane Franklin wrote to her husband of the 'Corroberry—their Arranmilly, or dance' which reminded her 'of the kickers and spinners on the Opera Boards'. This locating of the corroboree as ballet or opera reflected the non-Indigenous sense of displacement, of inhabiting an insecure, still Indigenous, space. It defined their sense of distance that here (in the colonial space) the ballet, the theatre was Indigenous, or more ominously, still Indigenous, as settlers looked forward to the establishment of metropolitan forms of theatre and dance.

This imagining helped settlers perceive the land of the corroboree as, after all, not so outlandish; as assimilable, since what was happening was a form of their own metropolitan experience. The colonists at this time sought the perception of sameness, not difference. As Manning Clark (1963:II 21) commented, 'so what did it matter if the white man's social gatherings left much to be desired: what did it matter if nothing like the splendour and gaiety of a ball in England could be exhibited in NSW for many years to come, when they had their own source of pride, and joy, and wonder, and mystery?'

No doubt Indigenous performers picked up, and played to the 'opera' and 'ballet' references. By 1856 in Victoria, the corroboree, having already been imagined as pantomime and ballet, was brought onto the stage by theatre producers of Christmas pantomimes.

The Ballarat review of the 1860 Ararat Aborigines' corroboree performance at Ballarat's Royal Theatre, reproduced in the Melbourne Argus also favourably noted that 'strict time kept together with their various steps, completely astonished the audience'. But, like that of the Queen's Theatre performance, the Royal's corroboree appears not have been repeated. Whatever the cause, there is no question that the socioeconomic environment of these independent players was restrictive.

Mission policy depended upon having sedentary Indigenous groups firmly under their control. The dangerous independent livelihood that corroboree performances potentially provided was compared to rabbit-shooting, and had a double danger by reinforcing the notion that traditional cultural practices had value, and should be upheld. Indigenous peoples were seen as requiring 'protection' from engaging in such free trade in their cultural capital. It would take until the end of the twentieth century for Indigenous dance-theatre groups, such as Tjapukai Aboriginal Dance Theatre and Bangarra Dance Theatre to stage regular corroboree performances in mainstream theatre settings. According to the latter's Russell Page, 'The Bangarra Dance Theatre is a modern day corroboree'.

The missionaries were assisted by the changes in public perception as to the 'authenticity' of 'traditional Aboriginal practices' by those Indigenous residents of settled areas. As Spencer's and Gillen's newspaper reports of their 1901 expedition to Central Australia confirmed, the 'true' corroboree lay beyond the northern frontier, where 'authentic' Aborigines could still be found (Register 5 July 1901; Advertiser 29 May 1901). In the meantime, in the southern settled areas, Aboriginal corroboree performers in the late nineteenth and early twentieth centuries were to occupy the theatrical domain equivalent to their increasingly marginalised social position. In settlement areas where Indigenous groups could hope to occupy only proletarian roles, corroboree performances were relegated to proletarian forms of theatre.

For Indigenous settler-corroboree performers, there were advantages in representing themselves using the new modalities of English music hall, American vaudeville and blackface minstrel entertainment. Like many settler-corroboree performances, both vaudeville and the exceedingly popular blackface minstrel shows of the second half of the nineteenth century included short recital pieces, nonsense songs, mimed scenes, short plays, and displays of agility, such as feats of dancing, juggling, contortion, and acrobatics. Moreover, the corroboree easily shared in the ethos of the minstrel show, which emphasised 'defying and mocking authority' and 'making fun of the rich and prominent' through skits and lampoons. Minstrelsy's morphology was also echoed by the temperance movement entertainments. Mission-dwelling Aborigines found that traditional forms of corroboree entertainment could be absorbed and reinvented in Blue Ribbon Army or Band of Hope performances. Short plays and sketches and recitals were also readily adopted as the format of such temperance entertainments. Thus we have the Mt Barker Courier's description (18 June 1886) of a commercial corroboree performance in 1886 being given by 'Salvation Army natives'.

In 1894 the Point McLeay Mission formed a Glee Club that, in December 1895, performed at the Aborigines Friends Association AGM where it filled the Adelaide Town Hall with record crowds (Jenkin 1979:226).

The Glee Club's popularity led to the Aborigines Friends Association AGMs continuing to be held in the Adelaide Town Hall. In 1898, a massive exhibition of mats and baskets and other local products was added. The sales success of these items led to mat and basket weaving becoming included in the Point McLeay Mission school curriculum in 1904. In 1908, weekly tours began operating to the Mission for summer holidaymakers at Goolwa, the tourists being treated to singing performances. Some 2000 tourists visited over the summer of 1908-9, and many bought traditional woven articles as souvenirs. In December 1909 there were more fund-raising concert performances at Adelaide, along with speeches by David Unaipon and Philip Rigney, which echoed the prevalent fashion for minstrelsy entertainment combining sentiment with heartfelt political speeches.

This 'peroration', said the Advertiser, 'fitted the situation, and should have been, if it was not, appreciated by the thoughtful in the audience'. It 'fitted the situation' because through Ruth's performance, it directly linked the 'pathos and sadness of the life of the colored people of another country' to the Indigenous experience.

As a political speech, remonstrating with the audience, it was also fitting in the sense of not being out-of-place in the minstrel format, a socially acceptable format for protesting injustice. In 1910, Point McLeay Mission Aborigines performed at the Tasmanian State Centenary celebrations, at the request of the Tasmanian Government. Claiming all the Tasmanian Indigenous population had been exterminated, the Tasmanian Government asked South Australia to provide an Indigenous group to act as Tasmanians in the pageant's reenactment of the first landing by Europeans at Hobart. Painted up and dressed in 'possum' skin rugs, the Ngarrindjeri reportedly most vigorously played their part in a sham battle corroboree opposing the planting of the British flag on 'their' soil. They also put on many other performances including boomerang throwing, contrasting them with magnificent choral singing in church services that 'astonished the Tasmanians'.

Perhaps it was the success of their Tasmanian tour that led to Point McLeay Mission's performance of a corroboree at the Commercial Travellers Club Charity Fancy Dress Football Carnival at the Adelaide Oval the following year. By 1911 the public was well aware of the new frontier of the Northern Territory and Spencer's and Gillen's eyewitness press reports on Central Australian corroborees revived public interest in the genre as it was felt a 'proper corroboree' cannot be seen except 'in the faraway haunts of the blacks'.

With 'twenty full-blooded natives' giving 'as perfect a reproduction of their old war dances as the laws of decency and their personal ability permit', the performance was meant to be a reminder of the dangers facing new settlers in the north of the State, but what in South Australia could only be an 'old-time corroboree', a 'novelty which should prove popular' as fancy dress football.

In such ways, marginal, mobile, gypsy forms of theatre were to dominate mainstream, sedentary forms for Indigenous performers for most of the twentieth century. Initially, non-Indigenous audiences saw corroborees as opera or ballet, when the Indigenous 'lords of the soil' were still in possession of their lands. But once displaced to become landless labourers, Indigenous persons were forced to turn to minstrelsy and vaudeville genres to re-frame their public performances. As vaudeville too became sedentary theatre for mainstream audiences, they shifted again to tour country towns at shows and rodeos and in sideshow boxing tents. These shifts acted to reinforce the representation of Indigenous peoples as 'nomads' and 'drifters', feckless wanderers over land, justifying and rationalising dispossession.

By the early twentieth century the corroboree performed in southern settled areas was often of the 'sham battle' kind. The playing out for non-Indigenous audiences of 'native war dances', far removed geographically and historically from the ever-present and real threat on the frontier, of an imagined threat, represented in a safe simulation. The corroboree was an incantation summoning up a lost frontier and its lost community.

On the other side of the frontier at the turn of the century, in Central Australia, in the wake of the Horn expedition and the growth of scientific interest in 'the Aborigine' as a remnant of the Stone Age, the demand for Aboriginal performance became subordinate to the rush to collect Aboriginal objects. These were mainly carved stone or wooden tjurungas, called 'corroboree stones', for sale to southern collectors and museum collections.

This interest saw a shift in South Australia, amongst those with a scientific or intellectual interest in Indigenous cultures, from experiencing intangible culture, such as corroborees, as collectable, to the construction of a collection of tangible objects, 'corroboree stones'. This shift created a secondary market, whereby tangible culture could be purchased or stolen by non-Indigenous wholesalers on the frontier for on-sale to non-Indigenous retailers and other buyers such as museums. Even on the frontier, however, at the level of the wholesaler, such as the prospector R.T. Maurice whose chief interest was to beat his rival Gillen to the best specimens, the corroboree became a means of adding value to corroboree stones by according meaning to them.

But an 'eyewitness account' in this context was insufficient, a 'mere travellers tale'. Given the cutthroat market-place of tjurunga-collecting, proof was required. Photography provided the process of assaying the intangible cultural interpretation of tangible objects. The by-product of the assay, the photograph, as an object to interpret an object, itself became saleable. Indigenous peoples in Central Australia quickly adapted to this new market. As early as 1895, Gillen wrote to Spencer that a 'deputation of greasy Udnaorigurta' Aborigines had approached him with the offer 'that they are prepared to allow me to photograph a corroboree this afternoon in return for a blowout of flour, tea and sugar'.

'Corroboree stone' collecting was sometimes accompanied by forced disclosure by Aboriginal informants. This led to Aboriginal reprisals against those disclosing. For example, the Horn Expedition's Aboriginal guide, Racehorse, forced to reveal the location of Luritja 'corroboree stones', was later executed by irate traditional owners. As Mulvaney (1989:139) commented, it was ironic 'that those in positions of authority who attempted to administer Indigenous affairs with a rough sense of justice, undermined the authority of clan elders and the fabric of Aboriginal society'.

The pilfering of these objects, which played a vital role in the ritual transmission of knowledge, inspired the 'collection' of 'every one he could locate' in the region by M.C. Cowle on behalf of the Sub-Protector of Aborigines, Frank Gillen. While, in 1927, Spencer stated 'It is regrettable that the true nature of the objects thus hidden away in a cave was not known at that time ... The loss of Churinga is the most significant evil that could befall any local group', no effort had been made to restore possession since 1897 when Gillen had confessed to him that 'there must be no more ertatulnga robberies. I bitterly regret ever having countenanced such a thing'. But while he had told Cowle to return some of them, Cowle continued to collect for Spencer's museum, sometimes through the interrogation of prisoners and the use of prison labour.

Winnecke and Stirling used the corroboree precedent to rationalise the theft, stating that they had 'left a number of tomahawks, large knives and other things in their place, sufficient commercially to make the transaction an equitable exchange'. Thus as scientific interest shifted from embodied cultural capital to objectified cultural capital, from person to product, a 'commercial' reckoning of the barter 'transaction' was readily imputed. In contrast, Indigenous groups mourned the loss of these objects as they did their relatives; a reckoning of product as person.

While the institutional, scientific and Governmental focus on collection of cultural materials was to be reflected by the tourism trade in souvenir boomerangs, coolamons, woomeras, spears, didjerdu and other carvings, it meant an opting out of the market for intangible cultural goods, such as the corroboree, which continued more firmly in the tourist domain. For hosts, this domain was relatively benign, affording an easier regulation over degrees of cultural disclosure.

Thus, even on the frontier, with its lack of a sizeable paying audience, by the end of the nineteenth century the word 'corroboree' became in equal parts guest convention and host invention. The true 'corroboree' was one Aboriginal people performed for visitors for a commercial consideration, as against the ceremonial and ritual dances they performed only for themselves. But as has been seen in Arrernte ltata songs, the latter could easily inform the former. That the former distinction was readily apparent by 1886, but the latter distinction not yet perceived, can be seen in the contribution by the South Australia Museum Director, E.C. Stirling, to the Report on the Work of the Horn Scientific Expedition to Central Australia.

In tourism terms, the response of Stirling, as an adventure traveller far 'off the beaten track', is understandable. Made aware that there are performances that outsiders, like him, may witness, and other 'secret' 'mysterious' performances that are kept hidden from outsiders, 'even Mr. Gillen', Stirling ranks the former as 'inferior'. But, as he finds himself only able to witness such performances, he goes on to reassure his readers that 'lest the statement of the inferior significance of these corroborees should unduly minimise their importance, that even these are very elaborate performances'.

Stirling's differentiation and his response to it encapsulated the in-built self-contradictions of antitourism in its urge to get off the beaten track in quest for an unattainable ideal. What is most superior to see is that which is prohibited from being seen. In the 'high degree of intimacy' situation, however, with its invitation to 'come share our culture', there is a certain, if uneven, guest expectation, that one is to be treated as an insider. Thus the difficulty occurs when hosts disclose or have disclosed to guests that what the latter are seeing is a partial disclosure, the one open to 'outsiders'.

The tantalising offer of 'forbidden fruit' may be a part of the chemistry of such interactions, but the revelation of exclusion accentuates the divide between host and guest and counters the sense of being hosted. Being kept outside the ring of those with inside knowledge, counters the 'authenticity' afforded by being on the other side of the frontier, and inside a guest-recognised Indigenous domain.

There is also the undercutting of the equilibrium of the capital exchange by the disclosure of nondisclosure. Stirling, for example, does not highlight but neither does he hide the fact that in performing for 'a few sticks of tobacco' or, as they did at Alice Springs, 'on promise of suitable reward', what his hosts were doing was to put on a show for visitors for a fee. But for Stirling the satisfaction of seeing 'a great show' performed in a dominantly Indigenous domain, offset the pangs of inauthenticity afforded by it being a staged paid performance.

Thus 'balletic' perceptions of corroborees by non-Indigenous observers remained active within the Indigenous domain, although they had long left the non-Indigenous 'settled' domain. In the late nineteenth and early twentieth century in settled Australia, dispossession, removal, denial of employment and self-employment through social control policies of government and mission agencies denied any possibility of independent Indigenous performers pursuing the mainstream theatrical stage.

The closure of options, acted to funnel and shunt Indigenous theatre into what was literally a sideshow tradition. Indigenous football and cricket players cum athletes cum corroboree performers found their niche in the rural fair, sporting or ploughing festival sideshows. Some Aborigines pursued acrobatic careers in roving vaudeville or burlesque bush shows. Some became famous as stars of touring colonial circuses, such as Ashton's trick rider, Mongo Mongo, and Combo Combo, the contortionist.

By the early twentieth century, stationary forms could be found in the Government settlement and Mission Station corroboree performances given to tourists. But the mobile forms—the circuses, tent troupes, wandering minstrel bands and travelling shows—provided an alternative forum of respectability, a locus of identity and, framed by exotic company, a measure of authenticity that was being denied to them by the advancing frontier. Indigenous performers were to affiliate socially and in some cases formally join such groups. This affiliation was to challenge, albeit not always successfully, the placing of a boundary around Indigenous and non-Indigenous geographical and social space.

Historically, the tourism industry, in its quest for experiencing the Other, has always encouraged an articulation of peoples with place, reinforced through destination marketing. This dove-tailed with the long European tradition that had it that, if inhabited, the most extreme places were occupied by the most extreme of peoples. The outlands were the home of the outlandish; the wilderness, the habitat of wild peoples. The inverse was seen to be equally true, with a place mirroring the perceived primitiveness of its inhabitants.

Thus for non-Indigenous settlers in early twentieth century Australia, the 'authentic Aborigine' was seen as one living beyond the frontier, not in the 'civilised' settled coastal regions. Consequently, the articulation of Indigenous peoples with wildness and wilderness in the non-Indigenous conception has left Indigenous peoples in more urbanised areas with the onus of proving their own authenticity, or being encouraged by the tourism market to emulate the accepted authenticity of 'The Outback Aboriginal'.

There has been an increasing recourse to using conservation areas to provide a link to the wildness and wilderness that has been lost or subsumed. For Indigenous communities seeking to demonstrate, gain or reinforce rights to their traditional lands, cultural tourism continues to combine the satisfying vision of economic self-reliance with a much deeper need. Cultural tourism has become a currency for Indigenous peoples to realise their land needs and to re-connect with their cultural heritage. Indigenous cultural tourism continues to express for both host and guest, in different ways, belonging to the land, and the longing to belong.

Rural mythology has historically provided an important focus for cultural explanations of Australian national identity. Since the early 1960s, however, rural myths-especially those represented through the Australian Legend-have been subjected to searching critiques from different positions within and outside the academy. Research using theoretical models interested in the politics of identity exposed the racial and gender bias of the rural legends associated with key Australian writers from the 1890s, in particular.

At the same time, the apparent adoption of a form of identity politics in government policies related to migrants and the Indigenous community, along with a simultaneous enthusiasm across the political spectrum for privatisation, deregulation, and globalisation, enabled a populist identification of the academic and intellectual class promoting these critiques with politicians, their policy advisers, and the forces of global capital.

Commentators in the metropolitan press and the academy have tended to argue that the new 'racist' and anti-intellectual political force mobilised by Pauline Hanson's One Nation phenomenon represented an outdated Anglo-Celtic conservatism, which could be sourced to provincial cultures and their affinities with the Australian Legend. Paul Kelly has characterised Hansonism as 'an echo of our Anglo-Celtic origins; the claims of the once mighty bush to define the Australian Legend; a descendant of the romanticism and racism of Henry Lawson whose hold on national identity was once so comprehensive ... the latest manifestation of our reflex to distrust authority, abuse our elites and damn our leaders'.

Phillip Adams called it a 'mess movement of bigotries, disappointments, indignations, resentments, neo-fascism, old fascism, Christian fundamentalism, conspiracy theories, hopelessness, hysteria and good old-fashioned belly-aching'. Adams's essay is rhetorically interesting because it uses the metaphor of a shopping-bag lady to ridicule Hanson and her supporters and, while the caricature is entertaining, it also suggests both an intellectual and a class-based contempt for 'ordinary Australians' which analyses of opinion polls, and the One Nation party itself, found were part of the problem that Pauline Hanson and her followers were addressing.

The academic response to One Nation and its claims upon the authentic traditions of the Australian Legend has sometimes taken a similar path to the metropolitan press by setting up an ethical opposition between Anglo-Celtic culture, and Aboriginal or multicultural Australia. The unfashionable identification of Anglo-Celtic Australia with an Australian Legend tarnished by the critiques of the last forty years has been played out at the level of discursive style where style, as it is in Adams, is a display of a linguistic competency that guarantees the subject's implicit claim to the forms of distinction required to participate as an intellectual in the public sphere.

Richard Nile's Introduction to The Australian Legend and Its Discontents, for example, deploys 'Henry Lawson' as a trope for a particular version of the Australian Legend, critiqued as a set of images that helped to licence a narrow and outdated version of Australianness. Nile's essay, 'Tell Them that Henry Lawson is Dead', includes subheadings such as 'He Died Without a Bottle of Beer in His Hand' and 'There's Something About Henry', and thus works rhetorically and logically to dismiss Lawson's contemporary value.

Lawson seems particularly unfashionable now, but it needs to be recognised that arguments against him have received regular airings from left-wing nationalists and their opponents since Lawson's earliest reception in the 1890s. The need to discredit Lawson through exposes that take the form of biographical anecdote or rum quotation has long been a symptom of the threat that his reputation has posed to preferred versions of Australianness.

The longevity of the Lawson Legend can, in some ways, be explained by the persistence of historical attempts to incorporate, or to erase, his potential for dissidence. The establishment's early assessment of the need for such incorporation recognised the political significance of the popular purchase of his reputation. A significant omission in more recent academic critiques of both the Lawson and the Australian legends has been an investigation of the detailed contexts of this popular reception.

Lawson's place in the Australian social imaginary has never had much to do with a consistent logic within his oeuvre, or the biographical and historical facts obscured by his myth, and his symbolic significance in this country is never going to be settled by a set of simplistic assertions. As Ghassan Hage points out, academic arguments lack the power to decide questions of social identity, because identity is the fantastic product of symbolic powers. The stature of Henry Lawson in the cultural history of Australia is due to the historical utility of his reputation for licensing different forms of social identity.

Hage's analysis of the causes behind the feelings of disempowerment that have helped generate the new racism suggests that it has much to do with a shift in the forms of cultural capital required to claim a governmental authority over the national space. His work is useful for my purposes because it understands the new racism as a spatial crisis related to the symbolic operation of social identity.

Those critics who have sought to silence the racism that

has sprung from this sense of disempowerment by seeking to ridicule their reliance upon a cultural heritage insufficiently useful for a (post)modern, cosmopolitan and multicultural country take a position in the debate that simply exacerbates the situation. The Lawson legend remains an important part of the national imaginary for some Anglo-Celtic sections of the Australian population who are denied the economic, cultural or political capital required to manage the pace of change in recent Australian society.

LOCAL CLAIMS ON AN AUSTRALIAN LEGEND

This region represents a suggestive sample of the contemporary popular use of Lawson's reputation and the rural mythologies that might be articulated with it for a number of reasons. This is where Henry Lawson spent his childhood, and the area provided the identifiable locations for many of his earlier works.

Mudgee is a regional town supported by a number of industries including wine, sheep and cattle grazing, fruit and vegetable growing, and tourism. It lies within the federal electorate of Gwydir, the seat of the National Party leader and Deputy Prime Minister John Anderson, where One Nation received 21% of the primary vote in the 1996 Federal election.

Local history in this region has often taken the form of a memorial to the famous writer. More recently, however, it has developed into a programme for the recovery of local memory and a related affirmation of a sense of community identity. These regional values sometimes run counter to the prevailing moods and intentions of the public memories of the nation, and the heritage tourism profile of the area consequently represents a process of negotiation between quite different constituencies—a theme that has been at the centre of much of the recent sociological work on globalisation and localisation.

The connections of the past of this region with a nationally-recognised rural mythology are put to a variety of uses by the local community. While there remains, here, much that I would still wish to critique, there is enough social value on show to suggest that some caution is needed before rural heritage in general, and its long suffering apostle Henry Lawson, in particular, are dismissed.

A celebrated pioneering history plays an important part in the commemorative activities of the area in which the famous writer was raised. The 'Roaring Days' of the great gold rushes represent one of the most significant in the national account of European settlement. During the 1870s and 1880s, the tailend of this significant historical period combined with the picturesque qualities of a specific local geography to inspire an exemplary son of the region. Henry Lawson and his work are both productive of, and the products of, a place, and these valued cultural relations provide that place with important associations. During this century, English-speaking cultures have made a habit of preserving regions as the immortalisation of their famous writers: Stratford has its Shakespeare, the English Lakes have their Romantic poets, and the United States's New England has its Thoreau. It is in this tradition that Eurunderee, the area of Lawson's youth and the subject of his work, has been remade as one of Australia's settler sites.

Lawson's habit of drawing upon the topography and social history of his youth in the Mudgee area has provided the region with rich cultural-historical associations. These associations allowed this space to achieve a particular place in debates over the status of the national culture in the period between the wars. After Lawson's death, the Lawson Societies, the Fellowship of Australian Writers (FAW), public intellectuals, and left-wing political interests were involved in campaigns to consecrate 'The Lawson country'.

The Lawson societies, the FAW, and public intellectuals such as Vance and Nettie Palmer, were motivated by a perceived need to respond to public and professional perceptions that Australia lacked the historical traditions required to sustain a sophisticated national culture. The promotional impetus provided by Lawson's State Funeral, the Domain Memorial Campaign, and his still significant public popularity, made him an ideal figure upon which to base a case for the national culture, and when the cultural nationalists' cause involved the national poet, they were able to secure aid from left-wing political figures for whom Lawson remained a useful political weapon.

Until recently, co-operation with initiatives from Sydney represented the characteristic mechanism of the Mudgee region's involvement in the preservation of its Lawson associations. In fact, the need to recognise a local connection with the celebrity of Lawson initially stemmed from a sense of shame caused by mistaken admiration from the metropolitan press. In 1921, when Mudgee opened Lawson Park as a memorial to William Lawson (no relation), the first European to stumble across and claim the land of the Wiradjuri people, it was incorrectly seen by some as a progressive recognition of Henry Lawson.

The local paper is quick to point out that it was fit and proper to recognise a dead explorer-settler before a living poet. The 'relative unimportance' of letters when compared to the 'finding and development and settlement of the Mudgee lands', and the 'gold ... sheep ... grain ... and the fortunes that have been made', meant that the Mudgee Guardian could safely reassure its readers that 'nothing so ambitious as an obelisk or a statue' need be contemplated. Not, at least, until the poet was actually dead.

THE SOCIAL PURCHASE OF LOCAL HISTORY

Some sixty years later another generation of Mudgee residents appeared to register the reluctance of the local establishment to recognise a poet while wine and honey were bringing in the money that really counted. Norman McVicker, Brendan Dunne, Betty McLean, Peter Mansfield and Carl Werchon formed the Eurunderee Provisional School Foundation, Inc. in 1989 to restore the small timber school that now occupied the site of the famous Old Bark School in which Lawson had been educated in the 1870s, as a memorial to the famous writer and the local community in which he was raised.

'Much of his best works were related to here', McVicker told the local press, 'and we ... wanted to save that'. The restoration was staged and conducted as a significant community event, and it used volunteer labour and local donations of money and of material and historical artefacts. In this way the one-room school was restored to its 'original' Federation colours, and an interior display established to represent the three important periods in its history: 1876, 1900 and 1970.

Although the building housed school memorabilia, McVicker was keen to distinguish it from a museum. It was to be a place that would permit the school children of today to 'imagine' themselves in the different historical periods that have formed the district, and the generations that have constituted its communities.

'Henry Lawson' is concerned to name the local pioneering families and catalogue their occupations, and this is a characteristic emphasis of the Foundation's commemorative activities. Lawson is valuable because of his national celebrity, and the potential tourist dollars associated with his fame, but he is also valuable as a repository of the area's forgotten social history. Fame can provide a powerful stimulus for local memories.

Celebrity gives quotidian things an enhanced significance, and often leads to the recollection of events more usually considered forgettable. Lawson's careful preservation by metropolitan, regional, and a number of interconnected familial cultures can thus be used by the locality to recover its own lost references. Through Lawson, Eurunderee might recover an authoritatively local sense of its past. Commemoration is, therefore, a familiar affirmation of the local settler history of pioneering families, and their establishment of a civil community.

The interest initially generated by the project led to a weekly column by McVicker in the Mudgee Guardian. Entitled 'Tales From the Wallaby Track ... In Search of Henry Lawson's Eurunderee', the column regularly reported the progress of the Foundation's restoration of the school complex and its rediscovery of the social history of the area. Writing in the column in November of the inaugural year, McVicker summarises the interests of the Foundation and its community activities: 'Our entire field of endeavour has been to establish and document the facts about Henry Lawson's Eurunderee years, the inter-relationship of the pioneer families and their association with Eurunderee as Lawson knew it and wrote about it'.

This mission is often interpreted as a monument to Lawson, within whose work Eurunderee is itself commemorated for posterity: 'Eurunderee is full of Lawson associations, its reality reinforced by the stories and poems which he wrote about the little world he knew. "Eurunderee", itself is his "Memorial". When our identifying signs are in place, Eurunderee will finally be recognised as "The Real Henry Lawson Country"'.

This shift in emphasis from Lawson to Eurunderee is a feature of the local initiative: Lawson and his work are memorials for Eurunderee. Remembering Henry Lawson thus adopts the form of the historical recovery of a local community history, and 'The Wallaby Track' accordingly thanked local residents and widely-dispersed expatriates for their regular donations of authentic artefacts, which had been safely preserved through the generations of a family.

Newer residents were also able to write themselves into the history of the area through their support for the Foundation and their respect for the community value of their places. One of the more interesting features of this recovery is a welcome sense of the multicultural character of original settlement, although it needs to be said that that character remains European, and hence fails to upset the articulation of local heritage with whiteness and its custodial role over the spatial imaginary.

The Eurunderee Provisional School Foundation, Inc. and the weekly 'Wallaby Track' column together orchestrated an ongoing community interest and initiative in the recovery of the forgotten stories of its past. They provided an occasion for remembering, and a safe haven for artefacts, records, and oral memory. Often the Foundation republished well-known texts, which it then recontextualised as the signs of the significant locale now safely in its keeping. Lawson's poems 'The Roaring Days', 'The Lights of the Cobb & Co' and 'Eurunderee', together with the story 'The Loaded Dog' were represented in a tourist pamphlet as markers of the area.

The national celebrity of Henry Lawson and his associated geographies are thus represented in local terms, according to local interests. In this way the citizenry of the region can acquire a particular type of local authority, which well arms them for any disagreements with the metropolitan expertise of professional historians and educators. When a staff writer for the Sydney Morning Herald chided the people of Mudgee for their belated recognition of Lawson, he drew a non-committal response. When the writer accused them of attempting to 'sanitise his life story', however, he was promptly rebuked. 'We are proud of what the Foundation has achieved' wrote McVicker, 'we have documented and recorded only facts'.

An important part of his defence was the restatement of the Foundation's purely local interest. Other agents have concerned themselves with Lawson's later life, whereas the 'entire field of endeavour' of the Foundation has been to 'establish and document the facts about Henry Lawson's Eurunderee years, the inter-relationship of the pioneer families and their association with Eurunderee as Lawson knew it and wrote about it.

Nothing more-nothing less'. Reporting on the Henry and Louisa Lawson conference, which was held in 1991 at the Prince of Wales Opera House in Gulgong under the auspices of the Centre for Australian Language and Literature Studies at the University of New England, McVicker was again concerned to position local authority in relation to professional disciplines.

'Some of the subject matter was, to the layman, unbelievably esoteric', he wrote. 'I left the conference wondering whether Louisa and Henry would have understood the discussions', he added.

TOURISM AND THE DARK PAST OF THE LOCAL

The Foundation's efforts to recover the social history of the region always stood side by side with an affirmed commercial interest in the tourist potential of this history's more celebrated associations. McVicker, who identified himself as a man who 'for thirty years was closely associated with the [tourism] industry', regularly reported tourist news in 'Tales From the Wallaby Track'. In October 1989, immediately following the restoration of the school, the column reported the opening of the newly signposted 'Wallaby Track' by the Mudgee Shire Tourist Officer.

Two weeks later the success was announced of the first minibus tour of the 'Track' with McVicker as guide. One year later, the columnist described his partipation in many subsequent tours, and the growing interest in 'the childhood days of Henry Lawson and the pioneer doings of the early settlers in Eurunderee'.

The Foundation's proprietary interest in the tourist value of Mudgee's Lawson associations is partly driven by the need to convince local authorities of its potential, and partly by the need to secure the identification of the Foundation with its inevitable success. It implicitly recognises that schemes for the generation of social capital need to connect with an economic bottom line if they are to secure material resources. The surprising need to establish the potential of history is due to the area's already affirmed tourist identity as the Land of Wine and Honey—an identity that potentially restricts the flow of resources to the campaign to identify the local geography as Lawson country.

This is not a case of a depressed rural town desperately turning to cultural tourism for salvation. The success of Mudgee as a wine area, and of its particularly wide range of rural industries, has drawn increasing tourism and significant development in the town. Therefore this drive to re-establish Lawson as a complementary tourist property expresses the anxieties of certain sections of the community about the overly commercial ways in which tourism was representing the area.

The success of the campaign for recognition confirms the Foundation's worth to the regional economy, and legitimises the cultural arguments it has used to justify its wide range of initiatives. The subsequent success of these representations has, in turn, provided social, political, and economic capital for the restoration of artefacts, and the recovery of the local memories through which they might productively be re-associated.

The limited multiculturalism of Eurunderee's late nineteenth-century social history is enabled through those forms of pioneering mythology that have been widely criticised as claims to a place that erase Indigenous peoples. While it may have been possible to erase Indigenous presence without fear of contradiction in times past, however, the ethical purchase of Indigenous issues make such practices increasingly dubious-particularly in those cases where the local is forced to cater to the global, in the interests of generating revenue from tourism.

Tourist trading of the local inevitably entails its representation for the cosmopolitan tastes and expectations of the traveller, and this means that it has to register their expectations. Therefore, when McVicker organised a tour of the Wallaby Track for a group of Country Press Association members and their wives, he was quickly confronted with the absence of Indigenous reference in the Foundation's tourist narrative.

The Press Association members' recognition of the priority of Indigenous possession and their associated curiosity about the Aborigines' associations of the area contradicts the settler claims of discovery and originality that so often feature in pioneering festivals, and McVicker moved quickly to produce a special issue of 'Tales From Along the Wallaby Track' on the Wiradjuri people. The Foundation's pamphlet, 'The Wiradjuri Story: Aborigines of Henry Lawson Country', represents a particularly interesting representation of black history.

In some ways it might be described in the (pejorative) words of Geoffrey Blainey, as a 'black armband' view of

Indigenous history. The early settlers' violent dispossession of a 'healthy, moral' Indigenous community, which was living in spiritual harmony with a Land they understood, is seen as indefensible. The affirmed ethical character of the Wiradjuri is considered a function of their sophisticated association with the local place, and the Foundation's own search for local origins can thus be represented as the expression of comparable ethical substance.

Tony Bennett has argued that Aboriginal sites and artefacts have been officially appropriated so that the national time might be extended into a deeper and hence more legitimate past. The Foundation's pamphlet can certainly be seen as an attempt to consolidate the local 'settler' claim to place by appropriating the legitimacy of the indigene, and it needs to be said that for all its good intentions, the Foundation fails to connect the Indigenous history with the claims of a contemporary Indigenous population.

Ultimately, the booklet reverts to Prime Minister John Howard's tactic of consigning settler atrocities and their undeserving victims to the past: 'Their lands, their kinsmen and their lifestyle had been ruthlessly destroyed by greed. In the wake of despair came the diseases of the white man, alcohol-and finally death.

By 1850 the Wiradjuri had been completely dispossessed and were virtually extinct'. The discourse of nostalgic lament has been a feature of the liberal response to Indigenous genocide since the nineteenth century, and the Eurunderee Provisional Foundation's representation of the local Indigenous claims to place ultimately remain conservative. Nevertheless, they stop a fair way short of the forms of red-necked regional racism that we saw associated with Hansonism's Anglo-Celtic Conservatism.

We are no longer living in the nineteenth century, and Indigenous claims are now regularly represented in the mainstream media as a part of an ongoing active political struggle. The Foundation's acknowledgment of the ethically desirable local associations of the Wiradjuri is there to be claimed by interested political agents. The potential for the reconciliation process of the conjunction of interest in erased Indigenous places and lost settler associations has been a theme of recent work by Australian historians such as Peter Read. The widespread experience of lost place which characterises immigrant cultures is a resource which might more productively be used in this way.

Heather Goodall's work on rural community history reveals some willingness by pastoralists to reconnect their history with those of Indigenous Australians in a self-interested effort to enable their own ongoing struggles with rival industries and environmental disasters. The need for local Mudgee interests to cater for a cosmopolitan taste in order to confirm the tourist value of their heritage paves the way for a similar recognition of native association. The articulation of the Indigenous past with the local project of reclaiming the lost settler history also associates the Foundation's activities with the moral legitimacy of the increasingly powerful metropolitan narrative of Indigenous dispossession. This is important, for in the sphere of tourism at least, the boot is on another foot, and the regional settler identities that have so often erased native association are now themselves being consigned to the cosmopolitan nation's colourful past.

Nevertheless, the tourist's interest in the Wiradjuri is not reported in 'The Wallaby Track' column because it is thought to disable the local claim to originality. It is used to confirm the importance of the Foundation's search after local truths. This is why McVicker is careful to point out that the trip was not a 'junket', but a genuine expression of interest in authentic local origins.

The need to make this argument is of course an expression of anxiety. The tourist presentation of the local social history is inevitably directed towards its involvement in the originating moment of the national literary heritage, and the mention of this origin is primary. The authentic origin of a national celebrity is the grand narrative, and it is only through the articulation of the local with such a narrative that local social memory is capitalised for the tourists.

THE COUNTRY AS ANOTHER TIME

In discussing the tourist promotion of the historical Rocks redevelopment in Sydney, Bennett argues that the area has been transformed into a 'centre of origins in the sense of being not merely the first area of settlement but one which contains the seeds of future and broader developments'. The transformation of the Rocks adopts the rhetorical forms of 'consensus nationalism which, in overlaying the various objects and buildings encountered, enables them to function as origins of the subsequent unfolding of the nation's history told as the gradual rise of a free, democratic, multicultural citizenry'.

If there is a comparable rhetoric for the transformation of the Eurunderee area into the Lawson country, it is the liberal pioneering myth. The Foundation gives little emphasis to the class struggle that was expressed through the battles over the Land Acts throughout the late nineteenth century, and the pioneering myth tends to work in conjunction with the conservative nationalist version of Australian literary culture to redeploy the political struggles of the settlers as a more familiar contest with isolation and environment.

The densities of local memories and their multiple authorial locations partially protect the local from the loaded forms of erasure practised by the official institutions of public culture, but the local is not immune from the flattering imaginings of a pioneering legend and its idealisation of quotidian struggles. The use of Lawson to get at local memories is reversed for tourists, who are presented with local memories as signs of the national celebrity. This reversal can shed the complicated idiosyncrasies of the local account, and allow the easy consumption of the region.

As recent studies of tourism and globalisation have shown, local significance can seldom function for the tourist in the ways that it might for the local citizenry. To make a tourist commodity out of a local past requires the adoption of the rhetorical tropes of the national heritage and these tropes, as Bennett describes them, are there to be found in both the literature of the local Tourist Information Centre, and the Foundation's packaging of local memories for tourist consumption.

In the discourses of tourist promotion that address the cosmopolitan consumer, the country becomes a pastoral form of the past that functions as a refuge from what Les Murray would call 'this metropolitan century'. As Bennett puts it, 'The more the structure of the past is subject to the exigencies of tourism, the greater the likelihood that it will focus on the country rather than the city, and on the nineteenth rather than the twentieth century. It will, as a consequence tend to offer the great majority of Australians an imaginative diversion from their present conditions of existence rather than affording a familiarity with the more immediate histories from which those conditions effectively flow'. Those local social memories would be appropriated through their articulation with the public memory and the marketing rhetoric of the tourism industry was rendered inevitable by the Foundation's need to find a place for their Lawson narrative within the region's already established tourism strategies.

The predominant tourist identity of the Mudgee area was, and largely still is, drawn from the region's distinctive rural industries: as noted, Mudgee is the 'Land of Wine and Honey'. Ruth Barcan has pointed out the way in which 'big things' (for example, the big cow, the big banana) 'create some regional identities at the cost of others, since tourist identities work best when they are distinct, relatively singular and easily reproducible visually'. Thus 'Difference gets subsumed under the marketing logic of brand recognition'.

It is easy to discern a note of self-justification in McVicker's celebration of the tourist triumphs of the 'Wallaby Track' and the Eurunderee Provisional School, which is perhaps directed towards local reluctance to accept that the land of wine and honey might at the same time be Henry Lawson Country.

Parochial rivalries and local tensions aside, the importance of a discourse of time and place to the marketing strategies of the wine industry meant that Henry Lawson was always going to be easily accommodated by the vignerons. It is the spirit of the place that was the genius of Lawson's art, and that same spirit of place is now creating the award-winning tastes of Montrose Wines' Poet's Corner. Wine is not a drink, it is a culture, and this culture needs to be distinguished by a geography that is rich in natural and historical associations.

The fusion of nature and culture provides a wine with a style, which it offers in the form of a taste. Style is the enabling trope of the publicity narratives of wine, because it represents a superior way of life. The national historical and cultural associations of the Mudgee area therefore provide Mudgee wine with the deep time and the rich place of a distinguished reputation. To buy and taste the wine of Poet's Corner is therefore a form of communion with a historically significant place. Montrose wine has Mudgee and Henry Lawson in a bottle, and both the local mythologies and the national heritage are in this way transformed into a commodity for consumption and exchange.

Tourist maps of the district's wineries are thus inscribed upon the historical map of Lawson Country, and the tourist cannot only travel, survey, imagine, feel, and experience the national heritage, they can taste it as well. It is therefore no surprise that the local wine industry has come to the Henry Lawson party as a prominent sponsor of the historical and cultural activities of the Eurunderee Provisional School Foundation and the Henry Lawson Society of NSW, which is based in the nearby town of Gulgong.

Montrose Wine's publicity narrative was printed on the back page of the entry form for the annual Henry Lawson Society of New South Wales/Montrose Wines Poet's Corner's Award for the best poem based upon a contemporary Australian subject or theme. The judging and the exhibition of entries was held at the Montrose Winery during the 1994 Mudgee Wine Festival in September of that year. This complementary relation between wine and culture is one that the 'Tales From the Wallaby Track' column comes increasingly to encourage, as history is gradually admitted to the tourist profile of the region. The role played by mythological figures such as Henry Lawson and pioneering myths similar to the Australian Legend in the constitution of contemporary Australian identities have much more to do with the strategic conditions in which local spaces encounter the cosmopolitan cultures of postmodernity than with privileged professional readings of the discursive detail of particular textual estates.

It is the strategic detail of these local contests that we are going to have to deal with if we are to follow David Carter's call to find 'new ways to make pluralism as popular as populism', and this study suggests that we are going to be much more successful at this if we find a way of engaging with a cultural heritage that provides a proportion of our citizenry with the symbolic capital required to feel a part of the nation. There is a disturbing similarity between the ways in which the local volunteer society consigned the native claim to place to a regrettable past, and the manner in which cosmopolitan Australia represents the times and places of its regional and rural cultures.

Questions of race, place and identity are always a question of capital, and if we are going to alleviate the racial tensions in this country, then we are going to have to find an innovative and productive way of capitalising the diverse forms of identity now party to the Australian social contract. For a politically significant number of Australians, that is going to mean a dynamic, creative and more specific critical engagement with rural mythology, the Australian Legend-and maybe even poor old Henry Lawson.

Chapter 8

Between Preservation and Tourism

Japan's folk performing arts (minzoku geino [text not reproducible in ascii.]) have long been considered as important cultural properties that must be preserved. Surprisingly, however, their relationship to tourism has not been considered in depth, even though the development of mass tourism and other social changes have markedly altered their form.

In particular, the 1992 Festival Law (Omatsuriho [text not reproducible in ascii.]) which promotes the exploitation of folk performing arts as tourist resources, clearly expresses the current situation of folk performing arts. Thus, before debating the pros and cons of the Festival Law, we should stop to reconsider the ways in which we have come to objectify folk performing arts

TOURISM AND FOLK PERFORMING ARTS

This chapter contends that Japan's folk performing arts have been objectified through tourism. By examining the history of folk performing arts studies, I demonstrate how the development of modern media, such as railway networks and travel magazines, has played a decisive role in this objectification process.

No matter what our views regarding Japan's folk performing arts, we cannot avoid premising them within the context of tourism. Some critics believe that tourism destroys folk performing arts as authentic cultural phenomena. However, rather than treat folk performing arts as authentic cultural phenomena existing as real entities, I consider them to be a type of culture that comes into being through the medium of tourism—that is, a form of tourist culture. By focusing on the practitioners of folk performing arts, I seek to decenter perspectives that stress the authenticity of the folk performing arts as cultural phenomena. Instead, I locate authenticity in practitioners' subjectivity, and in the creativity with which they adapt to new contexts.

As a case study, I take up the famous Mibu no Hana-taue [text not reproducible in ascii.] (Mibu Rice Planting Ritual). Though designated as an "important intangible folk cultural property" (juyo mukei minzoku bunkazai [text not reproducible in ascii.]), the Mibu no Hana-taue is a contemporary cultural phenomenon which continues to be produced/reproduced through tourism.

For example, when practitioners first began to participate in performance competitions, they discovered new sensations called noboseru (to forget oneself) and hazumu (to rise in spirits), which originated in the pleasure of performing and being observed. To help them sustain these sensations, practitioners have created two unique strategies, which they employ selectively in responding to two different contexts: that of the protection of cultural properties and that of tourism.

In maintaining the sensations of noboseru and hazumu, practitioners have engaged in a creative process that uses tourism as a resource to produce/reproduce (or interpret/reinterpret) Mibu no Hana-taue, and to provide themselves with a sense of purpose and identity. The authenticity of folk performing arts can be located precisely in this creative process. This chapter concludes that we should reconstruct the notion of authenticity by considering the experiences, attitudes, and feelings of the practitioners of folk performing arts.

What images does the reader have of the "folk performing arts"—Lion Dance, Kagura, Bon Odori? These examples may call to mind a pastoral and harmonious landscape. In recent years, the folk performing arts have received an increasing amount of attention. A crucial moment in this process was the passage of the 1992 Festival Law, which calls for the use of folk performing arts to promote tourism, commerce, and industry in specific localities. The purpose of the Law is thus to use folk performing arts to revitalize local communities. As a result, we can observe various contemporary cultural phenomena in which folk performing arts are transformed into tourist resources.

There are pros and cons concerning the Festival Law. However, the relationship between tourism and folk performing arts existed long before the promulgation of this law. Although the academic term "folk performing arts" was created after World War II, folk performing arts themselves can be considered as an objectified field produced through the medium of the modern tourism movement. Instead of questioning the rights and wrongs of the Festival Law, we must reconsider the perspectives that we have employed to objectify folk performing arts.

The history of folk performing arts studies most clearly demonstrates the process of objectification. From the advent of the modern age, Japan's rural population flowed into the cities in large numbers. Furthermore, as a result of the development of modern media, such as the railway network, the postal system, and radio, the public began to "discover" various local religious and folk performances—now called "folk performing arts"—which had previously remained concealed within each locality.

At the same time, the public developed a nostalgic view of the folk performing arts, which were identified with concepts such as "tradition," "simplicity," and "archaism." These views themselves also emerged and were widely transmitted through various modern media.

The rapid development of the railway network is especially significant as a technological and historical basis for the objectification of the folk performing arts. The Railway Ministry and related organizations published various kinds of travel guides covering festivals, performing arts, customs and manners, hot springs, and scenic spots located along each railway line.

The Railway Ministry also offered free train tickets to the media so that they might contribute to an increase in the number of travelers, and numerous travel magazines were published. A travel boom arose all over Japan. The travel magazines were not only sold as handy tour guides at the kiosks in each station; they were also sent out widely and directly tc consumers through the postal system.

This trend helped crystallize the field of folk performing arts studies, which began in response to the social trend that produced the concept of "folk performing arts." The same, in fact, can be said with regard to the field of Japanese folklore studies pioneered by Yanagita Kunio [TEXT not reproducible in ascii.]. Travel magazines, furthermore, played a decisive role in the development of folk performing arts studies and folklore studies.

For example, Tabi to densetsu [text not reproducible in ascii.] [Travel and lore], which was first published in 1928 as a hobby magazine and whose academic character emerged only later, offers us significant records of folk performing arts studies and folklore studies during the early period. In 1933 Kume Ryusen [text not reproducible in ascii.], known as a collector of love letters, began publishing Kyodo fukei [text not reproducible in ascii.] [Landscapes of local areas]. Although this journal began as one of the popular travel magazines, in 1933 it was retitled Kyodo geijutsu [TEXT NOT reproducible in ascii.] [Art of local areas], its contents were changed, and it began to feature numerous articles on the folk performing arts (Miyao Shigeo [text not reproducible in ascii.], a well-known cartoonist and researcher of folk performing arts, criticized Kume's facile approach, saying that he had merely published the magazine in order to obtain free railway tickets).

These early examples indicate that folk performing arts studies began with the utilitarian idea of using folk performing arts as a tourist resource, and that eccentric travelers and sightseers contributed to the development of folk performing arts studies through the print media. In particular, the title of the magazine "Landscapes of local areas" well expressed the characteristics of such folk performing arts studies during that period. In other words, the magazine articulated and produced the "landscapes" that were projected on the windows of trains running ahead to "local" areas.

Folk performing arts scholars, however, later sought to deny or conceal this origin. They not only disdained tourists and sightseers, but also considered people like Kume as secular dilettantes. Folk performing arts studies established its significance as an academic field by excluding the context of tourism, which suggested commercialism. The folk performing arts, originally discovered as a tourist resource, were thought to express values such as "tradition," "simplicity," and "archaism." Because of these authentic and inviolable values, researchers believed that the folk performing arts should not be used as tourist resources, but rather should be preserved as "cultural properties."

This view became increasingly influential, and, especially after the addition of the category "intangible folk cultural property" (mukei minzoku bunkazai [text not reproducible in ASCII.]) to the provisions of the 1950 Cultural Properties Protection Law, has long functioned as an absolute belief upon which not only folk performing arts studies but also the general objectification of folk performing arts has been premised.

Therefore, despite the intrinsic connection between tourism and folk performing arts, this relationship has not been considered in depth. And this is why folk performing arts researchers became almost hysterical in their opposition to the Festival Law.

However, social changes including mass tourism have altered the mode of existence of folk performing arts. Today, folk performing arts do not necessarily present pastoral and harmonious scenes, but rather stimulate awareness of a paradoxical situation. The Festival Law is the natural and inevitable result of the tendency to exploit folk performing arts as tourist resources, and as such it can be said to best express the present situation of folk performing arts. Thus, it is time for us to reconsider our perspectives on folk performing arts. Given the existence of the Festival Law, we must clearly state that folk performing arts are a product of objectification through the medium of tourism.

The conditions which I have described so far suggest that, regardless of our perspectives on folk performing arts, we must base those perspectives on the context of tourism. One perspective holds that tourism destroys folk performing arts as authentic cultural phenomena (the "corrupted folk performing arts" critique). This view has dominated the discourse among folk performing arts researchers since the passage of the Festival Law (minzoku geino gakkai hensho i'inkai 1993, 83-85).

While it contains a degree of validity, this critique reveals the researchers' preoccupation with the centrality of their own discipline, and tends to underestimate the role of folk performing arts practitioners themselves. As a result, it denies the subjectivity and creativity with which those practitioners can decide whether or not to use tourism as a resource to produce/reproduce the practices of the folk performing arts.

Therefore, I consider folk performing arts not as authentic cultural phenomena existing as real entities, but rather as cultural phenomena which emerge through tourism—in other words, as a kind of tourist culture. By paying attention to practitioners' sensations, I intend to decenter the perspective that views folk performing arts as authentic cultural phenomena. This idea may at first appear strange. However, even without referring to the Festival Law, one can find in the field of folk performing arts many examples of developments mediated through tourism. In the following section I will introduce one such example, Mibu no Hana-taue.

The Mibu no Hana-taue is the first example of a "nationally designated important intangible folk cultural property" (kuni shitei juyo mukei minzoku bunkazai [text not reproducible in ASCII.]) in Hiroshima Prefecture. Mibu no Hana-taue is one of the gaku [text not reproducible IN ascii.], or entertainments, that accompanied rice-planting, and which are widely distributed in the Chugoku area (shinfuji 1956; ushio 1968).

Although it has received national designation, Mibu no Hana-taue does not embody the idea of "preservation" of "cultural property." The present style, in fact, appears to have developed under the repeated influence of tourism.

Today Mibu no Hana-taue refers to an event that is performed jointly by two villages, Mibu and Kawahigashi, in Chiyoda-cho, Yamagata-gun, in Hiroshima Prefecture, on the first Sunday of June each year. The site is a privately-owned rice field in Take no Hana of Mibu, not far from the Chiyoda Interchange on the Chugoku Freeway. The current style of this ritual is very recent. Historically, Mibu and Kawahigashi have handed down separate rice-planting gaku called hayashi-da [text not reproducible in ascii.], or rice field songs. Hayashi-da were performed in the rice fields of large landlords, who sponsored the events and mobilized large numbers of participants.

The rituals featured shirokaki [text not reproducible in ascii.], in which a large number of bulls were paraded in the field in order to level the soil prior to planting, and songs called taue uta [text not reproducible in ascii.], sung by young women (saotome [TEXT NOT reproducible in ascii.]). After the middle of the Meiji era, powerful landlords gradually disappeared from both Mibu and Kawahigashi. Also, following a 1903 ordinance issued by the governor of Hiroshima Prefecture, the "Ten Point Programme of Agriculture," which prohibited outside singing, the hayashi-da disappeared temporarily.

In the early Showa era, however, a movement arose in both villages to revive the hayashi-da. In Mibu, the shokokai [text not reproducible in ascii.] (commerce and industry association) of a small shopping district in Mibu-cho interviewed people who remembered the way the ritual had been performed in the past and, with their help, recreated it.

They established the Mibu Dengaku Group (Mibu Dengakudan, originally called Mibu Nogakudan), and performed the hayashi-da as one of the community's annual events. In addition, Hiroshima Railway Company mobilized many sightseeing buses to bring tourists to see the Mibu hayashi-da, which thus gradually came to represent folk performing arts in Hiroshima Prefecture. A dengaku. (rice planting performance) group in Kawahigashi also successfully revived the local hayashi-da, but because theirs was a small village removed from the centre of Chiyoda-cho, this group focused more on reproducing the original form than attracting tourists.

A decisive moment in the penetration of the context of tourism into hayashi-da, not only in Mibu but also in Kawahigashi, was the spread of performance competitions, which had started during the same period and became popular throughout the Chugoku region. These competitions generally took the same form. Local shokokai invited groups of hayashi-da performers from each locality to compete for group and individual prizes. Mibu and Kawahigashi hayashi-da groups were regular participants.

Mibu was particularly highly reputed, and won first prize on numerous occasions. As the fact that they were sponsored by commerce and industry associations reveals, the purpose of these competitions was to revitalize local economies. By stirring up people's competitive and wagering spirits, organizers hoped to gather crowds and get them to buy local products. To put it bluntly, they wanted to make a profit from the competition.

The competitions brought significant changes to the hayashi-da of Mibu and Kawahigashi at various levels. Changes at the level of sensations were especially important. For example, since the competitions involved a ranking process, the main purpose of the ritual became to win. In order to obtain first prize (or at least a top ranking), each locality's hayashi-da developed showy acting styles and costumes designed to appeal to judges and tourists.

Groups also changed styles from year to year. Believing that the audience's applause would greatly influence the outcome, local cheering groups participated enthusiastically. Mibu and Kawahigashi, which were neighbors, became fierce rivals, and the competition between their cheering groups is said to have been quite intense.

The competitions were usually held at school athletic grounds. Under these conditions, it became impossible to bring in bulls for the shirokaki ritual, and most hayashi-da in the competitions came to eliminate this feature. As a new type of space, however, athletic grounds offered new possibilities. Originally, rice planting songs were performed in muddy paddy fields, where movement was difficult and a simple line formation was the most performers could hope to achieve. In contrast, athletic grounds permitted exuberant performance movements and offered limitless possibilities to create new styles.

The competitions were suspended during World War II, but soon after the War they were restored and continued for a few years. However, because local shokokai faced financial hardships, the competitions eventually disappeared. Thus, these competitions can be considered particular phenomena limited to a specific period.

The changes mentioned above emerged only within the framework of the competitions. But we must remember that the context of tourism had spread beyond this framework, even into the hayashi-da performed in the rice paddies. Furthermore, since the same people participated in rice paddy performances and competition performances, hayashi-da as a whole rapidly assumed the character of a show. Also, by leading participants to experience the pleasures of performing and being observed, the competitions can be said to have drawn hayashi-da into a new domain of sensation.

This type of hayashi-da, however, was also framed within the new category of "cultural property." The Kawahigashi hayashi-da, which was regarded as having preserved the original form, was designated as a "cultural property" by Hiroshima Prefecture in 1959. And the Mibu hayashi-da, which had early on turned into a show, also received this designation in 1975.

In the same year a partial amendment of the Cultural Properties Protection Law provided for the designation of a new category of "important intangible folk cultural properties." This development had various repercussions throughout Japan. In Hiroshima Prefecture, the Mibu and Kawahigashi hayashi-da, united under the new name of Mibu no Hana-taue, received the honour of becoming the prefecture's first "nationally designated important intangible folk cultural property" on 4 May 1976. The reason for uniting the two performances, which were originally distinct, was that this would facilitate national designation. Thus, Mibu no Hana-taue today refers to the combination of hayashi-da from Mibu and Kawahigashi.

In fact, however, the Mibu and Kawahigashi performances unite only once each year, on the first Sunday in June. On this day, the ritual is performed in the rice paddies, without the showiness seen in the old competitions. As an example of a "nationally designated important intangible folk cultural property," Mibu no Hana-taue is performed in the original style, using a large number of bulls.

Nonetheless, even if one focuses only on the first Sunday in June, it is still not possible to treat this as an authentic cultural phenomenon existing as a real entity. As I noted earlier, if one looks at the line of tourist buses, the pamphlets distributed on the site, and the broadcast explanations for tourists, one is compelled to acknowledge that even this particular day's proceedings have become deeply embedded in the context of tourism.

Today, the main activities of Mibu no Hana-taue have been shifted to various events at which the Mibu Dengaku Group and the Kawahigashi Dengaku Group perform. For example, in 1987, the Mibu Dengaku Group participated in the Folk Life Festival held by the Smithsonian Institute in Washington, D.C. Because they were expected to represent Japan's "authentic" rice culture, the group was asked to present the original form of their performance, and a rice paddy was temporarily constructed on the National Mall.

Nonetheless, the group gave up on the idea of transporting bulls to Washington for the performance, most likely due to the high costs involved. Even after the disappearance of the old competitions, many opportunities still exist to participate in various events located within the overarching context of tourism. In other words, the first Sunday of June is not the only and absolute opportunity for Mibu no Hana-taue to take place. Folk performing arts called Mibu no Hana-taue are contemporary cultural phenomena that are ceaselessly coming into being through the medium of tourism.

BETWEEN PRESERVATION AND TOURISM

What kind of sensations do the practitioners of Mibu no Hana-taue experience under the contemporary conditions described above? Hayashi-da originally offered an opportunity to appraise both the bulls and the bull-handling techniques used in the rituals. However, after World War II, the rapid development of agricultural technologies rendered bulls obsolete as farm animals, and many were slaughtered. The most basic conditions requiring the use of bulls in rice farming have already disappeared.

Nonetheless, on the first Sunday in June each year, Mibu no Hana-taue is performed in the original style, with large numbers of bulls. This is no doubt due to the fact that the ritual has received national designation as an "important intangible folk cultural property." The bulls used in the performance, however, must be borrowed from all over the region, and no longer possess the qualities that would stimulate participants' sensations.

In this way, new agricultural technologies threaten not only the existence of the bulls, but also the raison d'etre of the hayashi-da itself, which was closely related to earlier agricultural technologies. Today, however, practitioners have discovered the meaning of hayashi-da not in the original style, but rather in the new style of performing seen in various events conducted without the use of bulls.

For example, following their participation in the Smithsonian's Folk Life Festival, the members of the Mibu Dengaku Group edited and published a small commemorative booklet in which they recalled the wonderful memories of their trip, and their great satisfaction at having traveled at the government's expense and performed before an American audience in Washington, D.C. It is precisely these kinds of sensations that assume major significance. Practitioners have come to experience sensations of forgetting oneself (noboseru) and rising in spirits (hazumu), which seem to have originated in the pleasure of performing and being watched at the old competitions. These terms (noboseru and hazumu) are frequently used and have gained currency during the rehearsal process among the community of practitioners.

They function as a practical language, that is, as a craft language, which contributes to the process in which a practitioner learns to perform and thus acquires an identity as a performer. This demonstrates the creative process by which participants, while using tourism as a resource to produce/reproduce Mibu no Hana-taue, acquired their own sense of purpose and meaning. In addition, practitioners have devised extremely unique strategies to contribute to the preservation of these kinds of sensations.

Practitioners have thus devised two strategies that they apply in two different contexts: preservation and tourism. At the core of these remarkable strategies lie the sensations of noboseru and hazurnu. These sensations apply only to practitioners of Mibu no Hana-taue, and cannot be generalized.

However, the fact that practitioners, experimenting with the disparity between preservation and tourism, continue to interpret/reinterpret Mibu no Hana-taue in order to secure their own sense of purpose and meaning, requires us to decenter our perspective on authentic cultural phenomena. In other words, it is in the process itself that one can discover an authentic cultural phenomenon.

In his well-known collection of essays, Utsukushii mura [text not reproducible in ascii.] [The beautiful village], the poet and folklorist Ushio Michio described the scene of hayashi-da being performed within a literally "beautiful village," but lamented the absence of a "beautiful village" as he imagined it (HASHIMOTO 1989c, 10-14). I disagree with this assessment. A "beautiful village" does in fact exist: that which even today does not cease to be inscribed on the map of the senses by subjects who experience noboseru and hazumu. We must thus decenter the concepts of "tradition," "simplicity," and "archaism," and instead learn to decode an entirely different set of expressions from folk performing arts. Now, because of the existence of the Festival Law, we must seek to understand the sensations experienced by practitioners of folk performing arts.

Chapter 9

Mass Tourism and the Third Reich

Four days after Hitler was made Reichskanzler, he outlined his agenda in front of military commanders: the first objective was to gain total power by abolishing democracy and "eradicating Marxism root and branch." In doing so the new regime proved to be a master in political staging. Implementing an old demand of the labour movement, the government declared the first of May a holiday. Union-leaders were pleased and encouraged their members to participate in the processions during the "National Labour Day."

The following day, ten o'clock a.m., SA and SS stormed the houses of the Free Unions. Soon there were no trade unions and no political parties except for the National Socialist German Worker Party (NSDAP) and the German Labour Front (Deutsche Arbeitsfront). The coup against the unions had been launched by Robert Ley, organizational director of the NSDAP and later also chief of the Arbeitsfront, including its organization for the leisure time, "Strength through Joy" ("Kraft durch Freude").

At the first anniversary of the coup, two luxury liners left Hamburg and Bremerhaven for the Isle of Wight. One of them had Robert Ley on board, celebrating the beginning of a "new era" of tourism: "German workers" at the Seven Seas. And again, two years later Ley held a ceremony which was to mark a "new era." On May 2nd 1936, amidst a crowd of workers and men in uniform, he laid a foundation stone at

Prora Bay on the Island of Rugen. It was the start of a gigantic construction: "the most colossal seaside resort of the world." Millions of Germans were to recuperate here at the Baltic Sea and so to demonstrate the superiority of the "Socialism of Deed."

The "seaside resort of the 20,000" never went into operation. Nonetheless, the project serves as an outstanding example of the basic concepts—and ambiguities—of modernity. Linking social, political and cultural history, this chapter attempts to analyse this project in the light of a universal precondition of the consumer society: the grammar of rationalization. In linguistics a grammar is a limited set of rules which allows the production an unlimited number of sentences. The grammar of rationalization engended such inventions as different as the slaughterhouse, the computer, or mass tourism.

"MODERN TIMES"

'Metropolis'—the machine-like city of the year 2000 shocked the audience. When in 1927 Fritz Lang's lavish film came to German cinemas it proved to be a financial disaster; all too hopeless was his vision of the future world as a machinelike organism. Maybe Lang was a bit ahead of his time. In 1936, 'Modern Times' was released in America: the tragicomic parable about depravation through technology. Charlie Chaplin's film was a huge success. He succumbs to the rhythm of the assembly lines; the machinery runs faster and faster, culminating in an apocalypse. 'Metropolis' and 'Modern Times.' as different as they were, dealt with the same topic, a topic that was the subject of much controversy on both sides of the Atlantic: rationalization.

This controversy was not only about new forms of factory organization. 'Rationalization' had entered consciousness as something that permeated all 'spheres' of life, as Max Weber put it. The attitudes towards this phenomenon were extremely divided. Some, such as Max and his less known brother Alfred Weber, saw rationalization as a fatal destiny: "Until the last ton of fossile fuel is burned out," capitalism and bureaucracy force humanity into an "iron cage" of dependency, ushering in the "domestication of the world."

However, others, such as Frederick Winslow Taylor and Henry Ford, saw rationalization as the vehicle that would transport humankind into a happy future of full department stores and order books. There is no such thing like the "terror of the machine," Ford claimed. Also, if not with even greater vigour, Communists, like Antonio Gramcsi, praised the blessings of rationalization—the Soviet science of work dreamt of transforming the whole working class into a "social machine." Thus, in Aldous Huxkey's Brave New World, there were two gods: Marx and Ford.

Heated as it was, the global discourse on rationalization was characterized by a remarkable lack of a sense of history: the structure of this controversy was anything but new. It can be traced back at least as far as Rousseau and Voltaire. It is the debate on the costs and benefits of the "civilizing process" (N. Elias). At the dawn of modernity—especially in the second half of the 18th century—the perception of an acceleratetly changing world became common among the educated classes. This gave room for both fears and hopes. "Society" in this view was the result of a growing distance from "nature."

The "natural" state of mankind, however, could be conceived as hell or as paradise—just as the discoverers reported on fierce cannibals on the one hand, and on Gardens of Eden, on the other. The course of history, correspondingly, could be seen as principally good or principally bad, as "progress" or as "degeneration."

Therefore it is a fallacy to regard enlightenment and romanticism as subsequent phases (as in the common periodization of philosophy and arts); rather, they represented simultaneous, opposing attitudes towards modernity—inseparable like the two sides of a coin. Since then at times a modernistic, at times an anti-modernistic zeitgeist has prevailed but both of them have always been present at the same time, often mixed in ambiguous ways.

The interwar period gave new vigour to this old and lasting controversy; 'rationalization' dominated thought with tremendous force. A typical quality of such terms, however, is their vagueness. Instead of compiling the innumerable connotations, let me distinguish four levels of meaning according to the range they cover, to the degree of abstraction:

- A logical meaning referring to the basics, the universal principles of efficiency; this was a topic of mathematics and logic, partly of economic theory and philosophy. Though rarely speaking of a process (i.e. rationalization), the first level provided the others with criteria of an ideal state of a system (i.e. rationality).
- A historical-philosophical meaning referring to the interpretation of the long-term processes of "Occidental rationalization" (M. Weber), or—hardly less far-reaching—to the emergence and structure of capitalism. This was a field especially of sociologists and politico-economists (from Comte to Marx, Durkheim and Weber).
- A technological or economical meaning referring to the most recent stage in this process, in particular in respect of the organization of factory work and human engineering. This was the field of engineers, scientists, psychologists, and economists who formed the emerging science of work (Taylor, Munsterberg, Ford, Gilbreth, Bedeaux, Mayo and others).
- Finally, a psychological meaning, namely the use of pseudo-rational justifications for irrational behaviour as defined by Freud (in a wider sense also the substitution of supernatural explanations by scientific ones).

Admittedly, these levels were often interwoven in many ways; it is just this hidden unison which makes a discourse. But although used in so many venues, ranging from arts to arithmetic, the public debate mainly referred to the third level, meaning mass production and assembly lines.

Rationalization, in this sense, was just another word for 'Taylorism' and 'Fordism.'

While Taylorism was associated with inhuman (and on the long run contraproductive) restraint in the factories and used mostly in a disparaging intention, the broader term of Fordism made a brilliant, though also controversial career. Its meaning was twofold: the rationalization of production and its economic and social results—be it levelling, alienation and unemployment or be it good profits, high wages and cheap products; in this positive sense, moreover, Fordism comprised a whole ideology of mass consumption and of social engineering: the "white revolution."

In this connection 'rationalization' was the catch word which stirred up the public, frightened the workers, inspired the managers and divided political parties and trade unions. The underlying principle, however, did not move the masses (except for the scandals that art exhibitions of the avantgarde provoked). But it proved to be highly universal—the grammar of rationalization became visible.

This grammar is based on the idea of decontextualization and of disassembling and recombining: Isolating complex processes from their context, breaking them down into their individual components, then combining them again to form a new structure. That which is superficial can be discarded; that which is mixed can be separated. The processes, laden with significance, with meaning and morality, with traditions and arbitrariness, can be melted down to the pure scaffolding of relations—as translucent as crystal and as unsurprising as doubleentry bookkeeping.

This grammar, as everybody knows, provided for the victory of capitalism, step by step conquering science, technology and economy, judicial systems and management, the arts and philosophy.

Fundamental aspects of this grammer had been formulated during the 19th century. Although a blind rationality obviously is something instrinsic to nature—and as such has always been a characteristic of humankind, as well—it now reached a new quality of man-made control.

Analyzing the change from craft to industry, none other than Karl Marx had perceptively revealed the principles. The only element still missing to make the factory a single "mechanical monster," he concluded, was the "constant transport of the work-piece."

Indeed, the practical application also requires internal transport systems and a "central clock" which coordinates the machinery. What Marx did not knew was that in America this problem was already about to be solved: assambly line work was introduced in gun factories and in Cincinnati's and Chicago's slaughterhouses—it started in association with killing.

Then, in 1913, this principle was implemented in Henry Ford's car works in Detroit. Coincidentally, Frank and Lilian Gilbreth decomposed the human movements into single "units" (they isolated exactly seventeen), and arts and architecture decomposed space and colour.

Walter Gropius—founder of the Bauhaus—praised the industrial construction: "exact forms, devoid of any randomness. (...) Lining up identical parts." Ford's assembly line was neither an application of avantgarde aesthestics nor of scholary theories; but in turn, it inspired the attempts to automate not only production, but also thinking: in 1936 the computer was born, the universal calculating machine.

Simultaneously, Turing, Post and Zuse designed their computer theories (and thus the basics of our computers). All three had the radical division of labour in the factories in mind when they were in search of the smallest, irreducable steps of arithmetic operations—like Taylor or Gilbreth who identified the atoms of movements, like Feininger or Mondrian who identified the atoms of forms, they identified the atoms of thought. Rationalization had exeeded a crucial boundary: proof was furnished that its principles are potentially boundless.

Thus, in this connection a further invention is associated with the year 1936: the holiday machine. The "seaside resort of the 20,000" was a project as modern as the computer. Such a task had nothing to do with the nostalgic ideology of "blood and soil." It required cold-blooded, highly universal solutions—it required a holiday from the assembly line.

"STRENGTH THROUGH JOY"

The project was to be a centre piece of Nazi social and tourism politics. In February 1934 the travel activities of "Strength through Joy" had a dramatic start. Special trains had rolled all through Germany, with flags, flowers and cheering masses at the stations. Within a week, ten thousand "worker-vacationers" were taken from the grey cities to the clear mountain air. This cheap travel was accompanied by an unbelievable torrent of propaganda and made the leisure organization popular within no time.

Under the bombastic name Nationalsozialistische Gemeinschaft "Kraft durch Freude" (NSG "KdF") it had been founded as a department of the Deutsche Arbeitsfront (DAF) in November 1933. This marked the provisional end of the harsh internal fights on the role of the Labour Front (although they lasted until 1935). Taking over the lower staff of the Social Democrat Free Unions and treating the Christian Unions gently, the DAF at first could appear as an overdue step towards a unified trade union.

Social-revolutionary circles indeed had tried to from a Nazi union out of the small "Works Cell Organization" (NSBO), while others had aimed at corporative structures, similar to Italian and Austrian Fascism, which would have vested Ley with an enormous power. But these plans were thwarted. By no means did Hitler and his allies from big business want to allow a "second revolution." Thus, the Arbeitsfront had to unite "all working Germans" in order to "guarantee the establishment of absolute economical peace." Although soon the biggest and wealthiest organization in the "new state," the DAF was reduced to a mere Party's instrument and a means for controlling the workplace.

On the other hand, it had to "win the hearts of the workers"—a difficult task without supporting their interests. For it had to keep out of the industrial disputes, so the Labour Front looked for another sphere of activity—and found leisure time. So Ley was not responsible for the bread but for the games.

Of course, Ley did not admit his defeat when he held his speech at the KdF's founding congress. Instead, he opened the prospect of a "people's community" (Volksgemeinschaft), where all Germans would have equal access to the cultural assets which still were in the hands of the bourgoisie. In his speech, Ley drew a line between the justified "envy" and the "inferiority complex" of the workers, fueled by "Marxist" ideology, on the one hand, and the ongoing debates on the perils of rationalization, on the other. Rationalization was a global, irreversible process that in future would even speed up—resulting in the loss of "joy" at work, in the "ruin" of physical and mental health, in the increase in "nervousness." Remedies were to expand leisure time and to care for its proper use.

Already in 19th century England, "rational recreation" had been a favourite idea of social reformers. Now, by offering the masses all sorts of once privileged leisure activities, Ley announced, KdF would become a decisive tool for overcoming class struggle as well as for improving health and performance.

Initially, holiday trips ranked low among the planned activities. KdF was primarily designed to fill and control the evening and weekend leisure time. Ley worried that otherwise "boredom" would emerge, leading to "stupid, rabble-rousing, if not criminal ideas." In order to fight this dangerous "boredom"—in other words: to offer the "homeless" workers a substitute for their smashed organizations—a whole array of activities was launched: sports, theater, movies, cabaret, classical and popular music, folk-dance, evening classes etc.

The intentions were ambitious. In particular, the head of KdF, Reichsleiter Horst Dressler-Andress, saw himself on a "mission" of bringing "culture" to the workers. KdF arranged highcarat concerts and exhibitions: Paul Hindemith conducted in factory halls and even works of "degenerated" painters like Emil Nolde were presented.

However, the focus of the activities was changed quickly after the first KdF trains had met with an overwhelmingly positive response. The initiators—Ley, Dressler-Andress, and the head of the KdF-travel department, Bodo Lafferentz—were themselves surprised by their success and promptly expanded the travel programme. They were pleased that they had stumbled into an enormous gap in the market.

From that point now on, the founding of KdF was traced back to a Fuhrer's order: "I want every worker to get sufficient holiday time, and I want everything to be done so that these holidays and his other leisure times become a real recreation." To Ley KdF offered the chance to upgrade his unpopular Labour Front. As the (partly compulsory) DAF membership automatically included that in KdF, the leisure organization finally stood open to the vast majority of the population.

And within KdF, it was tourism that counted: with four fifths of the enrollment, the travel department (Amt Reisen, Wandern, Urlaub; RWU) soon became the most important branch—many people regarded KdF as a kind of state-owned travel agency. In 1934, the journal Deutschland-Bericht of the exiled Social Democratic Party (Sopade) noted that the holiday trips made KdF an important propaganda tool, whereas the other KdF activities were hardly ever mentioned in everyday chats.

The idea of turning the holiday trip into a mass-produced article was not at all new. In the end it goes back to the first English package tour organizers in the 1840s, among whom Thomas Cook became the most successful. He was a genius in making travel a standarized commodity, and at the same time saw it as a means to overcoming the "distinction of classes" and rescuing workers from booze and apathy. "Cookism" preceded "Fordism."

The package tour, however, caused more a widening of the spatial scope than of the social scope of tourism. Although better off workers flooded the pleasure beaches on Bank Holidays, their "excursions" were far from decent bourgeois travel. The 'proper' holiday trip remained a privilege of minorities. Organizing 'bourgeois-style' tourism as a mass product was first put to the test on a large scale in Fascist Italy. From 1931, the Duce's leisure organization "After Work" (Opera Nazionale Dopolavoro; OND) sent "popular trains" through the country. In the first year more than half a million Italians took advantage of the discount of up to 50%. However, the living standards of the "masses" were too low to afford such a trip without substantial subsidies; after the initial euphoria had dissipated the number of participants declined to about 100,000 per year.

But the concept of "popular trains" remained promising. When the Nazis picked up the Fascist model, they did so with German perfection and rapidly overtook their prototype. Soon "Strength through Joy" became the world's biggest tour operator. Already the sheer size meant a market position of a new scale. The crisis-ridden hotel industry had to willy nilly accept KdF's offers of at least fifty per cent below the usual level.

With an average of 35 Reichsmark (RM) for an all-inclusive package tour in 1934 the KdF prices fell by two thirds compared to the "cheap" operators in the Weimar Republic—not to speak of the prevailing individual tourism. The programe was expanded vigorously until 1937, when in terms of figures nearly a fifth of the population older than 15 had booked KdF trips.

With that, the upper limit was reached; the capacities of the transport systems (in particular the railways which had to serve the growing needs of the Wehrmacht), as well as the spending power of the lower classes did not allow for a further increase. However, the figueres were unique at that time and are still impressive.

By the outbreak of war, some 8 million package tours had been sold by KdF, almost a tenth of which—more than 700,000—were spectacular cruises abroad with the KdF fleet. Taking all trips together, more than 45 million had traveled with KdF in the prewar years. Of course, only the holiday tours were really a sensation.

To provide some examples: A seven day all-inclusive

tour to Reit im Winkel in the Bavarian Alps cost 28 RM; ten days at the seaside resort of Heiligenhafen 44 RM; a seven day "reduced offer" into the Swabian Jura only 16 RM. In addition to those 'normal' holiday trips there were also 'special' tours, e.g., an eight-day skiing course costing 48 RM. In accordance with the global trend, the vast majority of the KdF trips went to domestic destinations.

An exception was tours to allied Italy after 1937. The absolute highlight, though, became the cruises. They were not included in the original programme. But after the first cruises proved to be so successful, KdF bulit up the world's biggest cruising fleet and launched two luxuury cruisers of its own: the 'Robert Ley' and the 'Wilhelm Gustloff.' The prices were unriveled: an eighteen day journey to Madeira, a traditional destination of the English upper class, cost about 120 RM, a sevenday cruise to Norway 42 to 63 RM. A Swiss novelist trumpeted: "A nation at sea!"

With great relish, propaganda reminded of the Social Democrats' promise that one day the workers will be aboard luxury liners and cited the planned travel programme of the trade unions for the year 1933: just twelve tours had been announced with prices ranging from 42 RM—a three day excursion—to 350 RM.

And now: workers strolling through chic resorts and spas, tanning on the decks of cruisers! In the beginning, many people hostile to the regime thought this was simply a fraud. But they soon learned that it was not quite wrong when posters lured: "Now you, too, can travel!" or more poetically and in respect to the KdF travel saving system: "Weave your own dream carpet!" The impression was so strong that the chief of the KL Dachau wanted to send a political detainee on a trip to Norway—for "he is an obdurate Communist and may be convinced by the facts."

No wonder the underground opposition was alarmed, worrying whether this could really work. The Sopade-Bericht was at least ambivalent: "Some get enthusiastic, some grumble." Summing up the local reports from all over the country, the editors wrote: "The judgements are divided."

This remained true in the coming years—considering the Sopade-Bericht was published by the resistance, positive assessments count double. In contrast to nearly all other fields of the social politics, the KdF trips were often reported to be a great success. Former union officials had to hear: "Now we see what our subscriptions are really good for." From Bavaria, e.g., it is said that "according to the concurring reports of all (Social Democratic) comrades, KdF is a positive achievement for the regime. These trips get more and more popular, and how cheap they are is astonishing."

While excursions and even short holiday trips were nothing new for manual workers, the 'proper' tourism had remained in the realm of the upper and middle classes. Although the travel intensity had increased since late 19th century—in particular among the clerks and teachers, male and female, as the harbingers of modern lifestyle—the boundary between blue and white-collar workers had not been challenged: the holiday trip functioned as a social marker. And now the propaganda could chime: "Travel is no longer a privilege for the wealthy classes. Thanks to KdF every national comrade (Volksgenosse) is now able to partake in tourism."

This was not only due to the cheap package tours—in addition, the holiday entitlements were greatly improved. Traditionally Germany (together with Austria) had the best arrangements in this respect; now it increased its lead. In 1938 more than 87% of the workers in the metal-processing industry enjoyed a yearly holiday of six to twelve days. Even the International Labour Office had to acknowledge not only "Strength through Joy" but also the holiday entitlements as exemplary.

SOCIALISM OF DEED

KdF provided indisputable evidence of how effectively the grammar of rationalization can be applied to the production of holiday trip—just as Henry Ford had demonstrated with his Tin Lizzie how to turn an unattainable object of desire into a mass-produced article.

The Nazi version of Fordism was the "Socialism of Deed" (Sozialismus der Tat). This term suggests that The National Socialism really improves the living conditions of the workers, and thus makes the working class and their "Marxist ideology" obsolete. The greatest trump in this connection was the decrease in unemployment which finally ushered in manpower shortage. But Socialism of Deed was more then having a job again: The "cultural mission" of KdF, Dressler-Andress wrote, is "to overcome the traditional contrast between work and man." A lofty mission, indeed. Probabely he really had a cultural "revolution" in mind which breaks with the curse of alienation. However, more often and less pathetically Socialism of Deed was simply defined in terms of "standard of living." In this connection, DAF experts demanded that the "traditional concept of wages" should be replaced by transfers in form of "organized consumption."

Along this line the regime concentrated on reducing the prices of prestigious goods to such an extent that they could symbolically represent the prosperity that the worker parties had failed to give the workers. Standarized mass production should provide all households with "popular" products like refrigerators or cameras (already in 1932 Agfa had marketed a Volkskamera); most spectacular were the Volksempfanger (two simple radio types), the Volkswagen (which was never delivered), and travelling—only here were really impressive achievements made.

Thus, when the KdF cruiser 'Robert Ley' was launched in March 1938, Hitler could say: "The National Socialist state, the National Socialist Volksgemeinschaft are trying to make everything accessible to our Volksgenossen that was formerly the privilege of a limited social class. (...) This is an objective that in the beginning appeared to be unimaginable. At that time there were many who believed: this programme looks so much like Marxist promises, that it cannot come true. Well, my Volksgenossen, it is on the way to being fulfilled!"

Travel became a substitute both for higher wages and for civil and social rights. As Kuhnl had put it: The Labour Front "was not to produce social justice but the illusion of social justice." The social politics were grounded in the abolition of democracy in general and of the right to strike and the participation rights in the work-place in particular. Instead, white and blue-collar workers were both labeled as "followers," bound to the "leader of the firm" by mutual "loyalty and duty."

Mitigating this paternalism, the regime spoke of "workers of the brow and workers of the fist," signalling the dissolution of the traditional status hierarchy: All Germans form a great community, the Volksgemeinschaft—except, of course, those of racial or other genetic "inferior quality" and those who were "stubborn" opponents.

The "orderly" German worker, thus, was ennobled by merely belonging to that community—hypertrophic aggravation of the basic concept of nationalism. The space in which this banishing of hierarchy within the Volksgemeinschaft should take place was conceived, however, as outside the crude sphere of power, politics and work: in the realms of culture, leisure and consumption. A truly pioneering concept.

Of course, time was all too limited for this to be really translated into action. The promised land of affluence was counterpointed by Hermann Goring's famous slogan: "Guns instead of butter!" The cash had to flow first into the producer goods and the military buildup. Wages had to remain low, both to safeguard the profits and to avoid an increasing demand for consumer goods, in particular for imported raw materials.

Holiday politics promised a solution to the regime's conflicting aims: taming the working class and preparing for war. Spending money in the domestic tourist industry reduced the demand for limited goods and imports. And improving the holiday entitlements contributed to keeping the wages low and thus also to reducing the spending power freely disposable.

And KdF tourism and paid holidays were indeed an improvement in the standard of living. Thus, both could function as a conspicious symbol of upward mobility. "There is probably no nation," the newspaper of the DAF commented on the first cruise to Madeira, "which takes so much care of the working people (Werktatige) as Germany."

To sum up: "Strength through Joy" promised to combine many different functions in an ideal way.

First of all:

- Winning "the hearts of the workers" or—less sentimentally—promoting the integration of the working class.
- Providing for consumption control along the lines of the autarky politics.

Further objectives were:

- Giving a push to the tourist industry which was in a severe decline due to the Great Depression. This goal was dropped or modified, resp., when tourism recovered.
- Strengthening the "love for Germany" and overcoming regional fractioning and hostilities, e.g., among Bavarians and Prussians—a widespread idea and already promoted by Friedrich L. Jahn a hundred years before. Nation building became a main objective in 1938, when KdF was employed to integrate Austria.
- Promoting the "strength," i.e. the health and performance of the work force; in this connection DAF officials loved to speak of the "achieving community" (Leistungsgemeinschaft). However, the argument that KdF "overhauls" the worker like a car motor primarily aimed at the skeptical business community and later also at opponents within the regime.
- Creating a safety valve for activists from the left wing of the NSDAP: In the first years KdF offered a playground to those who were frustrated by the regime's social politics and its alliance with big business.
- Offering incentive tourism for Nazi "bigwigs" as well as for workers—the "leader of the firm" could reward

diligent "followers" by awarding them a cruise to Madeira; this went of course well with the two main objectives.

- Finally, KdF functioned as an instrument for foreign propaganda, thus mitigating the grim image of the Third Reich.

The pictures of the classless luxury liners were a sensation. Moreover, together with Italy, the regime fostered the international leisure movement. In 1936 the second "World Congress on Leisure and Recreation" was held in Germany, gathering 3000 delegates from 61 nations. Rudolf He[beta] issued the motto: "A proper organization of the working people's leisure time is a decisive precondition not only for social peace within the nations, but also for political peace among the nations"—a masterpiece of dissimulation that sounded like the former programme of Thomas Cook. Bodo Lafferentz, director of RWU, praised his cruisers as "ambassadors of peace" and stated: the "class-concious worker has disappeared."

The congress' honorary president, Gustavus Town Kriby from the USA, was impressed: "'Strength through Joy' grew from a mere ideal to reality." Also an international agency Joy and Work was installed. As its president, Robert Ley was received in London by King George VI shortly before the outbreak of war.

Nontheless, foreign propaganda was a by-product of holiday politics. By and large, KdF was essentially domestic politics. Admittedly in a special sense: in the eyes of the regime's inner circle all domestic policy was to serve foreign policy agendas: expanding the "biosphere" according to the visions of the German master race. The regime therefore could not elude the self-created dilemma of "guns" and "butter"—or better: it postponed its solution for after the victorious blitzkrieg.

Until then, the Nazi version of a "white revolution" was curtailed by Hitler's secret order from 1936 that Germany had to be "ready for war" within four years. The regime was forced therefore to preach old-fashioned abstinence, too. A tight-rope-walk, especially since the prospect of a renewed war was anything but popular. Goring, responsible for this "Four-Years-Plan," expressed no understanding for the dilemma.

He regarded the DAF as an enemy that "spreads wrong social ideals among the workers" and theatened: "I will ruthlessly take action against every obstruction by the Labour Front." Certainly, Goring failed "to take away all raw materials and workforce" from the DAF. But to the inner cirlce of power, social politics was just a tool of "great politics," or as Ley put it: "The Leader does not speak of wages and prices, but of soul, race, blood, soil, and fatherland." No wonder, Ley had a difficult position.

Nonetheless, the Volksund Leistungsgemeinschaft was more then a mere phrase. The term 'Socialism of Deed' could have come from Henry Ford himself. Not only was he an ardent anti-Semite and backed Hitler, his paternalistic engeneering, designed to curb both Marxism and Conservatism, went well with this kind of Socialism. From pushing efficiency and destroying participation in the firms to the concept of defining the social status by consumer opportunities—the Third Reich certainly swam with the mainstream of modernization.

THE "SEASIDE RESORT OF THE 20,000"

Admittedly, in respect to the implementation of assembly lines, Germany was far behind the USA. Ferdinand Porsche, for instance, when he built up the Volkswagen works (1938 named KdF-Wagen) which were to produce 1.5 million cars per year, wooed away numerous experts from the Ford works in Detoit. But in the industrialization of travelling Germany took over the leading role. This takes us back to that 2nd of May 1936, when the foundation stone for the "seaside resort of the 20,000" was laid on the Island of Rugen. What were the grounds from which this ambitious project emerged?

The response to the cheap travel oriented towards middle-class standards was surprisingly positive, but unexpected problems also arose, specifically in two respects:

First, it became clear that unskilled workers, and above all whole workingclass families, were hardly in a position to come up with the travelling expenses without further subsidies—a flagrant violation of the widely-disseminated family politics. Second, the tourist industry proved to be rather ungrateful: Instead of applauding the fact that their spas and seaside resorts were suddenly filled with KdF-holidaymakers, the tourist associations complained that "Strength through Joy" was taking clients away from the commercial operators and chasing off the "solvent public" in the chic resorts.

No better demonstration of the "shattering of bourgeois privileges" was really required. However, in this conflict of aims, the KdF's head office was guided less by its egalitarian mandate, than by the complaints of the middle classes, the social backbone of Nazism.

The retreat from the luxury hotels began: KdF tourists were increasingly sent to undeveloped touristic areas, such as Eastern Bavaria; finally, former Austria became the main destination (with some 70%). Initiallly more than 60% of the KdF holiday trips led to traditional German spas and beauty spots, in 1939 less than 5%.

Nevertheless: At the seaside the strategy of "no friction" with established tourism could hardly be implemented—the capacities were limited. But the seaside holiday could not be entirely removed from the programme. Thus, the plan emerged to build its own tourist towns on the beaches and so make KdF independent from the private hotel trade—and also cement the spatial class distinction in tourism.

In 1935, Ley explained that the Fuhrer had given him instructions to "think through the possibilities of a mass seaside resort with 20,000 beds." Five such "mass resorts" were planned on the Baltic Sea: on Rugen, near Kolberg, Konigsberg, Kiel, and Danzig. In 1940 there was even talk of ten such resorts. Three to four millions would have been driven through these holiday plants each summer.

Rugen functioned as the pilot scheme and was to be completed before the war. However, in the beginning there was an embarrassing delay. On July 30th, 1935, with a handshake, Malte von Veltheim, Duke of Putbus, indicated his agreement to "hand over" part of his property at Prora Bay as a building lot—whatever "hand over" may mean in this context.

The document was legally hardly worth the paper it was written on since it stated neither the size of the lot, nor the price, nor even the new owner. It appears that Ley was in a hurry to snatch the uniquely lovely land away from the Duke: A gently curved bay, pine forests, a wide, white beach.

One of the signatories of this strange agreement was the architect Clemens Klotz. Acquainted with Ley since 1925, he had joined the NSDAP in 1933 and became Ley's favourite architect. As the wealthiest Nazi-organization, the DAF provided him with an immense market. Hitler, the maniac lay architect, made him Professor but did not think highly of him—Klotz once had been a member of the Werkbund. Alfred Rosenberg, the guardian of "blood and soil," was not quite wrong when he gibed, Klotz lacks "deepening." Indeed, this architect was able to master every style ranging from the cool elegance of New Realism to the impressive pomp of neo-classicism.

A day after Ley's handshake with the Duke of Putbus the headline of Der Angriff read: "Fuhrer's order: Five huge KdF seaside resorts!" The plans have "already been commissioned." The latter seems to tally with the truth: Ley could present a first draft of the blueprints in September; a month later, on the occasion of the second anniversary of KdF, there already was an exhibition of "plans and models" including a doll's house showing the standardized decor of the guest-rooms.

In February 1936, however, for as yet obscure reasons, a competition was suddenly announced. Albert Speer, head of the KdF-department "Beauty of Work" and Hitler's favourite architect, was entrusted with carrying it out. He selected eleven participants from quite diverse directions ranging from neo-classism to modernism, including such prominent names as Giesler, Bestelmeyer and Tessenow. Meanwhile, without the competition having been decided, Ley staged the laying of the foundation stone.

In August 1936—during the Olympics—Hitler officially viewed the draft plans on display in Berlin, only to announce that his choice was the design by Klotz after all. (As the only major modification, the festival hall was to be built according to the neo-classical design by Erich zu Putlitz.)

The concept was brilliantly simple and perfectly adapted to the given local circumstances: an arc, nearly five kilometers long. Here Klotz had picked up the basic pattern of a 'bourgeois' seaside resort: a promenade with hotels along the beach and in the centre a square or mainstreet leading to a pier—but he inflated this pattern by means of repetition into dimensions of a new quality:

The centre of the complex comprised a square of 400 by 600 metres, containing a tower with restaurant, the monumental festival hall, the elegant reception buildings and "large-scale cafes" etc.; towards the sea there was a massive quayside with two piers for KdF cruisers. Adjoined to the left and right side of the central square, however, were the six-storey accommodation buildings, the "residence wings," stretching 90 metres from the water line behind a promenade running parallel to the beach.

Each of the wings (technically divided into four segments) extended over more than two kilometers. As Prora is an evenly curved bay, this made geometrically for one sixteenth of an imaginary giant circle. The residence wings were erected in skeleton construction and contained more than 10.000 rooms, most of which were identical hotel rooms, all with seaview—a really "Socialist" achievement, considering that the privilege of seaview symbolized the elite in the resorts. In accordance with modern architects' term "functional room-cells," the guest-rooms—as the atoms of the complex—were called "living and sleeping cell units."

They "measure 2.20 by 4.75 m and are all identically furnished with two beds, a washstand with running water and waterproof curtain, wardrobe (...) table, chairs and a couch." Each pair of "cell units" was connected via a communicating door, so that a six-member family could be accommodated. Furnishings, kitchenware, bedding, even the complete set of beach utensils, right down to the bathing suit, were designed by the DAF according to rational principles.

At the rear of the residence wings, towards the woods, 96 stump-like wings were attached; they contained mainly the stairways and the bathrooms. Thus, from the backside one faced an endless row of backyards. Approaching from the ocean side, on the other hand, the sight was of breathtaking modernity.

Here, ten massived though slender "community halls" or "dining houses" protruded from the residence wings, each seating 2,000 guests. These tracts jutted into the water line and thus divided the beach into eight, just half a kilometre long segments—the vacationers' "home area." Here, calculations said, each guest was provided with five, or according to other calculations ten, square metres of the beach. The rounded ends of the dining tracts resembled the stern of a ship—with its plentiful light and glass this was a "cheerful" architecture with "elegant simplicity," praised the Baugilde.

The resort was to function as a modern entertainment centre, offering—besides the beach life—theaters and cinemas, bowling alleys, indoor swimming pools with artificial waves etc. In addition numerous secondary facilities were needed inland. Among them a train station, 5,000 underground parking lots, residential areas for 2,000 employees, hospital, power station—and a slaughterhouse. A complex of such dimensions required excellent logistics: The problems associates with "bringing, distributing and removing large masses of people," the Baugilde wrote, "were, with the aim of total efficiency, brought to a mature solution."

Ley managed to budget a fantastic 100 million RM for his project on Rugen. It became the second largest civil construction site of the Reich, after the autobahn. Up to 15,000 people worked there in the middle of a once untouched nature reserve. "This luxurious 'resort for the rabble' is a thorn in the flesh of German bourgeois conformists," as the

Sopade-Bericht enviously put it: "It is one of the most effective architectural advertisements for the Third Reich." By September 1939 the construction—except for the festival hall and the dining tracts—had almost been structurally completed. Nonetheless, production in the holiday plant never started up; the premature outbreak of war forestalled the opening planned for 1940.

Outside Germany, too, the project met with great interest. The plans went on display at the World Fair in Paris 1937 and were awarded a Grand Prix. Although in respect to the style and the building technique were partly rather conventional, it was an outstanding example of modern architecture, of an architecture which was essentially Fordistic. "Lining up identical parts" was exactly the principle which was praised by the trailblazers of modern urban planning and architecture, under headings such as 'International Style,' 'New Construction' or 'New Realism.' Their gospel became the Charter of Athens, initiated by Le Corbusier and approved in 1933 by the Congres Internationale d'Architecture Moderne (CIAM). The world has to be freed from the mess and arbitrariness of history.

Instead, an austere network of relations has to be erected, a utopia, ruled by the rational "disjunction of the functions." The basics sound familiar: "Each structure has to be decomposed into its single elements, in order to integrate them in a new way according to rational principles. As modern painting has shown, this method allows one to get rid of the whole burden of traditional forms, and to create a tabula rasa as the foundation for the making of a completely new world."

Adopting Sullivan's motto "form follows function," the CIAM had declared: "Urban development must never be influenced by aesthetical reflections but only by functional conclusions." Repelled by the sunless, cramped conditions in the cities, well-intended architects became obsessed with order.

Together with his cousin, Le Corbusier ran a planning office, proposing to tear down Algiers and to put the inhabitants into tower blocks; the two main buildings—comparable to the "residence wings" by Klotz—stretch along the beach for twelve kilometers. Similar plans were made for Paris (it was envisioned to consist of eighteen gigantic skyscrapers or of a vast triangle in the middle of nowhere). One might dismiss those plans as childish power-fantasies if they had not been so influential.

In 1946, Hans Scharoun, whom the Soviets made the chief urban planner in Berlin, praised the blessings of the bombing war: the air-raid damages allowed for an overdue urban renewal (a stance already held among architects of Speer's planning team). Scharoun's Berlin consisted of a grid of "functional zones" but was—due to the division of the capital—never realized for the most part. In countless other places those ideas came true. The CIAM general secretary, Sigfried Giedion, could herald a new age in which "mechanization takes command."

In this view, machine-like structures were not "mechanical monsters" (as Marx had called the factory), but they were beautiful because they were functional. Thus, the resort at Prora Bay was indeed a beautiful machine, namely a "dwelling machine" (a term coined by Le Corbusier). It was a machine for producing fun, health and loyalty, engendered by the grammar of rationalization. Even today, architects are impressed by the "consequently functional solution" and the "elegant figure" following the "principles of New Realism."

As modernism and anti-modernism are in a constant battle, such praise povokes protest. Since the seventies, the Charter of Athens is no longer the (only) architect's bible. In the past decade, the project of Clemens Klotz has been critizised harshly. But already to Alfred Rosenberg—not only a personal enemy of Ley's but also an ardent foe of modern "Bolshevist" architecture—the project was a contradiction in itself: the workers will be carted "from the urban crowd into a mass machinery even worse."

This leads us into the further fate of this complex. During the war wounded and bombed-out, after the war displaced persons were put into the Aryan seaside resort, until the Red Army plundered and partly destroyed it. After 1950 the National People's Army of the GDR used it and the whole environs was resticted area. After reunification the last soldiers withdrew—what should happen to "Prora" (as the complex was called now), to the ruins, the remaining 9847 rooms, and the 3.5 million squaremeters of land? Investors promised to rebuild the complex for the original tourist purposes, including marina and 15,000 parking lots. Luckily, historians and community action groups achieved a "pause for reflexion" and the complex was listed. Local actors would like to turn the remains, or at least parts of them, into a museum that denounces the inhumanity of the Nazi regime. To them Prora is a "word of stone"—a term coined by Hitler on another occasion.

Since the "only objective of KdF was to stabilize a criminal system," Prora is labelled a "place of offenders" standing for the "terror" of the Third Reich and thus must not become a holiday paradise. Instead, an "educational place" should be developed at this "authentic" scene, last not least to prevent a pilgrim's site for Neo-Nazis—although here "even a naive visitor" realizes that Nazism was nothing but "visible and touchable megalomania." As can be easily seen, there is some inconsistency in the arguments.

First of all, nearly all that was built during the Third Reich helped—in one way or the other—to "stabilize a criminal system." The term "place of offenders" does not make much sense, if applied to all sorts of buildings, regardeless of their function and history. In an emerging market of remembrance, local actors may tend to emphasize the monstrosity of "their" spot—and indeed, the complex might appear a monsterous colossus. But neigther was it designed to commit nor did it witness exceptional "actrocities."

Secondly, Prora is a poor example for the "inhuman," monumental "words of stone," as favoured by Hitler in connection with important public buildings. Instead its structure simply follows the cool principles of Fordist architecture as promoted by the CIAM or the Bauhaus (stylistically Prora was a compromise: the moderately modern residence wings—today, they resemble the housing scheme of the fifties—were contrasted both with the neo-classical festival-hall and with the ultra-modern dining tracts and cafes). Admittedly, nowadays many people feel that this sort of architecture is "inhuman"—but this is no judgement on a peculiarity of Nazism.

Finally, even if—at all costs—one counts Prora as part of the "Nazi architecture," one should keep in mind that symbolic attributions to buildings rather reflect their shape than their use. Suppose that the KdF town had been used by the GDR's "Vacation Service" instead of by the Army, it would be regarded quite differently today. In 1945, bombastic constructions like Berlin-Tempelhof Airport were taken over gladly by the new authorities, in particular by the Americans; in the collective memory Tempelhof is by no means associated with "megalomania and terror" but—since the Airlift 1948/49—with "freedom and democracy." Only long after the war, the alledgedly unique "Nazi architecture" became a mighty symbol of evil in the eyes of German intellectuals, thus at the same time ennobling and daemonizing it afterwards, surpassing its original psychological effects by far.

The debate on the "colossus of Rugen" can serve as a warning example for a restriced view on Nazism. What Prora actually "stands for" obviously differs from the prevailing assessments with their moralizing undertone. The complex was simply an uncompromising application of the basics of mass tourism—"standardization, mounting, serial production" (H.M. Enzensberger). Societies are of "incredible complexity" (N. Luhmann): they are related to other societies and consist of many "systems," of levels and ranges of experiences, practices, discourses, policies.

This means that "normality" can coexist alarmingly well with "barbarism" (D. Peukert). Since the "joy" produced by KdF was to serve all but innocent ends, there remains an ambiguity at Prora Bay, making all planning delicate. But refering solely to the "great politics" would be an all too narrow approach.

The "joy" experienced by the individual KdF tripper is of another quality and scope and is worth another historical perspective. And so are the technical means to produce it. The complex at Prora is no fit object for a condemnation as megalomanic "Nazi architecture."

Meanwhile countless beaches have been transformed into holiday plants. Many of them outrival Prora by far—to mention only Benidorm, "the most efficient machine of mass tourism in Spain:" the fishermen's hamlet was made a mass resort during the Franco era and today takes pride in more than 60,000 beds in its dwelling machines. Millions of vacationers love such arificial paradises. The "fantastic dreams" of the KdF stategists had come true—or rather turned into a nightmare. Among the middle classes, namely, instead of "mechanization," a "post-modern" cult of individuality, naturalness and rootedness "takes command."

The shape of tourist organization and architecture is partly changing. But here is much confusion because the refinement of "mechanization" tends to result in concealing the underlying grammar. Flexibility does not contradict rationalization—but follows from it. Present-day computers, for instance, no longer force the users to struggle with highly formalized input standards—you may even talk to them; nontheless, they are based on the very same logic architecture as the former "electronic brains."

Already in the 1920s Ford's original system was replaced by more refined applications: General Motors president Alfred P. Sloane Jr. introduced flexible mass production in order to speed up the model cycles and to offer a range of marques from Pontiac to Cadillac—each with a different image although substantially composed of the same elements. But there was no "Sloanism," since it was just another phase of "Fordism." The grammer of rationalization is an all too powerful device to be abolished just by a change in zeitgeist.

Therefore—and not only for the socially biased perception of vacationing—it is a fallacy when tourist experts and sociologists herald the dawning of a "new," a "post-modern" or "post-Fordist" age. Like Sloan's cars, the holiday trip is a commodity which consists for the decessive parts of intangible goods, such as "fun," "recreation," "nature," "freedom," "flair," or "status." Consumption in general, but tourist consumption in particular is an active practice.

On the personal level, tourist experience always combines standarized supply with individual appropriation. Accordingly, on the social level, tourists consume and produce an enormous scope of experiences.

Tourist places are both stage and mirror, they document and require "taste" (P. Bourdieu). Right from its origins in the 18th century, tourism served as a prominent field of "distinction"—a never ending game, especially driven by the educated classes. "Post-modern" tourism, thus, is new wine in old bottles. Although tourism is regarded and sold to us as a counterpart to our frantic, mechanized everyday life, as a realm of "freedom," of playful values and individual practices—as a mass phenomenon tourism and tourists are inevitably part of the very same machinery which they try to elude.

What Prora "stands for" is less typical for a certain regime than for a certain stage of "modern times." In this connection, admittedly, the complex is a "word of stone:" an index fossil which confirms to George Orwell's famous notion that the "machine civilization" aims at total control to assure the "paradise of little fat men."

Amittedly, on the one hand, the terror of efficiency rules independently from application fields and political systems. But on the other hand, it was directly linked with political terror. Among many advocates of rationalization there was the strong belief that only heavy-handed policy can pave the way to an orderly, wealthy, egalitarian society. The Charter of Athens demanded: "the private interest will be put under the public interest" and everybody shall have "access to the fundamental joys" ([section] 95).

This comported well with the Nazi slogans; but even better was the call for "a political power of the sort desirable—clearsighted, sure and determined" ([section] 91). No wonder, Le Corbusier both admired the Russian revolution and the French Fascist leader Pierre Winter. Together they dreamt of the destruction of Paris to build it anew with mathematical precision.

Making tabula rasa and creating a Brave New World—such high-flown visions demanded the Great Central Clock, the political framework of a revolution from above. But where else if not in the USSR and in Germany was the way clear for the efficient doers—into the most far-reaching planning areas imaginable.

What were the effects of the Nazi holiday politics? A quantification of tourism suggests that "Strength through Joy" achieved at least a ten per cent share of the German travel market. Also roughly one out of ten workers was likely to have at least one time traveled with KdF; in particular the skilled male workers in the towns—often former Social Democrats—took advantage of the programme. These proportions are appreciable, but they are, at the same time, not a social breakthrough. Tourism as a whole was dominated by the middle and upper classes. Even among the KdF vacationers the (new) middle classes formed the majority—and their share increaed (in particular the famed cruises were dominated by white collars and "bigwigs").

The "seaside resort of the 20,000" was to reverse this trend. Calculations allowed for a holiday there costing 12 to 20 RM. This would have put it within the reach of unskilled workers or entire families. The test-tube town on Rugen might thus have been able to increase the travel intensity in the working class nearly by half! But even this would still not have done a lot of good: with at best some 3%, their touristic travel intensity was not substantially higher than in several other countries.

KdF failed to push working-class tourism to a new level. "For official use only," this was voiced by the Institute of Work Science of the DAF (AWI): KdF was the futile attempt "to use organized intervention to achieve effects that are in conflict with the existing social structure." A sobre analysis of the Socialism of Deed. No wonder, the hope that thanks to KdF the worker will be transformed into "the most dedicated follower of the Leader" did not come true. In the beginning, the propaganda effect was considerable, but the more KdF lost the aura of sensation, it ceased. Again, the stick, and not the carrot, became the decisive political tool.

While in 1935 the Sopade-Bericht had "no doubt that the vast majority [of the workers] is not aware of the political objectives the dictatorship pursues" with KdF, in 1938 the all clear could be given: "The attitude toward the regime is not essentially influenced"—the workers would just make the most of it. Accordingly, officials, too, complained about the vacationers' shallow consumerism, seeking trivial "fun" instead of "real joy."

But Sopade also feared an increase in "petit bourgeois self-esteem." Indeed, of significance in the long run was not the political but the mental impulse that had bred this dream machine. The figure of eight million KdF vacationers was large enough for that: A lot of Germans partook in 'proper' tourism for the first time in their lives—and could enthusiastically tell their family, colleagues and friends about it, thus reinforcing the impression that now every Volksgenosse has the chance to travel. "In particular the women," a Sopade correspondent grumbled, "for months report on the beautiful journeys and get their surroundings enthusiastic about it." KdF officials were fully aware of that phenomenon: "If you enjoyed your holiday trip, be happy about it.

However, we ask you not to keep this joy to yourself, but to tell it to your workmates, too." In this sense, KdF indeed "helped a mass desire (...) on its road to success," as a dissertation put it.

In doing so, "Strength through Joy" established a new level of tourist experience in Germany: the hedonistic holiday style, as to speak between the proletarian excursion and the distinguished bourgeois travel. KdF started as a copy of the latter; but transforming the production from a craft into an industry inevitably changes the product itself, physically and symbolically. The propaganda was right in calling the KdF vacationer a new type of vacationer and the KdF holiday a new type of holiday: less formal, less costly, less individual.

This trend must certainly be seen as entrenched in a long-term development, starting before World War I, and it is not a German peculiarity. In the thirties, the social scope of tourism was widened by means of cheap package tours, be it on non-profit or commercial grounds. In England—it was the year 1936—William Butlin started his first holiday camp. Three years later some 300,000 "Butliners" could be accomodated in two hundred camps, one of them designed for 5000 guests. Like the projected KdF camp, it was a modern styled holiday factory—partly even more "modern:" Group pressure was far more intense than at the average KdF trips: from dawn to evening red coated animators produced a total fun society of Orwellian proportions. In many other countries attempts were made to overcome the social boundaries, as well as the travel style of the bourgeoisie as the traditional 'leisure class.'

To mention in particular France, where the Popular Front introduced holiday entitlements and railway fare reductions in 1936, and Switzerland, where the tour operator Hotelplan offered "holidays for everybody." Looking at Europe at the eve of the war, it is obvious that holidaymaking was on the road to becoming an integral part of the life of broad sections of society.

Although still this was chiefly a matter of the white collar workers—the "horizon of chances" (G. Schulze) had been widened durably. In this connection, KdF represents a turning point in the history of tourism, both in psychological and engineering terms. Acceding to the grammar of rationalization, the tools of modern mass tourism had been tried out on largest scale and at the same time inhibitions among the lower classes to partake in "bourgeois" travel had been overcome. The "dams of pent-up demands" (R. Spree) were shaken—and they gave out as soon as purchasing power permitted after the war.

This was when Ludwig Erhard, the Federal Republic's

Minister of Commerce, in 1957 called for the "will to consume." He saw it as the precondition for his Social Market Economy: a truly white revolution which promised "prosperity for all" and at the same time curbed all Socialist "experiments." Mass consumption would "finally overcome the old conservative social structure," the "traditional hierarchy" with its "resentment between 'rich' and 'poor.'"

And indeed: both the bourgeois high culture with its claim to define morals and taste and the proletarian culture with its ties, ethics and ideologies, were finally buried under the piles of consumer goods. The old "class structure" gradually dissolved and the affluent society of 'little fat men and women' was born—the modern fun and event society with their patchwork of 'milieus.' Regarded in this way, Robert Ley was not entirely wrong when he declared: The best thing that the Fuhrer gave his nation—is a "new lifestyle."

TOURISM, DEINDUSTRIALIZATION, AND STORE-HOUR REGULATIONS

At first glance these statements appear to have very little to do with the issue of deindustrialization. Neither quotation employs the term nor both concern retail sales rather than industrial production. Moreover, both quotes are from the 1950s rather than the 1970s and early 1980s—the period traditionally identified with deindustrialization in North America.

And yet these quotes represent opposing sides involved in a series of debates in Victoria, BC, that were shaped by the local community's divided response to deindustrialization—debates on the regulation of store hours. This study explores these debates and examines the impact on the local community of Victoria's increasing dependence on tourism—a dependence brought about by the fact that Victoria's place as British Columbia's leading industrial centre had been usurped in the late nineteenth century by its mainland rival, Vancouver.

A key issue in the debates was the extent to which the

local community should be catering to tourists. While some elements of the local community argued that doing so was the only way to secure economic prosperity for the city, others countered that the city was catering to outsiders at the expense of the living standards of its own citizens.

In exploring this tension, the study reveals the tangible manner in which Victoria's economic transformation from an industrial to a post-industrial city affected the local community—in this case by challenging the legitimacy of the city's half-day mid-week holiday, which had been created as a bulwark against the growing power of consumption to colonize leisure time and, thus, dictate the rhythms of daily life. Victoria's emerging post-industrial reality pitted visitors' leisure time (increasingly spent enjoying the fruits of a consumer society) against retail merchants' and workers' attempts to preserve their common leisure time.

By no means were debates about store-hour regulations confined to Victoria. Communities throughout BC and, indeed, elsewhere in Canada, grappled with this controversial issue throughout the twentieth century. What distinguished the debates in Victoria from those occurring elsewhere was the central focus on tourism expenditures. It would also be too much to argue that deindustrialization directly caused Victoria to abandon store-hour regulations.

The city did so only in 1958—long after city officials had recognized the industrial primacy of Vancouver, which was also embracing six-day shopping. But recognition of the city's post-industrial reality by employers, employees, politicians, and the general public directly affected the manner in which these groups understood and experienced the economic transformation that was taking place and certainly assisted opponents of store-hour regulations in their campaigns to eliminate such restrictions. And for these reasons it is important that we explore these debates.

My aim in this chapter is to examine the connection between tourism and the social and cultural impact of deindustrialization. In doing so, I highlight the extent to which the literature on deindustrialization can expand our understanding of social and economic history for the period before 1970. But I also use these store-hour debates to argue for a more flexible understanding of deindustrialization, one that recognizes the term not as an era per se, but as an inherent characteristic of capitalism.

Adopting this approach allows us greater insight into the manner in which employers, service-sector workers, and the general public understood the economic and cultural forces that were affecting their lives during the twentieth century.

In some ways Victoria seems to fit perfectly into the traditional post-industrial thesis. After an unsuccessful attempt at sustaining industrial development, the city turned to the service sector (in this case, tourism) as an economic alternative. Indeed, back in 1986 Peter Baskerville went so far as to assert that Victoria was well suited for "a leadership role in the post-industrial world."

And yet the timing of this transition, which occurred in the first half of the twentieth century, flies in the face of so much of the literature exploring the relationship between tourism and deindustrialization. This literature emphasizes the extent to which North American communities turned to tourism as their last best chance to secure economic security in response to industrial collapse in the 1970s and 1980s.

To reconcile these contradictions, and to illustrate the complex ways in which the local community was affected by, and responded to, this economic transition, one needs to break free from the traditional understanding of the timing and impact of deindustrialization and to see the connection between tourism and deindustrialization as less a product of a specific moment, the 1970s and 1980s, and more as a long-standing relationship that informed the social, cultural, and economic experience of Canadians throughout the twentieth century.

One way of doing this is by broadening our notion of deindustrialization. As John Lutz perceptively notes, the very term deindustrialzation is problematic: "With its prefix of 'undoing,' and suffix 'becoming,' it is a word unravelling itself" and it implies "the existence of a single process of 'industrialization,' ... that no longer has credence." In his study of the decline of British Columbia's boiler and engine industry at the end of the nineteenth century, Lutz explains that his use of the term is meant to indicate "an economy changing specialization towards resource processing and away from secondary manufacturing."

In focusing on a later time, this study also examines the economic shift away from secondary manufacturing, but toward tourism and the service sector, rather than resource processing.

The dominant understanding of deindustrialization owes much to the work of Barry Bluestone and Bennett Harrison, who pointed to the end of the postwar boom in the early 1970s as a turning point in economic history in which the postwar Fordist compromise came asunder and management employed capital mobility, most visible through plant closings and relocations, as a strategy for increasing productivity and decreasing production costs. As Jefferson Cowie and Joseph Heathcott explain, "The dominant method of studying deindustrialization" has been "to trace the death of mills ... and workers' experiences of that process." And yet more recent work has begun to question the traditional definition of deindustrialization.

According to Cowie and Heathcott, "Deindustrialization is not a story of a single emblematic place ... or a specific time period," but instead a "much broader, more fundamental, historical transformation." After all, they admit, "The industrial age is alive and well, even if the locations have changed, and even if the rules of investment have shifted."

Most illuminating on this issue is Mike Wallace. For Wallace the term deindustrialization is problematic in a number of ways—two of which are important for the purposes of this chapter. First, it tends to invoke a "stages-of-development-theory" in which "pre-industrial gives way to industrial, which then moves on to a service (or, as it is often called, a post-industrial) economy." Such an understanding of history, he reminds us, leaves very little, if any, room for human agency.

Community debates and decisions about economic priorities seem hardly worthwhile if one assumes that the transition to post-industrial society is simply inevitable. Second, the very terms pre-industrial and post-industrial fail to "illuminate the key characteristics of the epochs they seek to describe, other than by reference to some other period." Rejecting the limited notion of deindustrialization, Wallace encourages us instead to think in terms of the "global reorganization of capitalism." "Industry ... has not been surpassed," he explains, "it has just moved."

From a global perspective, what we are witnessing is not deindustrialization, but "capital flight" in which corporations have become more mobile in their pursuit of "tax breaks, cheap land, or the muscle needed to repress the economic and political organization of labour." Informing this mobility, Wallace reminds us, is the logic of capitalism: "The point of industrial production under capitalism is to make a profit for the firm, not simply to produce socially useful items." Failing to seek out such opportunities to increase profits would be illogical.

It is the tangible edifices of industrial capitalism that make this last point somewhat counterintuitive. Physically imposing structures such as factories, lumber mills, and auto plants obscure what Wallace terms capitalism's "quicksilver reality of mobility and relentless transformation." As Cowie and Heathcott explain, "The aura of permanence that surrounded the industrial culture of Europe and the United States throughout the twentieth century has made the experience of deindustrialization seem more like the end of a historical epoch." "The solidity of factories and tenements and steeples," they explain, "masked a fundamental impermanence; it obscured the forces that both created this world through investment and broke it apart by withdrawing investment."

Similarly, Sharon Zukin underscores the limitations of terms like deindustrialization and post industrial precisely because they fail to capture "the simultaneous advance and decline of economic forms, or the sense that as the ground shifts under our feet, taller buildings continue to rise."

There is an important lesson here for historians of the twentieth century, for what is true of capitalism in the late twentieth century was true in the decades before the 1970s and 1980s: its capacity for creative destruction made modern life contingent and provisional. But this lesson can be appreciated only if we bridge the historiographical divide between the earlier decades of the twentieth century and the post-1973 era (or the "post-postwar period" as Sharon Zukin mischievously labels it).

As Steven High reminds us, "Plant shutdowns did not begin in the 1970s, but have always existed alongside industrialization. Plants open in one place, only to close in another." Similarly, Cowie and Heathcott challenge the binary opposition that posits a stable postwar era against a period of decline in the 1970s. In fact, they remind us that "the process we call deindustrialization was uneven in its causes, timing, and consequences, and the effects rippled through all aspects of society."

This point is echoed by High, who refreshingly suggests that "the 'golden age' of the 1950s was far less stable and not nearly as prosperous as has been commonly supposed." To understand this we might follow the lead of Max Page who has called upon urban historians to recognize the impermanence, or provisional nature, of urban centres by placing "the process of creative destruction at the heart of the story of urban development."

Recognizing the provisional nature of the period before the 1970s helps us to see the social and cultural impact of deindustrialization on what appears, on the surface, to be a stable period of economic growth—the calm before the storm of the 1970s.

One way to overcome the existing divide between scholarship on deindustrialization and that focusing on the pre-1970s era, is to recognize that some communities embraced tourism in response to declining primary industries well before the 1970s and 1980s. For example, in his study of Ketchikan, Alaska, Mike Dunning points out that this city, which began as a supply centre for a mining boom in the early twentieth century, endured cycles of industrial development and industrial decline, which opened its eyes to the importance of tourism by the middle of the century.

Similarly, James Overton demonstrates that Newfoundlanders turned to tourism in the late nineteenth century as an alternative to the periodic crises of the fishing industry. Historians of Nova Scotia have also highlighted the manner in which that province's government embraced tourism in the 1920s as a response to deindustrialization.

In the case detailed below, Victoria embraced tourism as an alternative to industrial development well before the 1970s, and the manner in which the local community responded to this economic transition can tell us a great deal about local responses to deindustrialization; at the same time, the vibrant literature on deindustrialization that focuses on the 1970s and 1980s provides important new ways to understand the economic and social reality of the pre-1970 period.

THE STORE-HOUR DEBATES

Today Victoria's economy relies primarily upon its tourism, service, and government sectors. During the 1880s, however, civic leaders could be forgiven for believing that the city could look forward to a promising future as a manufacturing centre. During that decade, Peter Baskerville explains, the city's "gross value of manufacturing production increased 3.5 times" and "when ranked by per capita value of manufacturing production, Victoria stood fifth out of the twenty Canadian towns and cities with a population in excess of 10,000." But the tide quickly changed.

Bolstered by its newfound position as the CPR's western terminus in the 1880s, Vancouver quickly supplanted Victoria as British Columbia's leading port, and throughout the 1890s Victoria's economy was outpaced by its mainland rival. "By 1901," Baskerville notes, Victoria "had dropped from fifth to twentieth place in per capital value of manufacturing output." "The prospects of Victoria becoming an important and diversified manufacturing centre, so bright in the 1880s," he explains, "had been severely dashed by the turn of the century." And it was in this context, he notes, that "manufacturing and wholesale trade gradually took second place to tourism and government as the mainstays of the city's economy."

Even during the economic boom leading up to the Great War, the city's economic expansion occurred without substantial industrial and manufacturing development. The quest for industrial development did not end; even during the post-World War Two era some members of the business community argued "that the city must take a more active role in attracting industry."

The results, Baskerville notes, were hardly encouraging: "Even tiny Moose Jaw had had success in attracting industry from Victoria to its prairie site." Victoria, like North America more generally, "was becoming deindustrialized," and "the pace of deindustrialization in Victoria put the city in the forefront of a major social and economic trend in North American urban life." Victoria's economic response to its increasingly post-industrial reality focused largely on tourism promotion.

Ironically, Victoria first turned to tourism promotion as a method of boosterism that would attract deep-pocketed investors to the city with the hope that they would return in the future to reside in Victoria and contribute to the city's industrial development. Only later was tourism identified as an important means of attracting outside expenditure to keep the local economy afloat. Victoria's response to deindustrialization, then, focused firmly on catering to outsiders.

Visitors to the city needed to be presented with a positive view of the city's possibilities. Early in the century this meant ensuring that potential investors and settlers saw the city as a vibrant and productive centre that offered attractive investment opportunities; later the key concern was ensuring that visitors keen to spend money in local shops were not inconvenienced and were given ample opportunity to part with their cash. A central concern in both campaigns was the city's store-hour regulations.

Victoria's store-hour debates began in earnest in the first decade of the twentieth century when local store clerks petitioned city council for a common half-day, mid-week holiday. Periodically the debates would include the issue of evening store hours, but for the most part the fate of the half-day holiday remained paramount.

Embraced by many merchants in the city, the Wednesday half-holiday was enshrined in provincial legislation in 1916. Because retail clerks were otherwise unaffected by the province's Hours of Work legislation, they worked a five-and-a-half-day week. The Lord's Day Act ensured they did not work on Sunday, and the province's Half-Holiday Act guaranteed an additional half-day off each week. In the absence of any specific hours of work legislation affecting retail clerks, store hours and hours of work became, for many employees, one and the same.

Despite growing opposition in the 1920s and 1930s from merchants and other commercial interests (especially those in tourism-related businesses), the provincial government retained the Half-Holiday Act and amended it as needed to ensure its continued efficacy. The half-holiday in Victoria remained a controversial but workable compromise among consumers, merchants, employees, and larger commercial interests into the 1940s.

The extension of the retail half-holiday to a full day of closing during the Second World War on the grounds of conservation and patriotism proved the undoing of this compromise. Victoria adopted all-day closing on a voluntary basis during the war, and the elimination or retention of this temporary war measure became a key issue for civic voters once the war was over.

In 1946 Victoria residents voted to return to half-day closing. Seemingly decided once and for all, the issue of store-hour regulation was revisited in an angry and divisive manner almost annually until the early 1960s. A 1954 Vancouver plebiscite eliminating Wednesday closing in that city placed even more pressure on Victoria to embrace a six-day shopping week. Finally, in 1958, faced with the decision of the neighbouring suburb of Saanich to eliminate all of its store-hour regulations, Victoria declared retail stores "wide open," and left merchants to set their own hours.

Throughout the period under study proponents of tourism squared off against other members of the local community on the issue of store-hour regulation, with each side claiming to represent the community's long-term interests. Opponents of store-hour regulations focused primarily upon tourism's economic benefits. Supporters of these regulations, and hence those who took issue with the pro-tourism lobby, emphasized instead the social and cultural advantages that the store-hour limitations ensured.

In particular, they championed the common half-day holiday that allowed community members to participate in shared leisure activities and insisted that store-hour regulations protected retail clerks from overwork and exhaustion. Both sides voiced their positions fully aware of Victoria's post-industrial reality, and the debates that resulted offer us a window onto the concerns that this reality engendered—particularly the ongoing worry that even during the ostensibly stable postwar era Victoria's economic prosperity was fragile and provisional.

My larger project, of which this chapter forms a part, explores the complex and multi-layered nature of these debates in Vancouver and Victoria. Store-hour debates in these two cities reveal a great deal about popular attitudes toward consumerism, religion, gender relations, government regulation of economic activity, and, of course, as I argue in the following pages, competing visions of the ideal recipe for civic prosperity.

Not surprisingly, the relative centrality of these themes to public debate was not static; nor was these issues integrated into the debate in a consistent manner. In the early decades of the twentieth century, for example, gendered arguments about the need to protect female clerks from unfair working conditions appeared quite frequently in local newspapers. By the 1950s, however, the once-dominant trope of the victimized female clerk had been replaced by that of the unfortunate housewife who lacked easy and consistent access to consumer goods.

And yet a close reading of the debates suggests that gender does not appear to have intersected very much with the specific issue of Victoria's dependence upon tourism. In short, in order to offer a coherent article-length exploration of the links between these debates and the theme of deindustrialization, one must recognize that not all of the varied issues that informed these debates (gender and religion, for example) appear in the pages that follow.

TOURISM AND THE OPPOSITION TO STORE-HOUR REGULATION

As early as 1908, Alex Peden, president of the local Merchants' Picnic Association, signalled his opposition to a common midweek half-holiday on the grounds that he and other local business people "were of the opinion that it was not business-like and besides the fact that merchants lost trade, it gave outsiders, who might happen to be in town, a very bad impression of the energy and progressiveness of the city."

Arthur Lineham, a key proponent of the city's developing tourist trade, was more forceful in asserting his opposition to the half-holiday. In 1923 Lineham explained to his fellow citizens that over the previous eighty years Victoria had proven itself incapable of luring traditional industry. Drawing upon an understanding of tourism promotion that equated it with immigration literature, Lineham argued that the tourist trade was the key to creating the right conditions that would, in turn, promote settlement and attract industry.

To this end, Lineham attacked the city's half-day holiday with vigour, arguing that "to close the town up tight any day in the week but Sunday is business suicide, and makes us the laughing stock of every stranger entering our gates.

Every business man and patriotic citizen in Victoria will endorse me when I say that the time has come when we must wake up and use every means of securing additional population and money to meet our obligations."

For Lineham, proponents of the half-holiday were putting their own interests ahead of the community's well-being. The half-holiday, he explained, allowed "retail clerks and small storekeepers to have what they term a good time, not caring whether it is a loss to the majority in the community or not." "I, personally, have no objection to any person playing any game he or she likes best on Sunday or any other day that suits his or her convenience," he continued.

"There is no necessity, in my opinion, to turn the town into a morgue one day in the middle of the week on this account, making us a subject of ridicule to all visitors and helping to ruin the retailers and responsible tax payers, who carry the burden of the day."

Given that local tourism promotion in Victoria was originally understood to be a means of attracting industry and population, it is not surprising that into the mid-1940s, tourism's propnents attacked store-hour restrictions on the grounds that such regulations damaged the city's desired reputation as a progressive and modern business centre that was eager to attract new customers and industry. Hence Dale Johnson's 1925 complaint that the city's half-holiday prevented visitors from seeing Victoria as a "business-like and attractive" urban centre.

A similar position had been voiced eight years earlier when the Victoria Board of Trade opposed what one of its members termed "grandmotherly legislation" that was giving outsiders the impression that Victoria was "a village of lotus-eaters." Even as the rationale behind tourism promotion was transformed from one that emphasized attracting investment to reverse the city's trend toward deindustrialization, to one that reluctantly accepted this development and focused almost exclusively on securing tourist expenditures instead of new investment, the concern that Victoria's civic image suffered because of store-hour restrictions remained prevalent.

On the eve of a local plebiscite in 1946, the Victoria Daily Times railed against the possibility of all-day Wednesday closing by charging that such a move would present an image of complacency to the outside world. Outsiders, the Times charged, would reach the conclusion "that the capital city of British Columbia is so satisfied with its present and future business outlook that it can afford to cut its retail week from five and a half days to five." Such concerns were echoed by individual citizens.

In a December 1946 letter to the Times, J. H. Davidson argued that closing stores during the tourist season did not "betoken Victoria as an up-and-coming city," while Elizabeth Davidson similarly argued that doing so "indicates a distinct lack of business acumen and puts a stamp of a small town upon a growing city." Economic growth, of course, required investment capital—capital, these observers argued, that would be increasingly difficult to solicit if potential investors found themselves questioning the community's work ethic.

By the 1920s, and increasingly in the 1930s, however, tourism's proponents were beginning to embrace a new rationale—one recognizing that Victoria would never be able to compete with Vancouver for traditional industry. As Victoria Mayor David Leeming put it in 1934, Victoria's consistent failure to attract investment now meant that "the only hope of the City was to extend its tourist trade."

Once it was recognized that reversing the trend toward deindustrialization was no longer possible, and that a new approach to economic development was required, tourism was increasingly championed as an effective method of increasing consumer demand for local retail goods. Where tourists had once been understood primarily as potential long-term settlers and investors, they were now increasingly thought of as short-term visitors who could be relied upon to infuse the local economy with their disposable income.

As tourism promotion came to be equated with the campaign to secure not industry but expenditure, the call for decreased store-hour regulation underscored both the central contribution this cash infusion made to the local economy and the potential damage the city's current store-hour restrictions did to this external source of expenditure. In later decades, as Victoria came to rely on tourism for a direct infusion of expenditure rather than as a back-door route to settlement, secondary manufacturing, and agricultural development, many argued that the city's prosperity was now even more reliant on tourism than ever before. In making their case, opponents of store-hour regulations pointed to tourists' complaints as well as to the concerns of a sizeable element of the local business community.

Opponents of specific store-hour regulations, along with those who led a determined effort to eliminate such regulations entirely, could point to a good deal of direct and indirect evidence that tourists, themselves, were frustrated by the half-day holiday, limited evening hours, and other restrictions. Indirect statements on behalf of tourists ranged from examples voiced by individual citizens, to more general complaints levelled by the business community.

In a 20 May 1925 letter to the Victoria Daily Colonist, local citizen Dale Johnson argued against the city's Wednesday half-holiday by pointing out the inconvenience this posed for visiting tourists. When the Kathleen arrived in port the previous Wednesday from Seattle "with several hundred passengers all ready and eager to avail themselves of the opportunity of purchasing several different kinds of merchandise," he lamented, they "were disappointed to see all our stores closed." A similar incident was relayed to the larger community by "Observer" who, in June 1927, informed the Times of the plight of several frustrated American tourists.

Having been told by "Observer" that the store they wished to enter was closed for the half-holiday, and not for lunch as they had assumed, one of the tourists responded sharply, "I always heard Victoria was dead, now I know it. We came here on purpose to get certain things which we are allowed to take over the border to the value of $100. Now we must go without them."

More frequently, the tourists took their complaints directly to the local tourist office, which publicized these laments within the local community, while endeavouring to limit such adverse publicity from reaching other potential visitors. In 1956 local tourism promoter George Warren endorsed the idea of six-day shopping so that there would be no repeat of the recent Fourth of July scenario in which US visitors found themselves unable to spend money at local shops. "One of the reasons they come here on a holiday is to shop in our stores, and then they find them closed on a weekday afternoon," he complained. Such claims were buttressed, at times, with statistical evidence purportedly demonstrating that tourists were now avoiding Victoria on Wednesdays.

While opponents of store-hour regulations seized upon tourists' views, the debate was primarily within the local community and focused increasingly on how to maximize much-needed tourist expenditure. And tourist-dependent businesses were among the most vocal participants in this debate. In 1951 Alan Vizard of the Victoria Gift House charged that supporters of the half-day holiday were short-sighted and failed to recognize tourism's central place in the city's economy. "You would not get holiday centres like Banff and Jasper closing down in early afternoon during the tourist season," he explained, "and the sooner Victoria realizes it is just a massive tourist resort and acts accordingly the better."

Vizard's position was echoed by the city's mayor, Claude Harrison, who in 1953 bluntly asserted his opposition to Wednesday closings by stating, "This is a tourist town." Harrison's successor as mayor, Percy Scurrah, offered a similar explanation for his own opposition to a campaign to bring back full-day Wednesday closing: "It is crazy to suggest that a city which depends on tourist trade for survival should close down all day Wednesday."

Victoria Chamber of Commerce president Stickney Harris Jr.'s 1957 declaration that six-day shopping was a necessity in Victoria was sparked by his concern that such a relaxation of store-hour regulations was necessary, given "the continued departure of industry to the mainland." Informing these concerns, as Stickney's comments illustrate, was the recognition that Victoria's early efforts at developing secondary industry had been undone by the rise of Vancouver and the outflow of industry to that city.

A fear that the city's tourism industry might fall victim to a similar fate convinced many opponents of store-hour regulations that outside competition, in the form of more relaxed store-hour regulations, might well prove the final nail in the city's economic coffin. Hence the position voiced by the chamber's Tourist Trade Group (TTG) in 1954 that the expansion of store hours was now an urgent necessity because both Vancouver and Seattle boasted six-day shopping. Even allowing six-day shopping during the summer months, TTG member Sam Lane suggested, would place Victoria on an equal footing with Vancouver, if only temporarily.

Central to the campaign to eliminate such restrictions were the assertions that tourism brought a significant amount of economic prosperity to the city, and that this prosperity was widely shared throughout the community. Opponents of store-hour regulations consistently pointed to the central role that tourism played in bringing "new" money into the local economy.

In 1953, for example, A. E. Newberry pilloried city council, and the citizens of Victoria more generally, for viewing antique shops with "a condescension almost bordering on superciliousness or disdain." In fact, Newberry asserted, such shops "attract more tourists, probably than anything else the city has to offer." As such they made an important if chronically unrecognized contribution to the local economy by bringing "new" money into the city. "The tourists do not come here to admire the beauty of the civic architecture or the excellence of the garbage trucks," Newberry maintained.

"They may stand in awe for a few minutes to gaze at the Parliament Buildings and the Empress Hotel, but they have to pass these buildings anyway on their road uptown from the ferry boats." Their key aim, according to Newberry, was shopping. Limiting tourists' access to antique shops and the like was a foolhardy and unfair move. R. A. Mackie, general manager of the CPR hotel chain concurred, arguing that Wednesday closings were denying the city much-needed revenue.

While Newberry and Mackie were content to assert tourism's importance in quite general terms, others offered more specific estimates of tourism's economic contribution to the local economy in the hope that this might win support for the dismantling of store-hour regulations. In 1936 proprietor Montague Bridgeman argued that the city's half-day holiday cost him between $300 and $400 a year. Ten years later, George MacDonald, then chairing the retail merchants' section of the city's Chamber of Commerce, urged Victorians not to adopt all-day Wednesday closing, by arguing that such a move would negatively affect the city's tourism business.

In making his point, MacDonald pointed to a 1938 survey that suggested that each tourist visiting the city spent $132. In 1951, officials for the CPR's BC Coast Steamship Service and the Black Ball Ferry Line produced statistical details of auto and foot passengers, to support their assertion that each year half-day closing cost Victoria "hundreds of thousands of dollars."

The desperation to cater to tourists by expanding the city's shopping hours was motivated by the belief, among many prominent citizens and civic officials, that with the loss of traditional industry the city's economic future was increasingly dependent upon tourism, and the pro-tourism lobby remained a consistent opponent of store-hour regulations. However, the rationale behind tourism promotion changed during the 1930s and 1940s and, as a result, so did the content of the tourism lobby's arguments. Once motivated by an "investment imperative" that viewed tourism promotion as the most efficient means of boosting the city and attracting long-term settlement and investment, tourism promoters now found that the economic dislocation of the Great Depression encouraged them to embrace the "expenditure imperative," which viewed tourists primarily as a source of outside expenditure to be lured to the city to boost local aggregate consumer demand.

From the tourism lobby's perspective, store-hour regulations remained anathema to tourism promotion, even though the tourism lobby's specific complaints changed over time. What remained consistent, however, was the notion that tourism had come to replace traditional industry as the city's economic lifeblood. Faced with Victoria's failure to challenge Vancouver as an industrial centre, these proponents of tourism promotion were anxious to ensure that the city was as tourist-friendly as possible.

And that view, in turn, informed their campaign to eliminate store-hour restrictions that raised the ire of tourists and placed the city's economic future in jeopardy. Like the more recent tourism proponents who view tourism as a panacea to the complex social and economic problems that plague post-industrial communities, Victoria's pro-tourism lobby was anxious to protect its ability to lure outsiders to town. But of course not everyone in Victoria agreed with the suggestion that tourism was the best, or even an unproblematic, approach to securing the city's economic future.

Opponents of store-hour regulations boasted representation from a wide variety of subgroups within Victoria, including employers, employees, consumers, and even some labour organizations. But each of these subgroups also included an alternative voice that embraced restrictions such as the Wednesday half-holiday, even in the face of the growing power of the pro-tourism lobby.

Some supported store-hour regulations because they didn't benefit directly from tourist expenditures and, in fact, argued that expanding store hours would simply increase operating costs. Others pointed to the social costs that expanded store hours might bring. In particular, they sought to preserve the retail clerks' mid-week respite and opportunities for common leisure time.

Tourist-dependent operations such as hotels, restaurants, transportation companies, and souvenir stores railed against the injustice of restricted store hours and came together, in particular, in support of a six-day shopping week. In this endeavour they were opposed by department and retail stores who did not benefit to a great extent from tourist expenditure. Instead, these operations pointed to the added costs that reduced store-hour restrictions would bring.

On one side of this fissure were the tourist-dependent stores. The Chamber of Commerce's Tourist Trade Group was their most vocal champion and consistently worked to undermine the legitimacy of store-hour regulations. Central to the TTG's 1946 arguments against restrictive store-closing regulations was the assertion that the entire community benefited from tourist expenditures. Hotel owner James Neely summed up this position nicely in 1951 when he asserted that "what is good for the hotel association and the tourists is also good for Victoria."

Significantly, such arguments could find support among local labour leaders. In 1953 Retail Clerks' Union representative John Aubry signalled his organization's willingness to see the end of Wednesday closing, so long as retail workers were guaranteed a five-day, forty-hour week, with a ringing endorsement of the notion that all Victorians benefited from tourist expenditures. "Whatever is good economy for the employers," he explained, "will benefit the store workers also and the shopping public at large."

Aubrey's Retail Clerks' Union faced opposition on this issue from a splinter group of employees that joined the Five-Day Week Action Committee, led by Peter MacEwan. In their attempt to garner support for a return to all-day Wednesday closing, MacEwan's group went so far as to seek out an alliance with the city's department stores—an indication, perhaps, that workers' class identity was occasionally trumped by their occupational allegiance to either small tourism-dependent operations or large retailers.

Arguments in favour of eliminating store-hour regulations, then, did not go unchallenged. And, as

MacEwan's decision to pursue an alliance with department stores suggests, the local business community was divided on the issue. In fact, retailers whose clientele did not consist primarily of visitors countered that not everyone benefited from tourism, and that the general interest of the community was being sacrificed to serve the interests of tourism-dependent businesses. In response to Alderman Brent Murdoch's claims that the half-day closing was hindering the city's prosperity, Courtney Haddock, store manager of the city's Woodward's department chain store pointedly asserted, "The business you get on Wednesday is not worth the powder to blow it to hell."

Tom Denny, manager of Standard Furniture and a past president of the city's Chamber of Commerce, offered a more quantitative argument when he used provincial Department of Trade and Industry figures to assert that Wednesday afternoon shopping would put just $3 in the pockets of each of the city's merchants. Factoring in the additional operating costs that the afternoon opening would require meant that abandoning the half-day closing was, in fact, unprofitable. Denny's claim was clearly rather selective and somewhat facetious. Some store owners were certain to benefit more than others, and it was unlikely that tourist expenditures would be spread so widely across the city. But of course that was an important part of the story.

The debate over store hours in Victoria did not always pit the business community against the workers. Nor did it simply pit externally controlled chain stores against independently owned local stores. It frequently divided the local business community itself. Hence, Denny charged the TTG with "being dictatorial to the retail merchants" and asserted, in a clever play on the usual pro-tourism rhetoric, that "what is good for the retail merchants is good for Victoria."

The division over tourism's impact was not based solely upon careful calculations of where tourist dollars were going. During the 1920s and 1930s, some observers began to voice concerns that the city's single-minded determination to preserve its tourist business was placing store-hour regulations, and the half-holiday in particular, in jeopardy, and that this, in turn, would have negative affects on the community's social and cultural well-being.

For the Hudson Bay Company's A. J. Watson, public debates about store hours in the mid-1920s boiled down to the question of whether or not tourists should be dictating local bylaws. As the pro-tourism lobby pushed for expanded shopping hours, a spokesperson for local retail clerks reminded city council in 1929 that longer hours came with a social cost for the clerks, which could include "a discontented body" and the "break up [of] home life."

A 1936 letter to the Times from G. W. Robinson urged the city to place the clerks' welfare ahead of other concerns, while challenging the Chamber of Commerce's perception that the half-day holiday threatened the city's tourist trade. Improved roads, he argued, held the key to expanding tourism, not longer store hours.

Not surprisingly, as the pro-tourism lobby stepped up its rhetoric in the 1940s and 1950s and embraced the expenditure imperative, the champions of local autonomy and the retail clerks' welfare responded in kind. In voicing his support for continued Wednesday closing, Reg Williams, president of the local Meat Retailers' Association, accepted the view that tourist expenditures were desirable, but argued that the concerns and welfare of local residents must continue to be the city's first priority.

Williams's arguments were echoed by furniture retailer Roy Denny, though in a more forceful manner: "We live in the city, not the tourists. We should have things the way we like." Peter MacEwen, not surprisingly, offered a similar view by asking rhetorically, "What we would like to know is this—who is running the city—the tourist trade group or the city council?"

Such concerns were not voiced solely by clerks' representatives or retailers, such as Williams and Denny, who had little contact with tourists. During the 1940s and 1950s the Colonist returned repeatedly to this issue in its editorials.

Acknowledging, in 1949, that "anything so firmly entrenched in the business life of the community as the weekly half-holiday cannot be disturbed without the strongest of reasons," the Colonist took its arguments a step further in 1951 by focusing directly upon the welfare of the retail clerks. Asking clerks to give up their weekly half-holiday, it argued "would be a lot to ask of them merely for the convenience of tourists."

The following year the Colonist expressed frustration that no solution had emerged that reconciled the welfare of the local population with increased shopping opportunities for tourists. Recognizing that the city's store-hour regulations were undoubtedly hampering its tourism promotion efforts, the newspaper nevertheless insisted that the common half-holiday was worth preserving. The holiday, it explained, provided a rare opportunity for communal recreation and allowed "one set afternoon" each week "so that friends may go places together" or "engage in organized sport and recreation." The welfare of retail clerks, the Colonist explained, was under threat and the city as a whole had a moral duty to protect their interests.

"These are the people who make up the 'we' who have to live in the city." At least one retail clerk concurred with this view. In 1953 H. A. Napper argued that what was being overlooked in the current controversy was "the right of retail clerks to take part, if they wish to, in group activities, such as cricket, football, baseball, or any other game they may fancy." "It took our fathers a long time to win this right," Napper explained, "and some of us don't want to lose it."

These observers recognized that Victoria's post-industrial reality left it reliant on outside forces, but they refused to accept that this situation necessitated abandoning the half-day holiday.

Central to the campaign to preserve the half-day holiday was the defence of common leisure pursuits. In a reversal of Arthur Lineham's earlier arguments that a small number of clerks and merchants were putting their own needs ahead of the larger community, local citizen Harold Gray wrote to the

Daily Colonist in 1953 castigating opponents of store-hour regulations for attempting to increase their profits by denying "some nearly 6,000 retail clerks ... the right to enjoy together and with one another their weekly half-day holiday."

Retail clerk A. G. Kinnis concurred and argued that the abolition of the half-day holiday would mean that "groups would not be able to unite for sports or outings." Rejecting a popular pro-tourist lobby proposal that retail clerks stagger their days off to suit the needs of their employers, Kinnis argued that "a staggered holiday system" would prevent workers from undertaking common recreational pursuits.

Kinnis's position was endorsed by fellow letter-writer Alex McLeod Baird, who argued that the Wednesday half-holiday had "grown to be a recognized day on which all store employees gather together and enjoy themselves collectively." Collective leisure, Baird argued, should not be allowed to fall victim to "the exploded wolf cry—'Tourist.'" Forcing retail clerks to abandon their half-day holiday, yet another letter-writer argued, placed these workers in a unique, and unfair situation.

"Today all banks, offices, all types of laborers, work a five-day week and none of them would consider a shift system," argued George Robinson in a 1953 letter to the Times. "Why then compel the store clerks to work a shift system which would not allow any group activities[?]" The answer, for opponents of store-hour regulations, was Victoria's increasing dependence on tourism—a dependence brought about by the flight of industrial capital from the city in the late nineteenth century and the city's failure to re-establish itself as a leading manufacturing centre. The result was a seemingly unending and uncomfortable search for economic stability.

Victoria's industrial decline in the late nineteenth century convinced the city to embrace tourism as a central component of its future economic development. In the long run this has proven to be a successful endeavour. As the store-hour debates demonstrate, however, this was a controversial enterprise. The campaign to cater to tourists divided the local community. The pro-tourism lobby campaigned relentlessly for the modification and elimination of store-hour regulations so that the city could meet the demands of tourists.

In doing so tourism's proponents argued that, because the city had lost the battle for traditional industry, it was imperative that the city embrace tourism promotion—first as a last-chance method of luring deep-pocketed investors to the city, and later as a means of increasing consumer demand for local retail goods. Central to the latter argument was the assurance that everyone in the community benefited from tourist expenditures.

Challenging these arguments were other community members who, like the pro-tourism lobby, were drawn from a wide range of backgrounds: employers, employees, civic officials, and consumers. They disputed claims that tourist dollars were spread evenly throughout the community and insisted that the social benefits—in particular, common leisure time—that the community accrued through institutions such as the half-day holiday should not be sacrificed to serve the interests of outsiders. Both sides were fully aware of Victoria's post-industrial reality; but both offered very different evaluations of tourism's role in alleviating the contingent and provisional nature of the city's economic fortunes.

The recent literature on deindustrialization is helpful in illuminating the lessons these debates hold for historians. First, as historians such as Hal Rothman have noted in other contexts, Victoria's reliance on tourism brought with it unexpected complications—in this case, a growing demand that the city's agreed-upon store-hour regulations be sacrificed on the altar of economic necessity. Second, as was the case in larger centres such as Atlantic City in the 1980s, the reliance on tourism brought with it a growing sense of unease within the community—one that expressed its concern that the interests of "outsiders" were being served at the expense of local citizens.

Third, we can see in Victoria, as in other instances of deindustrialization, a shift in power from within the community to without. In the case of Victoria, however, this change happened indirectly. Instead of large, faraway, multinational corporations seizing control of the city's economic future though hotel or casino development, the power to influence local bylaws shifted in favour of tourists indirectly and local tourist businesses directly.

The constant desire to craft the city's reputation as a tourist-friendly destination helped to sustain the campaign to reduce and eliminate store-hour regulations. Finally, the fleeting and provisional nature of post-1970 economic life that has been documented so well in the literature on deindustrialization points to an important element of Victoria's story throughout the twentieth century: these debates were the product of a community uneasy with its economic reality and desperate to pursue any means of securing economic stability, even if that meant transforming the rhythm of daily life and allowing individual consumer demand to colonize common leisure time.

And what lessons do Victoria's store-hour debates hold for historians of deindustrialization? They suggest that some assumptions about deindustrialization need to be modified and questioned. First, and most obviously, tourism certainly emerged here as an economic alternative to traditional industry, but much earlier than the current literature on deindustrialization would suggest.

These debates, then, point to the possibilities of comparative studies of deindustrialization that focus not just upon the post-1970 period, but upon earlier periods as well. Second, while much of the literature on deindustrialization focuses on the tension between community and capital, the debates underscore the extent to which deindustrialization in Victoria nurtured divisions within the local community. Moreover, these divisions did not fit into tidy compartmentalizations such as workers versus employers, or outside chain stores versus local entrepreneurs. Instead, the divisions emerged primarily within the business community but also, at times, among retail clerks and between their labour organizations.

Third, Cowie and Heathcott argue that changes brought

about by deindustrialization, unlike those ushered in by industrialization, "were more disorienting than overtly political, tended toward the elusive rather than the tangible, and marked a confusion of power relations that had seemed significantly clearer under the old order." These debates challenge that assumption.

After all, the issue here was a tangible one: a growing momentum in favour of eliminating store-hour regulations that affected when and how retail employers and employees worked. What was at stake here was a tangible reorientation of leisure time—a reminder that we must continue to factor leisure into our analyses of workers' lives.

If the store-hour debates are any indication, Victoria's failure to retain traditional industry haunted the city well into the postwar era. Some community members championed tourism as the most effective alternative economic strategy to industrial development and, in doing so, fought to eliminate the city's store-hour restrictions. Others strenuously opposed the elimination of these restrictions on the grounds that they served the interests of the local community, and local interests should not be sacrificed in favour of outsiders.

Recognizing that Victoria's embrace of tourism as an economic strategy was contested is an important indication of the complex nature of community responses to deindustrialization. Recognizing the fact that Victoria's post-industrial reality confirms some patterns unearthed by historians of deindustrialization, while challenging and modifying others, is an important indication of the extent to which historians of the late twentieth century and those focusing on earlier periods of economic disruption and transition can learn a great deal from each other.

Chapter 10

Modern Tourism Change in Ladakh

Ladakh is a typical example of an internal periphery in a centralised State, where an ethnic minority isolated from a lowland majority is facing the challenge of being integrated into a national identity different from its own. At the core of this phenomenon is the ongoing process of modernisation and the linkage of a traditional subsistence economy to regional and national markets.

Several authors have successfully highlighted the close relationship existing in similar Third World situations between the implementation of activities linked to tourism, the appearance of new economic operations or attitudes, social change in traditional hierarchical structures and identities, and the important role played by the State in the regulation of the actors involved in these activities.

TIBETAN ENCLAVE IN INDIAN KASHMIR

Ladakh is a complex of Himalayan valleys on the western edge of the Tibetan plateau. Located between the Great Himalayan range to the south and the Karakoram range to the north, the enclave is a vast rocky desert where only a few islands of vegetation bear witness to a human presence. The inhabited part of the territory is 3000 to 4500 meters above sea-level, with several summits rising to more than 7000 meters.

As of the 9th century A.D., way stations appeared in the area to tend to the needs of the caravaneers and their animals plying trans-Himalayan trade routes. Since that time, Ladakh has helped maintain the commercial traffic which uses the valley of the Indus as an access route into Central Asia and Tibet.

Religion in Ladakh developed as a blend of Indian Buddhism and the indigenous Bon-Chos faith, producing an original synthesis which progressively took root in the whole of the Tibetan plateau, and eventually became modern Lamaism. This religion has melded with the Ladakhi way of life in a harsh ecosystem to forge a lasting association between the native peoples of these high plateaux.

Today, Ladakh is the most sparsely populated area in all of India. Indian census figures for 1981 establish the population of the district at 132 000 inhabitants, dispersed between one town and close to one hundred smaller settlements. The language used by the population is Ladakhi, a local Tibetan dialect, written with the same alphabet. The use of classical Tibetan persists among former nobles and the clergy but its use outside religious life is decreasing rapidly.

Seasonal merchants and Kashmiri civil servants stationed at Leh (8500 inhabitants in 1990), the capital of Ladakh, have brought Kashmiri with them, while Urdu, a mid-oriental version of Hindi, is used in business and administrative communications with the rest of the country. English, a constitutional language considered transitory at the time of Indian independence, is employed by an enducated minority of Ladakhis to communicate with the exterior. Understandably, this latter language is quickly growing in popularity amongst entrepreneurs and guides involved in international tourism, as well as Indian-educated youth eager to connect with the outside world.

The so-called traditional structure of the work force - i.e., that prevailing roughly up to Indian independence in 1947 - was overwhelmingly tilted towards agriculture, with 90% of the population, exclusive of the Buddhist clergy, involved in agricultural production in a rural milieu. Agriculture still dominates the Ladakhi economy. Farming-related activities are concentrated in the period from May to October when all able-bodied people pitch in to assure the survival of the family, which is directly dependent on this one summer harvest. During the winter, below-zero temperatures render the use of water for irrigation and as an energy source impossible. It is during this period that people take care of domestic chores in their homes, which are heated by burning dried dung or, often today, coal.

Patrilineal, patrilocal and polyandrous, the family is the village economic unit, and is led by the oldest male in the child-bearing generation. The rule is that each household looks after its needs. Practically all the villages in Ladakh today still produce the basic foodstuffs of the traditional diet in sufficient quantities to satisfy most of the local demand.

The estimated percentage of the population engaged in religious life varies from to 2% to 8%, sometimes more, the majority being men. Monasteries are the spiritual, political and geographical centres of their respective villages. They act as information broadcasting centres and comment on changes and innovations in all sectors of Ladakhi life. Spiritual power is vertically stratified in three hierarchical levels.

At the top, the abbott, whose soul is considered immortal, is responsible for the monastery; monks are second in the hierarchy; and the general population is at the lowest level. The physical layout of the village corresponds to the spiritual hierarchy: monasteries are built on the highest ground, the monks' cells along the flanks and villagers' dwellings at the base. As major landowners, the monasteries administer the profits from rents collected on the lands belonging to them.

Aside from agriculture, almost all other economic activities were concentrated in the city of Leh. Situated at the junction of the Indus and a minor tributary, Leh was well established by the beginning of the 16th century, and is favourably situated with respect to irrigation and efficient communication networks.

The city grew up around the monastery and the royal

palace, built when the city was founded. Until the beginning of its decline in 1948, caravan traffic was an important element of the Leh economy. The caravan market was also a major physical landmark in the city around which were grouped merchants, inn-keepers, horse-dealers, etc. Most of the remaining 10% of the Ladakhi population not active in agriculture or the clergy lived in Leh: the commercial caravaneers, the aristocrats and the lower castes.

LADAKH'S LOCAL ECONOMY AND POLITICS

In order to facilitate better understanding of the origins and the sense of social developments in contemporary Ladakh, this section presents a more specific picture of the history of economic and political organization in the region. Most authors have divided this history into three periods: the monarchical age (10th century to 1841); the era of Dogra and, subsequently, British colonization (1841 to 1947); and the Indian district period (since 1947).

For the purpose of our expose, the latter period can be sub-divided into two parts, the first beginning with the establishment of the Indian State in 1948 and the second with the debut of tourism in 1974. The following presentation draws heavily on the historical accounts of the above named authors.

FEUDALISM: THE MONARCHICAL AGE

Ladakh has been intimately linked to the Tibetan world since the installation in the 10th century of the first monarch. Despite numerous Muslim raids and subsequent attempts to convert the local leaders to Islam, the cement of Lamaistic Buddhism has proved to be resilient and has contributed to the maintenance of friendly relations with Tibet for twelve centuries. The apogee of the kingdom of Ladakh came at the beginning of the 17th century.

This period was distinguished by a flourishing caravan trade, several territorial conquests, the erection of numerous monasteries and the active participation of the clergy in political life. It was during this period that the traditional hierarchical structure of Ladakhi society became fixed. At the summit, the royal aristocracy and nobility, whose members lived mainly in the capital, represented about 3% of the population. The rural base for this group was composed of local village chiefs responsible for collecting land rents, administering local justice and seeing to military obligations. In second position on the social ladder were the tenant farmers who guaranteed the continuity of the social structure. At the very bottom of the social scale, making up about 3% of the population, were the lower castes, subjected to the taboos of pollution and even more isolated from society than were the tenant farmers from the aristocracy.

Parallel to the secular social ladder was the Buddhist clerical order. The relationship of dominance between the two hierarchical systems could not have been any clearer: "Le religieux l'emporte toujours sur le profane: le monastere sera toujours plus haut que le palais et les lama s'assoient toujours avant les laics dans une cuisine, quels que soient leurs rangs respectifs".

Gifts of land awarded by sovereigns in exchange for religious favours have, throughout the centuries, helped turn the clergy into major landowners, leaving entire villages in their hands and adding rents and statute labour benefits to the revenues derived from the sale of spiritual brokerage to the population. The monasteries are interrelated in a complex sectarian fashion, and a clergyman recognized as particularly enlightened will sometimes have had a determining influence on the reigning sovereign, a relationship which will lead to advantages for himself and his monastery.

Muslims also have a long-standing presence in Ladakh, the origins of which can probably be attributed to a gradual overflow of population from Kashmir. In the nineteenth century, significant numbers of Muslims were drawn to Leh by a flourishing commerce in fine wools. During this period, business gravitated mainly around the caravan trade.

Shorter haul transportation of goods between adjacent valleys was in the hands of their respective local populations and corresponded to the agricultural specializations imposed by the feudal regime. However, on the longer routes, the Muslims controlled caravan activities throughout Kashmir. Once Leh had become a regular stop-over for the long distance caravans, it was logical for a colony of Muslims to settle there.

Only the richest of the local Buddhist families were involved in caravaning, for the trade required a large number of pack animals and significant amounts of capital. The royal power derived most of its revenues from the flow of trade across its territory, both directly from the levying of import and export duties and indirectly from the fact that the caravan trade between Yarkand and Srinagar, the most important of the routes, was partly in the hands of the Ladakhis. According to Cunningham, the most important trader in Ladakh was the king himself.

DOGRA AND BRITISH COLONIZATION

In the nineteenth century, first Kashmir (1819) and then Ladakh (1841) came under the outside control of the largely Muslim Dogra. In what was to represent a decisive step towards a definitive break in Ladakhi political autonomy, the Dogra rulers set up an administrative and a commercial structure controlled by a few representatives of the raja and several local leaders in the pay of the interests of the Dogra dominion.

Although the royal family was forced out and economic administration was placed in the hands of outside managers, the Dogra reforms were nonetheless limited to a simple administrative restructuring of the system of tenant farming, leaving landowners' privileges largely intact. The political power of the Ladakhi elite, however, was weakened. In contrast, Singh (1977), who analyzed the immense areas of influence and the property of the great monasteries in Ladakh today, shows that the Buddhist clergy survived the Dogra reform without any major changes in their status, their capacity for survival, or their economic power.

The Dogra occupation also triggered a new wave of Muslim immigration to Leh in the wake of increased trade with the south and the implementation of the Dogra administrative reform. Little interested in agriculture, the new arrivals rapidly associated with their already established coreligionists, reinforcing and increasing the competitiveness of the Ladakhi Muslim community.

This group gradually replaced the former feudal money-lenders, and after obtaining land in payment for unpaid debts, accumulated property in and around Leh. Excess parcels of land thus acquired were then let out to poor Buddhists for rents in kind. In this way, Muslims rapidly accumulated merchandise capital which was in turn converted in exchange value on the caravan market. In fact, the process marked an important step towards making a firmer connection between Ladakh and the outside market.

As for the influence of the British colonization of India on Ladakh, there is little to be said, for there was never any formal occupation. Indirect rule maintained or made use of numerous intermediaries between the colonial administration and this distant district which, like other Himalayan kingdoms, was considered of little interest to the crown except as a buffer zone with China and Central Asia.

THE PRESENCE OF THE INDIAN STATE

From the moment that British India was partitioned in 1947, and for several years afterwards, Ladakh found itself embroiled in a border dispute with the then West Pakistan. The dispute led independent India to take notice of Ladakh, and its emerging geostrategic importance. Following the Sino-Indian war in 1962, the Indian army received a mandate to establish a permanent presence in the region and transformed the caravan route linking Leh to Srinagar into a road capable of handling military supply convoys. It also modernized a military airfield two kilometres from Leh, originally constructed during the first Indo-Pakistani war in 1948.

The Indian State then moved to consolidate its position in the upper Indus valley. It initiated local development projects, relieved the monks of their monopoly over education and built public schools as well as introducing such national services as mail delivery and policing. Furthermore, the Indian government authorized the regulation of traffic on the new road that was to be used to supply the residents and the military. At the political level, national legislation first passed by the British in 1941 to abolish the feudal system and landed property, polyandry and inheritance by primogeniture was enacted with mitigated success. Nonetheless, this same legislation did allow farming families with sufficient means to take ownership of the land they in fact cultivated, and also annulled their huge ancestral debts to moneylenders from within the clergy, the aristocracy and the commercial bourgeoisie.

The principal source of political unrest in post-partition Ladakh has undoubtedly been the introduction by the State of a democratic representative regime. Not only does this regime run counter to inherited feudal tradition, but it has transformed sparsely populated Ladakh into a tiny minority enclave with mere district status inside the Muslim state of Jammu and Kashmir, itself in a minority position within a de jure neutral but de facto Hindu Indian Union. Another important consequence of the consolidation of the State was the development of employment opportunities in the civil service.

From 1949 on, and even more so after 1962, younger men from the wealthier classes were increasingly drawn to the salaried positions available in Leh. where they were freed to a certain extent from the influence of elder family heirs; for the lower castes, the option of salaried jobs in construction or road-work helped offset their constrictive social position. And, in a similar vein, village farmers saw their younger sons, who had little interest in agriculture, polyandry or the monastic life, leave for the city.

Economically, it was the long-haul caravan trade that suffered the most in the aftermath of Indian independence, one consequence of which was the closing of borders with West Pakistan and Tibet. The abrupt interruption in trade caused by the closure provoked a considerable reversal of fortune for many merchant families in Leh; a good number of them liquidated their assets and left Ladakh in search of new fields of activity. As a result, many tracts of land in Leh and the outlying areas changed hands during the 1950s, and were bought back at discount prices not only by the few Muslims who chose to stay, but especially by the rich Buddhists who had never thought about leaving. Although the Buddhist aristocracy was also hard hit by the interruption in the long-haul caravan trade, its members had other sources of revenue. Deeply attached to their region, they pinned their hopes on a future economic recovery.

The arrival of the army and of State representatives in the 1960s offered partial rewards for their patience as Ladakh experienced a wave of relative prosperity engendered by the sale or rent of land and reinforced by investment in construction and transportation. In addition, some of the richest merchant families, both Muslim and Buddhist, were able to adapt to the wholesale trade by buying trucks. They hired salaried drivers and succeeded in carving a place for themselves in the lucrative and steady business of transporting foodstuffs, a business generated by the increase in population.

As for the other traditionally dominant group, the clergy, it has maintained a virtually unblemished reputation in the years since independence. The involvement of the clergy in politics at all levels is such that abbots were still unrivalled on the national stage in the 1980s.

The abbots of Spituk and Shankar, for example, represented the Ladakhis in the Indian parliament; the abbott of Thiksey directed the local Congress party; and the abbott from Phyiang was vice-president of the Ladakh Development Board at Srinagar. Some of these positions are filled by candidates elected by universal suffrage, a further illustration of the prestige that the population still confers on the higher religious offices.

SINCE 1974: OPENING OF THE REGION AND INTERNATIONAL TOURISM

In 1974, India decided to open parts of the Ladakh valley to the free movement of people. From Delhi's point of view, the geographical and political isolation of Ladakh between 1948 and 1974 had had the advantage of keeping military manoeuvres along the Indo-Pakistan cease-fire line and the Chinese frontier secret, a motive still invoked today to justify the maintenance of strict military control over the north of the Srinagar-Kargil-Leh route and the road from Leh to the east. Delhi's principal incentive for changing this policy was to promote a strategy of increased internal migration aimed at augmenting the civilian population in the area, for it was the lack of inhabitants which had resulted in an important loss of territory to the Chinese in 1962. Socially, the national government saw the possibility of keeping young Ladakhis at home, and also hoped to provide the spark for permanent migrations from overpopulated regions in Kashmir and India.

For Srinagar, the incentive was first of all economic: additional subsidies from the national government and the opening of "virgin" lands to international adventure tourism and aggressive Kashmiri merchants seemed very appealing. The Kashmiris, long aware of their competitive edge in the field of tourism, quickly realized that the business opportunities were attractive, and a lobby favourable to free movement to Ladakh was formed among the great entrepreneurial families in Srinagar.

In Kargil and especially in Leh, the local population had no choice but to take the idea under consideration. Ladakhi elders faced a steady stream of much deplored, and sometimes permanent outmigration, as young people left to study or take up salaried posts elsewhere in India. Furthermore, the changes in the mentality of those returning were troubling. Rooted in their land and traditions, the elders were desperately seeking solutions to strengthen the local economy, rendered precarious by the loss of the caravan trade.

Although there is no evidence indicating that the local population was consulted in the decision-making process, it is extremely likely that the Buddhist clergy was kept informed by religious representatives in the political apparatus, and it can be assumed they were fairly favourable to plans to open up Ladakh. The fear of seeing new-comers disturb the political, cultural and social order could not outweigh the prospect of new profits to compensate the losses incurred since the end of the caravan trade.

Pulled along by what Rizvi calls "the extension to Ladakh of India's ambitious programme of economic development", the inauguration or consolidation of services to the population also had the effect of favouring the development of tourist enterprises. In return, the influx of visitors further stimulated State participation in implanting services that would probably have been delayed without the impetus of tourism demand and wealth.

The Jammu & Kashmir Tourism Authority, with its services for entrepreneurs and visitors, was Srinagar-based, as were the Public Works Authority and the Jammu & Kashmir State Road Transportation (public transport). Furthermore, Srinagar was in charge of all regional administrative costs, which have risen considerably since 1974.

The economic consequences of tourism were quickly felt in the years following the arrival of the first tourists in 1974. In direct response to the rapid increase in visitors, there was an important summer migration of Kashmiri and Indian middlemen coming to do business with the tourists, especially in Leh. Tourist infrastructures developed rapidly and the number of young people holding salaried jobs or going into business for themselves visibly increased.

Furthermore, the direct introduction of foreign currency via tourism is encouraging Ladakh's integration into the Indian and world markets. The endless rows of trucks which arrive full of consumer goods and leave empty bear witness to this trend. Since 1962, the distribution of consumer goods has become increasingly important and has increasingly tended to displace traditional every-day objects and the activities inherent to their production.

Among imported consumer goods, radio and television sets are major vectors of national integration. Nonetheless, the influence of television will be severely limited as long as the local generator in the city of Leh continues to produce only four hours of electricity daily, as was still the case when I last visited in 1988.

ELEMENTS FOR AN ANALYSIS OF THE CURRENT SITUATION

The hierarchical organizational structure of political and administrative powers in effect in Ladakh reflects the current transition-in-progress from traditional local forms to the national democratic type formalism promoted by the Indian State. Ladakh district is connected to the nation through the vertically hierarchical networks of the State apparatus, with Delhi at the top, and the district at the bottom. However, at the local level, the structure perpetuates the traditional organizational pattern whose points of juncture with the State apparatus are subject to a play of influences where the key positions are coveted.

At the local level, where the weight of tradition can be observed, the official notion of democratic representation remains rather theoretical. Village power is still based on kinship and seniority, and, in order to circumvent the problem of democratic legitimacy, the State has opted to recognize the elective role of the clan in the choice of the traditional chief, who is chosen for a three-year mandate (assistants are mandated for one year).

This is equivalent to turning a blind eye to the issue of representativity, for today the title of village chief tends to be connected to the patronymics of some of the most influential families. It is highly unlikely that anyone could make a break with tradition in favour of the elective process by voting against a traditional leader.

Two new social groups that appeared on the Leh political chessboard in the 1980s should also be mentioned. The Ladakh Ecological and Development Group (LEDeG) and the Students' Educational and Cultural Movement of Ladakh (SECMOL) are involved locally without, however, being directly involved in the elective process and the open struggle for power.

The former group is composed primarily of mature Buddhist intellectuals, but has increasingly begun to seek out members among young intellectuals trained outside the region; the latter group is strictly composed of young Buddhist intellectuals often educated outside Ladakh. Although the membership and aims of the two organizations partially overlap, they function separately, each constituting an independent pressure group with its own network of alliances to lobby the establishment. The LEDeG is supported in part by a network of western ecologists and is close to the traditional and modem power base.

The SECMOL, for its part, has the backing of the religious authorities. The two groups have also set up their own enterprises and represent the new wave of Ladakhi mobilization allegedly seeking to contain tourism-related cultural disturbances through a strategy of participation in current social economic development.

TOURISM ENTREPRENEURS AND LOCAL POWER

The reason why attempts to set up an elective system to choose representatives at the district level have not yielded anticipated results is partly because partisans of the elective system are primarily Kashmiri and Sikh merchants from outside Ladakh. Heavily involved in the tourist industry and already familiar with democratic representation, they seek to increase their influence over local economic development, for they are generally excluded from the local decision-making process.

However, the traditional power-brokers, the lay and religious elites, have turned their backs on the electoral process, thus undermining its validity in the eyes of the local population and disenfranchising the outside merchants. The fact is that all the tourism entrepreneurs, including such endogenous merchants as the "nouveau riche" Ladakhis, intend to have an active say in the decision-making process at the local level in order to protect their vested interests.

But, motivation and stakes vary greatly with the identity of the actors. In an earlier analysis, I identified that the entrepreneurs' origins and religious affiliations were of significant importance in understanding their political positions. I would like to refer to certain results from that study.

Tourism-related business activities set up under the direct initiative of endogenous actors are concentrated in the areas of lodging, guiding and transportation, crafts, and to a lesser degree, the trade and the food business. These activities involve landowners, guest house owners, guides and their families, taxi drivers, musicians and women who produce saleable craft-wares. SECMOL and LEDeG must be added to this list as they only recruit among the Ladakhis. Exogenous entrepreneurs are, to all intents and purposes, those with no local permanent residence and whose business activities are concentrated in the tourist season from May to October.

These entrepreneurs are involved in the hotel business, in travel agencies, and in the sale of souvenirs. The majority are tenants, for example, hotel managers and shopkeepers. Other exogenous entrepreneurs include self-employed guides from outside the area who accompany small informally organized groups, and Tibetan merchants living in India. The great majority of these entrepreneurs are part of family networks whose members are already involved in the tourist business, mainly in Srinagar.

Whether endogenous or exogenous, entrepreneurs belong to several different religious groups; Lamaist Buddhism and Islam have been the principal faiths in Ladakh over the last several centuries, with the adherents of the former group far outnumbering those of the latter.

Buddhists comprise the majority of the landowners and tourist entrepreneurs involved in the operation of guest houses, restaurants and permanent businesses, as well as those working as taxi drivers, guides and craftsmen. For historical reasons, the group of landowners and operators of permanent businesses includes a greater number of Muslims than the other categories, but they remain a minority. The SECMOL and the LEDeG are also Buddhist. Muslims are principally involved in tourist activities associated with the

managing of hotels, the running of boutiques, guiding done by self-employed exogenous workers, and travel agencies.

Thus, onto a traditional power structure based on a strong clergy and an historically rooted monarchical regime was grafted a commercial bourgeoisie of tourist industry entrepreneurs. In turn, this has led to the emergence of a nascent new petite bourgeoisie composed of intellectuals and young people, mostly from the LEDeG and the SECMOL, who have had access to a western-style education through the Indian school system and foreign alliances. Partly because of tourism, the longstanding complementarity between the clergy and the aristocracy has diversified: the modern commercial bourgeoisie and the new petite bourgeoisie now constitute an enlarged but relatively homogeneous group in terms of economic, political and ideological aims.

The caravaneer commercial bourgeoisie, which has always been composed of a certain percentage of Muslims, has grown less religiously homogenous, a potential source of friction which, so far, seems to have been contained in favour of a more desirable common interest: economic and political stability.

The landowners, as a specific interest group, are defenders of the traditional Ladakhi identity, especially in the case of the clergy and the aristocracy. They are also the privileged partners of exogenous entrepreneurs, to whom they rent their facilities and from whom they derive what has become the greater part of their income.

The landowner group includes the majority of political leaders, both traditional and modern; in other words, they control endogenous participation in State activities at the local level, and are at the same time involved in economic activities in the formal sector. Ideally, this group could use its strong political influence to encourage the further development of informal endogenous enterprises trapped in competition amongst themselves.

The pretext of protecting traditional cultural heritage could be easily justified, and would correspond to the nationalist ideas group members support. But small-scale businesses in Ladakh are being weakened despite the fact that traditional elites and the new petite bourgeoisie advocate an alliance among natives with the objective of saving their cultural identity and limiting outside power. Exogenous Muslims operating formal enterprises are little affected by protective actions, but small-scale entrepreneurs and endogenous restaurant owners are paying a price that is increasingly high.

Consciously or not, local elites are currently putting the promotion of a native takeover of businesses second to the promotion of economic ties with the formal sector exogenous entrepreneurs, and this despite the potential for cultural preservation that such a takeover might offer. This attitude could undermine the informal sector enterprises that are too busy competing with each other to realise the long-term danger inherent in this reciprocal non-collaboration.

Can we speak, despite these contradictions, of a movement to protect Ladakh's cultural heritage? Young people and the intellectuals manifestly realise the dangers of acculturation, both the danger of integration into Kashmiri and Indian society and the danger stemming specifically from tourism. Strategies proposing alliances with politically aware visitors and "engaged travellers" to support cultural affirmation vis-a-vis the State, and alliances directly with Delhi to escape the influence of Srinagar do exist.

Yet socially, the traditional model has been to a large extent maintained. Although young people are rapidly becoming wealthy and acquiring power, a novelty in the local social landscape, the members of the elite are still the owners and leaders; the peasants are holding their own as well as they can; the clergy has not lost much of its former influence. However, globally, I suspect these adjustments would not prove to be all that original if they were compared to those of caravan age.

Indeed, it is tempting to draw a parallel between the present situation and that of the caravan era but the demonstration of such a hypothesis would require more documentation.